Urban Harvest

URBAN HARVEST

Roy Joslin

 EVANGELICAL PRESS

EVANGELICAL PRESS
16/18 High Street, Welwyn, Hertfordshire AL6 9EQ England

© Evangelical Press 1982
First published 1982

ISBN 0 85234-159-8

Bible quotations are from the New International Version.

Typeset in Great Britain by 'Altair', 83 Tilehouse Street, Hitchin, Herts. SG5 2DY.

Printed in the U.S.A.

Contents

1. Urban people: the working classes — 1
   '... crowds ... harassed and helpless, like sheep without a shepherd' (Matt. 9:36-38)

2. In darkest England — 10
   the working classes alienated from the churches — history and sociology explained

3. Battle for the mind — 47
   from God's mind to man's mind — how God has spoken and how the working man thinks today

4. A message for the millions — 79
   the gospel to be preached and the people to be reached

5. Winning them wisely — 103
   some New Testament principles of evangelism

6. Lessons from Lystra — 156
   the arrival of the gospel in a New Testament city

7. Growing together — 191
   the corporate life of an indigenous company of believers

8. Building an indigenous church — 222
   the importance of local membership, culture and leadership

9. Salt where it counts — 274
   the urban Christian in an industrial society

10. How long till harvest? — 298
    some hopes for the future

For a detailed analysis of the contents see page 324.

1.
Urban people: the working classes

Our study begins with a bang! Hear the report of an Anglican canon: 'It is in fact a broad truth, which multitudinous exceptions that might be cited do not disturb, that the "artisan class" constitutes by far the toughest identifiable core of resistance to the gospel today. Up to the present no dents at all have been made in its surface. It is a hard saying but a true one that until some more effective way of appealing to the artisan has been found there will be no real revival of religion in this country, since in modern post-war conditions this class has become socially more important than any other. No amount of success elsewhere will compensate the Church for failure here.'[1]

These words were written by Canon Roger Lloyd nearly thirty years ago. They appear in his book *The Church and the Artisan Today*. Although he uses the term 'artisan class' in preference to the term 'working classes', it is quite clear that he is speaking about the people who are the subject of our study.

Do we accept Lloyd's estimate as being true to fact? Is he overstating the case just to prove a point? Have the past thirty years brought about changes which call for a revision of the assessment? If Lloyd's statement is an informed judgement from within the Establishment, then let us add to it the verdict of an authoritative voice from within Nonconformity.

In 1975 the theme for the 'Westminster Conference' was *The Christian and the State in Revolutionary Times*. According to custom, the final paper of the conference was given by the chairman, Dr

D.M. Lloyd-Jones. His particular subject was 'The French Revolution and After'. In the course of the paper, the speaker made reference to the topic of the *status quo* and how it affects Christians. He said, 'The impression has gained currency that to be a Christian, and more especially an evangelical, means that we are traditionalists, and advocates of the *Status Quo*. I believe that this largely accounts for our failure in this country to make contact with the so-called working classes. Christianity in this country has become a middle-class movement; and I suggest that that is so because of this very thing. Nonconformity is by no means clear on this question. In the last century, and in the present century, far too often, as Nonconformist men have got on in the world, and made money, and become Managers and Owners, they have become opponents of the working classes who were agitating for their rights.'[2]

The canon and the doctor agree. There is an immense gulf between the Christian church and the working classes in this country. But is the outlook totally dark and depressing, or are there any slender shafts of light? In all fairness, we must acknowledge that over the past thirty years signs of change have been appearing. Evidences of interest and concern are to be seen where nothing was happening before. Could this be the end of the long, hard winter for the industrial areas? Has springtime really come to the urban churches? Green shoots breaking through the hard-packed soil signal hope and promise. But is our exultation premature? Could the late frosts of prejudice, fear, discouragement or even an unbiblical conservatism destroy the burgeoning hope? Many words are being spoken, many conferences convened, many committees formed and many books written. How do the deeds square up alongside the growing mountain of words? What are the realities of the situation we face? Why does it exist? How can it be changed? The exploration of these issues is the task we now begin.

We commence our study by trying to understand more about the people for whom we are concerned. We look first at what church history has to teach us, and then at what contemporary sociology tells us about life in urban communities today. Following a consideration of the way in which the working-class mind works, we then move on to two chapters on the major topic of biblical evangelism. A detailed study of the New Testament church at Lystra seeks to draw out helpful parallels with our urban church situations today. After two chapters on the local church — how it is to be established and nurtured in working-class communities, we investigate the final topic — the role of the urban Christian in today's industrial society.

Is it right for Christians to think in terms of 'class'?

Among some Christians, talking in terms of 'class' is regarded as either an improper or irrelevant thing to do. They feel a certain embarrassment when we talk in this way. We shall briefly consider some objections and how they may be answered.

Objection 1: It is unbiblical to talk in this way. Christians should be concerned to overcome and diminish distinctions between groups of people, and not to magnify them by making them a topic of special study.

Answer: We will only make progress in overcoming distinctions and divisions between groups of people when we understand why it is that these categories and groups have arisen in the first place. Sin does not go away if we choose to ignore it. We have to face reality in order to deal with the problem. If the Christian church chooses to ignore these distinctions among people it is certain that the divisions will remain and the church will continue to fail in her responsibility to some of these groups. We find no problem in accepting the reality of different racial groups among the nations of the world. Why should we find it difficult to accept the reality of different social groups within our own British society?

The apostle Paul recognized the various racial and social divisions which existed in his day. In the opening chapter of his letter to the Romans he says that he is 'bound both to Greeks and non-Greeks, both to the wise and the foolish' (Rom. 1:14). 'A study of Paul's sermons in the Acts of the Apostles shows that he adapted his presentation of the gospel to suit the particular needs of his listeners. (Compare Acts 14: 15f with Acts 17:22f.) The apostle was always careful to take account of differences in national character and cultural development (or the lack of it)...'[3] In recognizing the working classes as a definable group of people within today's society we are following a biblical principle.

Objection 2: The 'class' categories used many years ago no longer apply.

Answer: Since I write as a pastor and not as a sociologist, I must concede that my answer may be less accurate than that of the 'expert' in this field. It would appear that the social groupings within contemporary society are more blurred at the edges than used to be the case. There is now much easier mobility between the social groups. Also, it is now apparent that level of income is no longer a convenient guide to class. However, the term 'working classes' still gives us a pretty good idea of the kind of people we are talking about. There is no more accurate term to use. The 'blurred edges' of present day social groupings will in no way invalidate the general observations we shall make concerning the working classes.

Objection 3: When Christians talk about the working classes it often sounds condescending and patronizing. It may seem that Christians generally place themselves in a 'higher' social category and tend to pass judgements on the working classes. It may sound as though we are blaming these people for the problems they pose for the Christian church.

Answer: Unfortunately, Christians are at times guilty on this point. We must be careful in the words we choose and in the manner we adopt. Christians are generally in a *different* (and not superior) social group from working-class folk. Middle-class values are *different* from (and not superior to) working-class values. We must speak with humility and sensitivity. The Bible says that Christians should 'do nothing out of selfish ambition or vain conceit, but in humility consider others better than yourselves' (Phil. 2:3). This is how Christians are to regard one another. The same attitude must be carried over into a Christian's thinking and speaking about the working classes.

Who are the working classes?

It seems that there is not one universally accepted definition of the term 'working classes'. A few fairly obvious clues to the kind of people we are speaking about can be indicated. Working-class people are generally 'manual' workers. They work in 'trades' rather than professions. Most of these workers would receive a 'weekly wage' rather than an 'annual salary'. They work in factories, mills, mines, building sites, power stations, dockyards and other similar industrial locations. Some of the main industries in which these men serve would be coal mining, electricity supply, shipbuilding, the steel industry, building, road haulage, farming, the car industry, aircraft construction, the water and sewage industries, the postal service, public transport, food processing; they include local council workers, road sweepers, dustmen, those responsible for road repairs and so on. These examples are sufficiently clear for us to formulate in our minds an adequate understanding of the term 'working classes'. Geographically these workers would be concentrated in major urban and industrial areas — places such as Liverpool, Birmingham or London. They would also be well represented in council housing estates and new town developments. These men and their families make up the major part of that social group we call the 'working classes'.

The plural 'classes' is used because this social group can be further sub-divided in a number of ways. Sometimes the analysis is upper, middle and lower, within the general category of working class; sometimes skilled, semi-skilled and unskilled; sometimes deferential, proletarian and privatized. There is no need for us to dwell upon these class sub-divisions at this stage of our study although we shall see later that there is some link-up between these sub-divisions and the practice of church-going.

It can also be demonstrated that geographical location has some link with the practice or neglect of church-going. Information on church-going gathered in the Religious Census of 1851 showed 'a very high correlation between proportion of attendance and size of town: the larger the town, the lower the proportion. Such figures did indeed illuminate the "spiritual destitution" of the great cities.'[4] This correlation discovered over a century ago is still valid today. The proportion of the population attending church in the 'big city' is noticeably lower than the attendance in the 'smaller industrial town'. 'It seems that in a socially varied area working-class practice may not be quite as low as where the class affiliation is entirely monochrome. Patterns of observance within England are plainly connected with complex variables relating to region, class and size of town ... The north is more practising than the south, the south-west more practising than the south-east. The upper middle class is more practising than the lower middle class, and a large gap yawns between the lower middle and the working class.'[5]

What proportion of our current British population can be described as 'working class'?

'For sociologists there are two main classes: middle and working. In general, people who do manual jobs (and their families) are defined as working class. People who do non-manual jobs (and their families) are defined as middle class. By this definition, about 65% of people in Britain are working class, and about 35% middle class. (What used to be thought of as the upper class — the old landed gentry and aristocracy, for example — is now generally assumed to have merged with the upper reaches of the middle class.)'[6]

Other estimates of the size of the working class in Britain vary between 50% and 70%, although it is reckoned that up to 80% of our English population now lives in towns and cities.[7] These figures establish the fact that the working classes form the largest social group within our nation. They also support the claim of Roger Lloyd, which we noted earlier, that 'in modern post-war conditions this class has become socially more important than any other'.

What do we need to know?

We are not primarily concerned whether a man is a miner or a magistrate, a bricklayer or a bank manager, nor even whether the 'working man' gets a fair day's pay for a fair day's work. But we are, in the first instance, concerned to understand how these people *think*. Our observations so far about the working classes have identified them by occupation and geographical location. But these things are only clues to the 'class' of these people. The essential nature of class is something different: it is a question of 'attitudes'. K.A. Busia writes that, 'It has been observed that people who have essentially similar occupations, economic standards of living, become similar in other ways, mental, moral and behavioural. The economic and occupational bonds operate to produce certain similar social and mental attitudes.'[8]

What binds people together in a 'class' grouping is not so

much the type of work they do, nor the place where they live. It is that these common external circumstances operate to produce common *inward* attitudes and patterns of thought. It is these attitudes, as they are passed on from generation to generation, which produce the essence and the enduring nature of a social group. Richard Hoggart's book *The Uses of Literacy*, with its richness of colourful detail, provides a great variety of insights into working-class life. Hoggart claims that, 'One may fairly make generalizations about *attitudes* without implying that everyone in the working classes believes or does this or this about work or marriage or religion... The implication of my generalizations... is rather that this or this is what most working-class people assume should be believed or done about such matters... Within that majority there is obviously a very wide range of attitudes, and yet there is a centre at which a great number of people are represented.'[9]

Although Hoggart wrote nearly a quarter of a century ago, his observations and conclusions are not necessarily dated. Aspects of working-class behaviour may indicate changing trends, but the underlying attitudes are generally slow to change. The working class has not escaped the consequences of technical, occupational and social change over recent decades. But these changes do not necessarily imply a major disintegration of older class and culture patterns. 'Common patterns of residence and style of life, an oral tradition of culture transmission, and common experience of relative deprivation and the expectation of deference to one's "betters" preserve solidarity and an egalitarian ethos.'[10]

The 'very wide range of attitudes' to which Hoggart refers spans a variety of forms of mental material — opinions, ideas, suspicions, prejudices, fears, beliefs, half-truths, sayings, maxims and the like. These attitudes have to do with the way working-class people regard one another within the same social group, and also how they regard other groups in society. This will involve attitudes to the bosses, the government, and the Christian church. It is these patterns of working-class thought that we need to explore and understand.

But why is this necessary? The Bible shows us that it is the way in which a person thinks which determines the kind of person he is going to be. This rule holds good both before and after a person becomes a Christian. Ungodly thoughts produce ungodly behaviour (Rom. 1:21-25). At conversion the Holy Spirit illumines the darkened mind and this leads to repentance — a change of mind, disposition and affection. Thereafter the Christian is required to go on having his mind renewed according to the Scripture and no longer according to the thinking of this world (Rom. 12:2).

We need to know how the working man thinks in order to present the gospel to him intelligibly and effectively. If the person to whom we speak is representative of the social group to which he belongs, he will have barriers in his thinking which seriously hinder his grasp of the gospel. Because of this we shall need to exercise a ministry like that of the prophet Jeremiah. God commissioned His servant 'to uproot and tear down,... to build and to plant' (Jer. 1:10). The weeds of ignorance, prejudice and fear will need to be uprooted so that the good seed of the gospel can be planted properly. The mental blockages of error, distortion and sentiment must be broken down before the foundation of truth can be laid.

In presenting the gospel to the working classes we must start from where the people are in their thinking, and then work from that point to explain the good news of Jesus Christ. This surely was the principle that Paul applied in his evangelistic work. It is particularly noticeable in his sermons to the pagan Gentiles. When the apostle performed a miracle of healing at Lystra, the locals seemed to go into a state of religious ecstasy. They cried out, 'The gods have come down to us in human form.' Paul could have wished for no clearer indication of their religious thinking. It was a golden opportunity to preach the gospel. Demolishing their beliefs that Paul and Barnabas were Hermes and Zeus, Paul then proceeded to build in their minds an understanding of the 'living God, who made heaven and earth and sea and everything in them' (Acts 14:8-18). Similarly, when Paul was at Athens, a city 'full of idols', their confessed ignorance of the true God provoked him to preach. He observed their altar inscribed 'To an unknown god' and then declared, 'What you worship as something unknown I am going to proclaim to you' (Acts 17: 16-31).

Working-class views of the church

Some indication of the nature and extent of the gap which exists between the working classes and the Christian church may be judged by three typical working-class views of the church.

'In so far as the working man thinks about the Church at all he sees it on the other side of the fence from where he stands. It represents another class, not necessarily one he hates; his circle is outside; it is the done thing for his group not to go to church, and he is seldom prepared to break with the commonly accepted practices of his mates. He identifies the Church with the suburbs, with a different way of life and a different kind of speech. He knows that the lay people who serve in the councils of the Church are not drawn from his class. If he remembers anything about religion at all, he thinks of it as a pious moralism, at most all right for the wife and kids, but not really of much significance for the world in which his life is set.'[11]

'Their attitude towards the Church is coloured by their stiff class-consciousness. Because of this they regard Christianity with suspicion for it is a mark of middle-class culture. Churches are cold, dark and dull, with people singing dull hymns, saying dull prayers and listening to unintelligible sermons. The language of Christianity is foreign — so are its practices, and its people. It is associated with being 'posh', snobbish, and educated. Christians are people who own cars, have money, and are weak, timid and sanctimonious. To become a Christian means becoming one of 'them', and there is a very strong feeling that this would mean betraying their class.'[12]

' "Hypocrisy" is the main epithet applied to those with church affiliation and it is almost universally maintained that those who do not attend church are as good as those who do. "You don't need to go to church to be a good Christian" is the nearest thing to a fundamental creed amongst working-class people. It may also be suggested that what goes on inside a church is out-of-date mumbo-jumbo. This puzzlement at liturgical complication is very genuine and particularly concerns the Church of England, in which every new ritual quirk or even reform devised by the clergy only deepens the conviction that this is not designed for people "such as us". '[13]

2.
In darkest England

The Old Testament prophet Ezekiel received his call and commission from God in unusual circumstances. As a young man of twenty-five, in training for the priesthood, he was taken along with 10,000 others into exile in the plains of Babylonia.

In the early days, away from their beloved Jerusalem, the exiles would lift one another's morale by speaking of the time when the captivity would end and they would return home. Rumour and gossip could always hope and see their return to the homeland 'just around the corner'. After several years, doubts and questionings about the imminent return began to seep into their thinking. When was God going to do something? When was God going to say something? How long could this state of affairs go on?

Then, in the fifth year of the exile, God did speak. The thirty-year-old Ezekiel, among the exiles by the Kebar river, experienced 'the heavens opened', and 'saw visions of God' (Ezek.1:1). What did God have to say? Had He fixed the date of the return? He had. But to Ezekiel's consternation the people's optimism had been unfounded. They had got it all wrong. There was not going to be any immediate return. The exile was going to go on and on and on. They would be in bondage for the rest of their lives. They would live there and they would die there. They would not see Jerusalem again.

Before Ezekiel could bring himself to open his mouth and proclaim this unwelcome news, he had to let the awful facts sink deep down into his sensitive soul. He says, 'I came to the exiles who lived at Tel Aviv near the Kebar River. And there, where they were living, I sat among them for seven days — overwhelmed (Ezek. 3:15). Too emotionally stunned to speak, Ezekiel just sat and stared and pondered the misery and despair which God's message would bring to his fellow countrymen. It took a whole week for the reality to sink in. He was 'overwhelmed'.

Any Christian who is at all concerned to reach the working classes with the gospel must come prepared to understand the situation with head and with heart. An academic and detached study of the problem is bound to come up with superficial answers. An ignorance of the real conditions in these areas, together with a shallow grasp of biblical principles, can be yet another recipe for discouragement. Ezekiel could speak to his fellow exiles with authority and understanding precisely because he came 'where they were living' and 'sat among them for seven days—overwhelmed'. The complexity and the magnitude of the church's missionary task in working-class areas cannot be understood and appreciated with feeling from outside.

The saving word of the gospel does not come to man in some kind of spiritual vacuum. It confronts him in his own particular circumstances and at a particular point in his earthly pilgrimage. The setting in which the gospel is addressed to a person's need is something we must examine. The apostle Paul's adherence to this scriptural principle is something he spells out clearly (1 Cor.9: 19-23). To disregard this requirement because it is 'not part of the gospel itself' is to fly in the face of Scripture.

Further, it is to reduce man to the level of a 'soul-computer' which merely needs to be 'programmed' with the right 'salvation formula'! The working man is already subject to many dehumanizing influences in his daily life. The good news of Jesus Christ should reverse, rather than reinforce, this trend. The working man needs to know that a personal God, who can be personally known, loves him as an individual, knows his name, and fully appreciates the situation in which his life is set.

The purpose of this part of our study is to provide a survey, historical and sociological, of the people for whom we are concerned. If we take time to ponder the way of life of working-class folk, past and present, and to appreciate their desperate spiritual and social needs, we shall, like Ezekiel, be overwhelmed. To the clear eye and the compassionate heart such a reaction is unavoidable.

The legacy of history: an unbridgeable gulf?

The general picture

One of the major works of historical research in our subject is the treatise of Bishop E.R. Wickham, *Church and People in an Industrial City*. Although the title of his work contains the word 'city', and much of his research relates to his immediate situation in Sheffield, his study also encompasses the national picture. A few selected references from his book will indicate the general picture from the onset of the Industrial Revolution to the present century.

Writing of the religious conditions in this country in the latter part of the eighteenth century, and also more particularly as they applied to Sheffield, Wickham says, 'We see also the artisan group with its own identity politically unformed but no longer aptly described as "the begging poor", and capable of an ugly mood towards the more privileged groups when prodded by adversity. Their *general estrangement from all the religious bodies* will become more apparent as we trace their expansion into the nineteenth century.'[1]

Concerning the situation in the mid-nineteenth century, he writes, 'The national picture at the mid-nineteenth century, painted as it must be with a large brush, is quite clear in outline — a return to the church on the part of the upper classes, not unrelated to the strict example in morality, social etiquette and evangelical piety set by the Queen and her Court; continued religious habits of the growing middle classes with some of the superior, or respectable, and individualistic of the artisan class, although different denominations correspond to different shades in this middling section of the social spectrum; and *the labouring class, itself, capable of cultural sub-division, generally outside all the religious institutions.*'[2]

During the second half of the nineteenth century the churches passed through years of religious boom, but in spite of this it had

In darkest England

to be admitted that 'in respect to the working-class population the churches had made negligible gain.'[3]

By the turn of the century trends began to change and boom passed into decline. Apart from the first few years of the twentieth century the trend has been unrelieved decline. Writing in the concluding chapter of his book, Wickham says, 'From the eighteenth century and progressively through the nineteenth century, since the emergence of the industrial towns and the working classes, the labouring poor, the artisan class, as a class and as adults, have been outside the churches.'[4]

Writing in 1902 Charles Booth says, 'The great section of the population which passes by the name of the working classes, lying socially between the lower middle class and the poor, remains, as a whole, outside of all the religious bodies, whether organized as churches or as missions; and those of them who do join any church become almost indistinguishable from the class with which they then mix, the change that has really come about is not so much *of* as *out of* the class to which they have belonged... But meanwhile the bulk of the regular wage-earning class still remain untouched, except that their children attend Sunday School.'[5]

A man for the masses

An accurate historical assessment of the relationship between the Christian church and the working classes must necessarily take into account the life and work of John Wesley. Bishop Wickham appears anxious not to over-credit the impact of the eighteenth-century Evangelical Awakening and its influence on the working classes. He speaks of early Methodism as a 'purely religious-revival movement' and goes on to say that, 'The contempt in which the early Methodists were held, both by those who were well-to-do and by the masses of the common folk, is sufficient evidence of the social insignificance of their body.'[6] Over against this estimate we need to set the findings of Robert Wearmouth who has produced several volumes on the history of Methodism with particular reference to its impact on the working classes.

Writing of the century in which Methodism was born, Wearmouth says, 'Methodism gained its greatest successes among the socially distressed and ostracized among the labouring masses. Never claiming to be a class or partisan movement, always emphasizing the universal love of God, its most urgent appeals were addressed to the common people, to the multitudes who were as sheep without a shepherd. Methodist preachers and evangelists went out into the highways and byways to minister to the forsaken and the destitute, the poor and the neglected. The higher classes in English society were scarcely touched by Methodist influence but *the working men and women were profoundly affected.*'[7]

The locations and the occupations in which Methodism gained its earliest successes are detailed by John Wesley in his *Journal*: 'Societies sprang up particularly among the artisan and labouring classes of the manufacturing districts in the North-East, among the workers in the textile industries of the north Midlands and the West Riding, in the Potteries, among the Cornish tin miners and the domestic craftsmen of the West Country woollen trade, in seaports and fishing villages, and in agricultural areas characterized by extensive freeholding. Tradesmen, soldiers, and small manufacturers were potential Methodist recruits.'[8]

Even after the death of John Wesley in 1791 Methodism continued to go from strength to strength. By the middle of the next century it could be claimed that 'In spite of conflict and division within, together with opposition from various sources without, the *registered members of 1850 were six times greater than in 1800*. No other movement at the time showed such a continuous success. While it had practically no effect upon the upper portions of the community, its influence on the lower sections was almost phenomenal.'[9]

After the mid-nineteenth century the story is one of declining influence. 'From the middle years of the century, according to a Wesleyan historian, Wesleyan Methodism entered its mahogany age.' A rise in the wealth and social standing of many Methodists tended to carry the movement away from those among whom it had experienced its earlier successes.

We may justly use the word 'success' to describe the achievements of early Methodism. That is not exaggeration. These major advances in the work of the gospel were due to the sovereign power of God working in revival and also to the scriptural policies adopted by those human instruments through whom God chose to manifest His power. Any attempt to overcome the enduring alienation of the working classes from the Christian church must take careful note of the principles upon which John Wesley founded and directed the church life of the early Methodists. We shall return to John Wesley later in our study.

What about the Baptists?

Of particular interest to the writer is the question: 'Where do Baptists stand in the league table of concern for the working classes?'

In her book *Evangelicals in Action* (an appraisal of the social work of evangelicals in the Victorian era), Kathleen Heasman credits Baptists with no small achievement: 'In a very general way the different Evangelical denominations tended to appeal to certain social classes. The evangelical Church of England and probably also the Plymouth Brethren, though their numbers were very small in comparison, consisted mostly of middle-class people. Both the Congregationalists and the Presbyterians, with their intellectual approach, attracted people who had been successful in trade or industry and the lower ranks of the professions... *Only the Baptists,* whose tabernacles were to be found in the leading thoroughfares of the poorer districts, *and the Methodists,* who appealed largely to newcomers to the industrial areas, *attracted large numbers of the working class.*'[10]

Hugh McLeod, in his *Class and Religion in the late Victorian City,* would concur with Kathleen Heasman's assessment: 'The largest number of "converted working men" was probably to be found among the Baptists, who had a large lower middle-class membership and a few distinctly wealthy chapels, but also a considerable working-class element in most of their chapels. Though a few of the leading Baptists, such as John Clifford, were distinctly liberal Evangelicals, the "orthodoxy" of the denomination as a whole was proverbial: thus Charles Masterman, in a catalogue of suburban personalities drawn up in 1909, referred to "the Baptist chapel", where "the minister maintains the old doctrines of hell and heaven, and wrestles with the sinner for his immortal soul", and Charles Booth, saying much the same thing in less urbane language, reported that a sermon by Charles Spurgeon junior "was filled with all the usual crudities of the Baptist views". From the point of view of the working-class convert, the "usual crudities" were "the gospel", with no milk-and-water modern modifications, and the Baptist chapel provided the comradeship of men like himself who proudly proclaimed the 'old, old story of Jesus and His love', while middle-class neologists flinched and workshop bullies sneered.'[11]

Before we devour these crumbs of comfort too quickly, we need to set alongside the foregoing assessments the estimate of Charles Masterman. A Fellow of Christ's College, Cambridge, he was given the task of interpreting the statistics obtained through the Religious Census of 1903, and particularly as they applied to South London. His assessment concluded that, 'The working man does not come to church. A few communities of Primitive Methodists, Baptists and Salvationists, and similar bodies, as a general rule represent his contribution to the religious life of the nation ... The tradesmen and the middle class of the poorer boroughs exhibit an active religious life mainly gathered in larger Nonconformist bodies, especially the Baptists.'[12]

Since the Metropolitan Tabernacle church is located within that part of London which Masterman was analysing, it might be wondered how far C.H. Spurgeon was effective in reaching the working classes. For the duration of his ministry in London (1854 — 1892) his world-wide impact was nothing less than staggering: 'When a general census of church attendance was taken on an ordinary Sunday in London in 1886, the total congregations at the Metropolitan Tabernacle, morning and evening, exceeded 10,000 people! ... So great was the popularity of his sermons that one time there was even an attempt made, without Spurgeon's leave, to cable the Sunday morning sermon to America for publication in Monday's papers. By 1899 over a hundred million of his sermons had been issued in twenty-three languages.'[13]

Without doubt among his regular congregation 'large numbers of the working class' were present. And yet, in spite of this, Spurgeon is reputed to have said of Walworth (a densely populated and predominantly working-class community within the immediate catchment area of the Tabernacle) that it was 'breaking his heart'. Long before his death Spurgeon discerned an adversely changing religious climate. In his opinion, 'Compared with what it used to be, it is hard to win attention to the Word of God. I used to think that we had only to preach the gospel, and the people would throng to hear it. I fear I must correct my belief under this head ... We all feel that a hardening process is going on among the masses. In this vast city, we have street after street where the people are living utterly regardless of the worship of God. Those who attend church or chapel are marked men; and if you were to enquire for them, they would be pointed out to you as remarkable individuals ... It is a fact that thousands of persons live close to our notable sanctuaries, and never dream of entering them.'[14]

Iain Murray, in his book *The Forgotten Spurgeon*, draws our attention to a further aspect of biblical realism which became all too apparent to Spurgeon in the declining situation: 'Robertson Nicoll's idea that there was a kind of natural affinity between the working-class masses of South London and a firm Calvinism, is one which no one born in the twentieth century would care to own. Spurgeon himself would have disowned it.'[15]

What conclusion may we draw if we gather these observations together? At the turn of the century, after the death of Spurgeon in 1892, Baptist influence was considerable. Numerically, the 1903 census showed them to be the strongest of all the Free Churches both in Inner London and Greater London. Compared with other church bodies, their efforts and achievements were commendable. Even so, Baptist work and witness made no serious and sustained inroads into the *general alienation* of the working classes from the Christian church.

The true perspective

Apart from the achievements of John Wesley and the early Methodists, the Christian church has failed to bridge the gulf which separates it from the working classes of this country. It is easy to be wise after the event and, from our vantage point of a two-hundred-year history of the British working classes, to say what the Christian church ought to have done and ought not to have done. Of course, more could have been attempted, but a great deal that was done has now largely passed from view and memory.

During the nineteenth century a great variety of Christian initiatives took place with the specific aim of bringing the gospel to working-class people. Some of these ventures were exclusively evangelistic in emphasis, others combined gospel outreach with social concern. Among the better known of these endeavours were the 'Missions' (e.g.London City Mission, South London Mission, Tower Hamlets Mission, the Navy Mission, the

Railway Mission, Cabmen's Mission, etc.), the Settlements, (e.g. Toynbee Hall and others), Labour Churches, the Ragged School movements and the Pleasant Sunday Afternoon movement, to name but a few.

The most notable of these ventures was the Salvation Army. Beginning with an experiment in Whitechapel in 1865, the Salvation Army really became established in 1880. William and Catherine Booth had special reasons for creating this novel evangelistic agency. 'They created the Salvation Army because they were convinced that the poor could be made Christians only (as Mrs Booth put it) "by people of their own class, who would go after them in their own resorts, who would speak to them in a language they understood, and reach them by means suited to their own tastes". This conclusion was reached by the Booths only after wide experience in several Methodist sects.'[16] 'Nobody in Victorian England did more than Booth to put unconventional methods into the service of conventional Christianity. If he and his followers had not been so charged with passion to fill the gap between the churches and the masses, they could not have achieved the empire that was theirs by the time the founder died in 1912. It was clear long before then, however, that not even he had shown (in a phrase he loved) how to reach the masses with the gospel.'[17]

There is one final point which needs clarification before we complete this part of our historical survey. How is it possible to claim that the 'Baptists ... attracted large numbers of the working class' and then later to say that 'Baptist work and witness made no serious and sustained inroads into the general alienation of the working classes from the Christian church'? Is there not a contradiction here? Can these two statements be reconciled?

There is an explanation. In order to get a true estimate of working-class church-going two questions need to be asked. First, how many of the working class do attend church? Second, how many of the working class do *not* attend church? Church attendance expressed as a proportion of the total population provides a clear indication of the extent of working-class estrangement from the Christian church. For example, referring again to the 1903 Religious Census figures for South London, Masterman calculated that the figure of adult church attendance in Walworth, by the 'working-class people and the poor' of that area, was about 2% of the local community whereas, in a suburban area of Dulwich and Sydenham (only a few miles out from Walworth) church attendance was 30% of the community.[18] If these figures are substantially correct then it is true to say that the *proportion* of the local community attending church in the suburban middle-class area was *at least ten times* that of the local community in a working-class area. The disparity between the two levels of church attendance is very great, based on the figures we have indicated. However, the true perspective is not obtained until we also take into account the *total population* figures of the areas being compared. This will also explain how it is possible for 'large numbers of the working class' to be attending church even though the proportion of the local *adult* community was probably as low as 2%. With a population of around 99,000, Walworth had treble the population of the Dulwich-Sydenham area.

Inner-city areas today are densely populated compared with suburban areas. But at the turn of the century these areas housed some two to three times the population they do now![19] Post-war tower-block estates house less than half the number accommodated in the tightly-packed streets of small terraced houses and tenement buildings in which the working class lived at the beginning of the century. Observers in the inner-city churches at that time might have drawn the conclusion that Britain was a Christian country. Suburban churches were well attended. Inner-city churches could also number their congregations in hundreds. The fact that the inner-city churches were largely supported by people who formerly lived in those areas but had now moved out to a 'better area' might have escaped the notice of our observers. A glance at a church congregation could easily lead to a false conclusion. But a glimpse into the streets and homes which surrounded these well-attended churches would speedily have dispelled the false notion. 'Most of the families who lived in the crowded back streets were poor working people. They lived in small four-roomed houses, "two up and two down", but often, although they were large families, they had to take lodgers in the upstairs rooms to make ends meet.'[20]

The alienation of the Christian church from the local adult population was almost total. The hope and promise, signalled by the existence of many flourishing works among children and young people, failed to materialize. The churches grew weaker, rather than stronger. They had failed to find or provide a 'bridge' whereby growing teenagers could cross over from interested adolescence to committed adult Christianity. Here were the pagan masses. This was darkest England. The 'unbridgeable gulf' remains. The task which faces today's Christians is nothing short of overwhelming.

Exploring and explaining the unbridgeable gulf

The 'river of alienation' which separates the Christian church from the working classes continues to flow on in full spate. Its origins can be traced back beyond the emergence of the Industrial Revolution. Its course and character have been influenced by a variety of factors — industrial, social, economic, political and spiritual. Our purpose now is to take a brief conducted tour along the banks of that river so that we may identify certain features of its historical landscape. This should help us to understand better how we have arrived at 'the gulf' which confronts us today. In the previous section we sought to establish the *existence* of the gulf. Our aim now will be to discover *the reasons* for this gulf.

Our method of investigation will be to indicate trends, rather than events, which have a bearing on the purpose of our excursion. No attempt will be made to arrange these topics in strict chronological order, although it will be evident that some of them occurred at the onset of the Industrial Revolution, while others emerged prior to, or during the Victorian era. Since the emergence and development of evangelical Nonconformity is a dominant ecclesiastical feature of the period we are considering, our observations will be conducted primarily from the perspective of dissent rather than that of the Establishment.

Before we set off on our 'guided tour', some comments on the matter of Christian doctrine are appropriate. Belief determines behaviour. What we think conditions how we act. Applied to the history of the church and the working classes, this means that behind the historical events and trends that can be observed, there lie particular emphases or neglect of Christian doctrine. It is difficult to categorize and quantify the impact that these doctrines had on the relationship between the church and the working classes, in particular, as compared with that on the relationship between the church and society in general throughout this period. For example, during the mid-nineteenth century there was a resurgence of Romanism which led to the defection to Rome of a number of major figures in the Anglican Church - for example, John Henry Newman and Henry Manning, to name but two. This doctrinal change affected the relationship between the Church of England and the working classes. The High Churchmen of the Tractarian Movement, as it was called, had a particular concern for the needs of the poorer urban areas. Their success among the working classes, limited as it was, can be traced to 'compassion' and 'colour'. They had a genuine compassion for the masses, and their accent in worship was upon the visual rather than the verbal. It is said that the colour and movement of High Church worship has a particular appeal for the working classes, whose lives were continually surrounded by what was dull and drab.

A further example of doctrinal change was that which emerged in the final quarter of the nineteenth century. Incipient liberalism posed a major threat to historic evangelicalism. New views about the Scripture began to be expressed. The significance of the 'inspiration' of Scripture was questioned. The meaning of the atonement was challenged. The doctrine of eternal punishment was undermined. These views, which can all be traced back to a defective view of Scripture, were those against which C.H. Spurgeon fought in the 'Downgrade' controversy in the last few years of his life. Late nineteenth-century evangelicalism was seriously weakened by these inroads of alien thought. To what extent this had repercussions on the witness of the churches among the working classes it is difficult to say. The deviations which emerged and developed in the latter part of the nineteenth century paved the way for a more general doctrinal flux in the twentieth century.

A mine of valuable and very detailed information for our excursion has been the book *Religion and Society in Industrial England* by Dr A.D. Gilbert. I am grateful for permission to quote from his work. In this section of our study, except where otherwise stated, all quotations in the text are attributable to Dr Gilbert. It has been possible to identify *twelve* factors which have 'in some way affected the force and flow of the river of alienation'.

Progressive industrialization

The change from an agrarian to an industrial society had many repercussions. The comparatively stable order of an agrarian society, with its occupational and economic dependence on the land and its social structure built around the manorial system, had to give way to an entirely new pattern of occupational and residential relationships determined by the needs and the potential of the new industrial society. The geographical redistribution of the population continued steadily and irreversibly. 'The proportion of the population engaged in non-agricultural occupations had risen from around twenty per cent at the end of the seventeenth century to well over fifty per cent by the beginning of the nineteenth. It was sixty-five per cent in 1811 and over seventy per cent in 1831.'[21]

The rapid expansion of manufacturing and mining industries in the last quarter of the eighteenth century required a similar rapid expansion of the labour force in the midland and northern regions of Lancashire, Cheshire, Nottinghamshire, Leicestershire, Northumberland, Durham, Yorkshire, Derbyshire, Warwickshire and Staffordshire. It was in these areas and among their fast-growing social groups that the Church of England found itself ill-equipped to cope with the responsibilities and challenges that these situations presented. During this period as Anglicanism declined, nonconformity achieved remarkable expansion. But even nonconformity, which had its chief impact on artisans with strong links with pre-industrial economic patterns, was later to discover that factory workers in the industrial cities were much more difficult to mobilize than craftsmen employed in domestic industry.

Although the gulf between the Christian church and the industrial workers became increasingly apparent, it would be wrong to imagine that an agrarian society was necessarily, by nature, any more religious than the industrial society that followed it. David Martin observes that, 'Most people suppose that our comparative indifference to religious practice nowadays has its root in the effects of the industrial revolution. Substantially they are right. Yet the evidence is conflicting. Rural societies are not necessarily given to unanimous practice, as many areas of disaffection in the nineteenth-century France show, and we know that the overgrown bulk of London harboured indifference as well as heresy even in the 'religious' seventeenth century. Indeed, the historian Christopher Hill has suggested that in the seventeenth century the very lowest social strata were largely outside both Church and Dissent.'[22]

Urban revolution

Urbanization and industrialization were virtually two sides of the same coin. The change from a mainly rural society to a predominantly urban society brought unavoidable social upheaval. Traditional authority structures began to disintegrate and social cohesion tended to break down. Forsaking the rural life with its smaller and more stable communities, many families came to the developing towns in the hope of better wages and increasing prosperity. But they could not have known beforehand what life would be like in the 'relatively unstructured world of the industrial shanty town or industrial city'.

'Organized religion', as it is sometimes called, and urbanization have not proved to be compatible. Almost invariably, since the onset of urbanization, where the populations are greatest, there the churches are weakest, rural areas excepted. Is there an explanation why this is so? A sense of community proved difficult to establish in the densely populated urban areas. In the smaller rural communities there was a sense of belonging and members of the community knew one another by name. But these social assets were forfeited in the move to the cities. Instant community could not be created anywhere. But the new 'mass' aggregations of people in the expanding urban areas found it the most difficult of all. The socially monochrome nature of these developing areas also highlighted another social asset that had been forfeited in the move from the rural communities with their variety of classes and cultures. The loose aggregations of the urban people lacked natural leaders able to develop a sense of community. The inhabitants of these areas did not form coherent communities which could be mobilized to sustain local churches.

The day of the big city had arrived. In 1695 when the population of England and Wales was 5,200,000, that of London was 500,000. Only Norwich and Bristol had populations over 25,000. Birmingham with 12,000 people was the only other city with over 10,000 inhabitants. By 1750 Liverpool, Birmingham and Manchester each had populations in the region of 25,000 but the period of rapid growth in population size was yet to come.

The process of urbanization, we have contended, involved considerable population movements from the older rural areas to the new expanding urban areas. This seems a reasonable explanation of the way that the urban areas gained a rapid increase in population. However, this view is challenged by Peter Lane in his book *The Industrial Revolution*. He claims, 'We know that in the second half of the eighteenth century there was a continual and rapid growth in the population of England's industrial towns. In the past this rise has been explained by a "migration of labour from the countryside to the town in search of employment". We know now that there was little such migration; indeed we know that the population of the rural areas did not decline at the time when the population of the industrial centres was rising. What appears to have happened is that there was a higher than average increase in the birth rate in the industrial centres.'[23]

It is difficult to know how much weight to put on this claim. There seems to be some lack of synchronization in his case. He points to the rapid growth of industrial towns in the second half of the eighteenth century. The chief reason given for this is a 'higher than average increase in the birth rate'. But that does not appear to harmonize with the population growth statistics. In the sixteenth and seventeenth centuries the rate of population growth was slow. It also remained slow during the eighteenth century when the social process of urbanization advanced considerably. The *rapid increase* in birth rate did not appear until the dawn of the *nineteenth* century. The population of England and Wales doubled between 1801 and 1851 and again between 1851 and 1901.

Ecclesiastical inflexibility

At the onset of the Industrial Revolution the Church of England found itself seriously handicapped by a parochial machinery designed to function satisfactorily in an agrarian society, but unsuited to meet the needs of a population progressively being redistributed according to the evolving social pattern of the new industrial society. It took several decades for the unwelcome truth to sink in. It was several more decades into the nineteenth century before a constructive response was forthcoming. The

Established Church had lost the monopoly position. Its structures were proving more and more anachronistic. Its role had to change. But that was easier said than done. In the relatively stable pre-industrial society the Church of England had not only catered for the religious needs of the people; it had also acted as a conservative and integrative influence within the nation.

'In the new industrial areas, where the Church of England lost physical contact with large sections of the population of early industrial England, the great problem was the lack of *proximity* to potential adherents. But in many rural parishes where proximity was no problem the Establishment faced the problem of widespread alienation among its nominal constituents.'[24]

These changed social and spiritual conditions of the early industrial period were pressurizing the Church of England towards a changed role in society. But it was not until the 1830s that Anglicanism became sufficiently motivated, or desperate, to initiate reforms which were appropriate to the changes that had occurred. Eventually, reforms were implemented. They concerned matters of parochial reorganization — the creation of new parishes and the sub-division of unwieldy and over-populated parishes, financial rationalization of the parochial system, a church-building programme, a major recruitment of more clergy and a re-examination of their parochial and pastoral duties. As a result of these reforms, the Victorian parochial system functioned far more effectively than the 'system' had done in the early industrial period. But it must also be said that urban parishes still proved difficult to operate.

Social migration

A term which has come into the vocabulary of the 'science of missions' is the word 'lift'. It is associated with the phenomenon of upward social mobility, but the term itself describes the social and cultural estrangement of members of a religious group from the social environment in which they were recruited. David Martin says, 'In most of the Nonconforming bodies we can trace a process whereby they have evangelized a segment of the less prestigious social strata (usually not the very lowest) and have then lifted this segment to a higher position on the social scale. This process has sometimes emasculated their capacity to repeat the task of evangelization, so that a new group has been needed to repeat the process a second and a third time. Thus the Salvation Army partly took over from the Methodists and the Pentecostalists from the Salvation Army.'[25]

As the years passed the social process of 'lift' was to have serious consequences for the Christians and the churches in industrial areas. 'Lift' appeared to trigger a number of unwelcome trends in the realm of evangelism. Aggressive *outreach* steadily waned. This was replaced by 'a concentration of evangelistic activity among people already on the peripheries of organized religion'. Lay involvement in gospel witness declined. What had been the general responsibility of all believers gradually became the particular speciality of the minister. The chief area of evangelistic effort changed progressively from adults to children. As we shall see, 'lift' also had repercussions on the style of worship and in church life generally.

Religious formalism

In the early industrial period evangelical Nonconformity was characterized by three particular features: the priority of aggressive evangelism, the importance of itinerant and open-air preaching and the heavy reliance on laymen in the overall evangelistic strategy. In time, however, the earlier enthusiasm noticeably cooled as the process of social migration continued. By the beginning of the Victorian era some marked changes had occurred in the general character of Nonconformity. David Martin points to the seeds of spiritual decline which almost inevitably appear to be associated with social migration. He says, 'A correlative process has involved cooling of religious zeal and an intrusion of formality, perhaps even of high culture.'[26]

'This tendency towards professionalization and institutional order gradually altered the essential character of the Wesleyan movement during the period between 1791, when John Wesley died, and the 1840s.'[27]

Patterns of worship, methods of evangelism, the respective roles of ministry and laity were all deeply affected by this trend towards formalization. As these changes came, church life generally became more a matter of organization than organism. The preoccupation with 'order, respectability and style' tended to accentuate the gap between the Nonconformist churches and the social groups from which their members had formerly been recruited. As the spiritual temperature fell it became increasingly difficult for the churches to avoid the glacial slopes towards spiritual decline and decay. The warning signs were there. The route to extinction was plainly marked: evangelize, catechize, popularize, institutionalize, fossilize!

Ministerial professionalism

The trend to religious formalism within evangelical Nonconformity inevitably had its effect upon the ministers of the churches. When the industrial age dawned the churches were generally outward-looking and ministers were chiefly involved in equipping and mobilizing the laity to carry the gospel forward on a wide front. By 1840 a distinct change had come about in the respective roles of the ministers and the laity. In the early days of the rapid advance in evangelical Nonconformity the churches were characterized by aggressive outreach and their ministers might have been described as 'rugged'. By the onset of the Victorian age the churches were becoming progressively inward-looking and their ministers might then be described as 'refined'. Just as social migration gave the impetus towards religious formalism, so this religious formalism gave the impetus towards a change in the role and character of the Christian ministry. The 'vocation' became a 'profession'. 'Enthusiasm' gave way to 'expertise'.

Dr Gilbert tells us how the Nonconformist church member viewed this changed role of the minister and how he, as a church member, was affected by it: 'He tended to become less and less preoccupied with the prospect of sharing in the evangelistic, pastoral or liturgical functions of the chapel community; his basic values and expectations altered in subtle but important ways, and far from resenting ministerial specialization in religious matters, he welcomed it. There was a change, in short, in the character of his commitment, and it was reflected in a heightened regard for orderliness, taste, refinement, and for a minimum of old-fashioned "enthusiasm".'[28]

The colleges preparing men for the ministry were necessarily directly affected by the aspirations of the churches, and this affected what was expected of the ministers. In assessing and developing the spiritual gifts of men submitting for preparation for pastoral ministry, less and less emphasis was placed upon the need for plain and powerful preaching and consecrated pastoral care. Increasingly the emphasis was on a man's ability to lead 'dignified' worship, to preach erudite sermons, to cultivate a 'theologically informed' congregation, and generally to produce 'refined and respectable' Christians.

The 'professionalization' of the Nonconformist ministry only served to widen the gulf between the churches and the alienated working classes. Kathleen Heasman says, 'Charles Booth was of the opinion that the average working man would have little to do with church or chapel, not because he really believed in free thought, but because he despised the professionalism of the clergy, the class consciousness of the conventional church or chapel-goer, and the benevolence of the social worker.'[29]

Introverted evangelism

Operating in parallel with the changing roles of ministers and laymen, a marked change can be detected in the focus and the importance of evangelism. As the social process of 'lift' continued, the churches became increasingly distanced from the social constituency in which they had gained their earlier recruits. This common trend placed the churches in something of a dilemma. Should they now turn their evangelistic endeavours towards the social group with which they were newly identified? Or should they, as a matter of Christian duty, still attempt to evangelize the social group from which they had come, and which it was all too easy to abandon?

There were no easy answers. Often there could be a failure on both counts. Some churches found themselves unable to evangelize the more prestigious social strata with which they were newly aligned and in which they had yet to feel fully 'at home'. Other churches found they were losing the battle to stay in touch with the social group of their own origin. For those willing to face facts squarely there was inevitably a responsibility to walk an evangelistic tightrope.

There was nothing essentially wrong in the social process of 'lift'. At best it could be curbed or slowed in order to give realistic attention to the demands of evangelism in the working-class communities. Dr Gilbert puts his finger upon the very careful course that had to be steered. He says, 'Only when a religious body can recruit new members quickly enough to retain much of its original social character can *lift* be combined with continued recruitment from its original constituency. In

Evangelical Nonconformity, for example, although, as Wesley recognized, *lift* was occurring well before the end of the eighteenth century, recruitment from artisans, mining and labouring sections of the population was continuing unchecked. It began to diminish significantly only in the late 1820s and 1830s when the vigorous itinerancy — lay as well as clerical, chapel-based as well as connexional — which had been the instrument of early Nonconformist recruiting was either abandoned or adapted to other ends, notably to pastoral supervision rather than evangelism, and to the recruitment of children rather than adults.'[30]

Churches which failed to apply the policy we have just outlined tended to become introverted in their work of evangelism. The tendency to give increasing attention to reaching children with the gospel, and particularly the children of church members, is an understandable policy where there is a general inability to evangelize adults in the working-class communities. 'Reaching the most reachable' is certainly a positive approach and infinitely better than doing nothing.

However, what became an acceptable spiritual expedient for the immediate situation in Victorian working-class neighbourhoods was not necessarily appropriate as a longer-term evangelistic policy for the same areas. What began as an expedient became established as a tradition. This evolving pattern of local church evangelism became the established practice carried into the twentieth century. 'There was a definite trend during the period from around the beginning of the Victorian era to the First World War, as the crisis of plausibility weakened the religious *a priori* of the wider society, for the effective evangelistic activities of the churches to be confined increasingly to internal constituencies. This shift to endogenous growth both reflected and accentuated the widening cultural gap between the Church and the "world".'[31]

The progressively introverted evangelism of the Victorian age did not augur well for the future. The zealous evangelizing of church members' children, other young people, adherents and all in the general church 'fringe' category, though wearing an appearance of success, was not to bring the results it seemed to promise. A flourishing work among the young in one generation is no guarantee of a thriving adult church in the next, as twentieth-century churches in working-class communities were later to discover.

Cultural estrangement

At the commencement of the Victorian age we can detect an ever-widening cultural gulf between the working classes and the Christian church in England, both Establishment and dissent. Anglican decline had been halted and reversed, but the encouragement which such a trend ought to have provided needed to be tempered by the recognition that this advance had been achieved largely within a particular 'culture-class' category, rather than through a more general progress among all social groups.

Contrasted with Anglican decline and recovery, we find that Nonconformity had made remarkable progress and particularly among the social category from which Anglicanism was most estranged. The achievement of Nonconformity was notable, not only because its impact was chiefly among the industrial workers, but also because it occurred at a time when there was a rapid increase in the size of the British population. In 1741 the population of England and Wales was 6,013,000 but by the year 1841 the population had risen to no less than 15,914,000.

As the early industrial period passed and the Victorian age dawned, changes in religious culture patterns began to appear. Whereas previously the Church of England and Nonconformity had tended to tread divergent cultural paths, the Victorian years signalled a converging of their cultural ways. Anglican links with the Victorian middle classes improved the quantitative position of the church. But, at the same time, evangelical Nonconformity had arrived at a position in which it was no longer prepared to play a Cinderella role. Was not the grown-up sister, Nonconformity, also entitled to be interested in the matters of taste, refinement, style, order and respectability? 'The very success of the struggle for religious equality provided Nonconformists with increased access to the social, educational, and political rewards of the wider society; and the higher levels of social status and material comfort typical of denominations experiencing *lift* brought with it new opportunities for "worldliness".'[32]

As Anglicanism successfully wooed the Victorian middle classes, so evangelical Nonconformity was similarly drawn to court their affections as well. Anglicanism saw the links with the middle classes as a privilege to which it was rightly entitled. Nonconformity saw these links with the middle classes as a new prize to be zealously pursued. Thereby, both the Establishment and dissent accentuated and deepened the cultural estrangement of the Christian church from the working classes. The significance of this estrangement becomes more apparent when we remember that, whereas there was an erosion of the strength of middle-class churches through the secularizing influences of the late nineteenth century, the dawn of the twentieth century has witnessed an ever-increasing influence of working-class cultural values reflected by, and reinforced through, the instrumentality of the popular media.

Economic parochialism

In the early industrial period there were those within Anglicanism who envied the freedom and adaptability of the younger, more vigorous and more flexible evangelical Nonconformity. The Church of England soldiered on into the nineteenth century with a growing awareness of the need for some reform of its structures. But, with the passing of time, there were those in Nonconformity who envied a particular feature of Anglicanism.

From the 1830s onwards, the Church of England developed a greater rationality of its financial administration. New work was initiated and established in urban areas. The commencement of the new causes in these areas was justified on the grounds of need rather than on the ability of a local cause to finance its own operations. This 'denominational' or 'inter-church' policy could be implemented because the Church of England, as a national body, was able to direct funds and personnel to industrial causes without too much regard to the availability of local finance. Evangelical Nonconformity did not have the same facility within its own approach to financial matters. Free Church principles, defending the autonomy of the local church, tended to emphasize the 'independence' rather than a voluntary 'interdependence' of the local companies of believers. This made it much more difficult for Nonconformity to inaugurate and sustain a Christian witness in the industrial locations.

'As the overhead costs of maintaining Nonconformist operations rose throughout the Victorian era, the tendency was for the denominations to flourish only where there was a clientele economically capable of supporting a minister and his family, and of acquiring a chapel sufficiently elegant to satisfy middle-class tastes and expectations.'[33]

During the same period the concern for chapel-building tended to direct money to material ends, and this necessarily limited the availability of finance to be used for the specifically spiritual purpose of support for Christian workers in the urban situations. 'Because it depended on the availability of considerable financial resources, the effect of chapel-building was to concentrate Nonconformist activities: it inhibited the kind of expansion characteristic of the early industrial 'religion of barns', and it threatened the survival of congregations too poor or too small to finance a chapel-building programme. Two recurrent themes in the councils of Victorian Nonconformity were the decline of Nonconformist representation in rural areas, and the failure of the movement to establish itself in the poorer districts of large cities.'[34]

Recreational diversions

As we have already noted, the rugged and outgoing Nonconformity with which the nineteenth century began changed in character as time progressed. By the end of the century a more refined and inward-looking Nonconformity had taken its place. When the nineteenth century dawned zealous believers were chiefly concerned for the *spiritual* welfare of those who were as yet outside their ranks. But the spiritual temperature cooled with the passing of the years. At the close of the period a more restrained Nonconformity paid much more attention to the *social* welfare of those already within its fold. The pagan masses were left largely undisturbed by this more 'respectable' brand of the Christian faith which preferred to look after its own interests rather than intrude its message into the lives of the multitudes who so far had shown no inclination to take the gospel seriously — neither the benefits it offered nor the claims that it made.

'Charles Booth in the 1890s and R. Mudie-Smith in 1902-03 observed that in London the social and recreational activities of Nonconformist communities often flourished and expanded while the services catering for the 'essentially spiritual' interests of the laity virtually disappeared. In a host of ways, from the establishment of denominational sporting clubs, music societies, debating groups, excursion and holiday associations, and similar ventures, to an increasing emphasis on entertainment in specifically religious services, the tendency was for Churches to cater for the new expectations of their members by attempting to compete with the burgeoning entertainment industries of the wider society.'[35]

C.H. Spurgeon observed this trend among Nonconformist churches with grave concern. He said, 'Another great evil of the times is the insatiable craving for amusements. That men should have rest from labour, and that they should enjoy such amusements as refresh both body and mind, nobody wishes to deny. Within suitable bounds, recreation is necessary and profitable; but it was never the business of the Christian Church to supply the world with amusements.'[36]

Spurgeon was not opposed to amusements as such. What he could not tolerate was the incongruous association of the 'trivial' with the 'eternal'. He cites a church which had organized a social evening with its 'various silly dissipations' as an introduction to a 'series of special services'. He castigated another church which advertised, with a special poster for a special occasion, a 'Punch and Judy show' next week! It was in this late Victorian period that the 'magic lantern' made its first appearance among the churches. There seems little doubt that the instrument was introduced more for its entertainment value than its evangelistic potential.

Undisguised snobbery

Many church-goers during the Victorian years seemed to be either unaware of or unconcerned with the warning of James, the brother of our Lord. He says, 'My brothers, as believers in our glorious Lord Jesus Christ, don't show favouritism' (James 2:1). It is unrealistic to pretend that social distinctions do not exist, but in no way should they intrude into the life of the church and prove a hindrance to fellowship.

Kathleen Heasman observes, 'The Evangelical Revival of the eighteenth century had left its imprint upon English society. Victorian middle-class families, with their large households of children and servants, all followed a very similar pattern of living. Each member, whether master or servant, had his own particular position with its appropriate duties and responsibilities, but together they presented a united front to the world. Such things as family prayers and family anniversaries held them together. They clung strictly to a system of rigid class distinction which had few dealings with a class below themselves, except in a spirit of benevolence and sometimes, unfortunately, of condescension.'[37]

K.S. Inglis confirms the foregoing observation: 'Pew rents, the rarity of working-class stewards and deacons, and the silent demand for middle-class dress were admitted by some Nonconformists to be signs that worshippers were unwilling to accept artisans and labourers and their families among them on terms of social equality.'[38]

Social injustice

'Am I my brother's keeper?' protested the guilty Cain when he denied knowledge of the condition of his brother Abel whom he had murdered. 'The Lord said, "What have you done? Listen! Your brother's blood cries out to me from the ground!"' (Gen. 4:10.) At the dawn of the twentieth century, how far were the Christians and the churches in the developing suburbs aware of obligations to their urban brothers? There can be guilt by omission, just as much as by commission. James, the Lord's brother, tells us, 'Anyone...who knows the good he ought to do and doesn't do it, sins' (James 4:17). Immediately following that statement, James exposes and condemns the harsh oppression and neglect shown by the rich farmers against their vulnerable and powerless workers. Such was the extent of their neglect that James charged the farmers with being implicated in the crime of murder (James 5:1-6). The vehemence of James' condemnation (5:1) of these employers is a reflection of God's deep concern for all who are the victims of exploitation and oppression (Exod. 1:11-14: 5:6- 6:8.)

For an application of this teaching to our present study, the Lord's question to Cain, with a minor alteration, needs to be put to the steadily expanding number of suburban Christians at the beginning of this century. 'What have you *not* done? Listen! Your urban brother's blood cries out to me from the ground of the inner city.'

C.F.G. Masterman describes the general outlook of what he calls '*suburban religion*' at the time. 'It upholds a decent life and a clean moral standard, with much individual personal piety. But it is far too content to limit its outlook to its own family or church, heedless of the great chaos of confusion and failure which lies at its very doors. It regards with disapproval and often with contempt this world of poverty with its dumb demand for aid; it is generous in charity, but no appeal for justice in the name of the forgotten poor goes forth with united voice from the churches of South London. It is content to cultivate its own garden, to save its own soul; it is loth to identify its interests with those of its less successful neighbours ... It draws the line tight round its border, and endeavours to satisfy with missions and gifts of money the obligation of personal service and of a campaign for justice to all the desolate and oppressed ... If the prevailing type of religion largely withers before such forces as these, (e.g. materialism, hedonism, and biblical criticism) it will be because it has set itself apart in comfort, content with a personal creed of salvation; because it has felt no passionate impulses to assert a common fellowship with the less fortunate who are lying at its doors — no call to right the wrongs which ... "cry continually into the ears of the Lord God of Sabaoth".'[39]

The twelve factors we have identified in our excursion constitute the major influences which have determined the course and character of the 'river of alienation'. But there were, in addition, many lesser matters which cumulatively also exerted a significant influence.

David Martin draws together a fascinating diversity of factors which contributed to the continuing gulf between the churches and the working classes in Victorian London. With this comprehensive summary, the historical part of our study is nearly at an end.

'Nobody could suppose this failure was due to lack of trying. The story of Christianity in London at this period is one of extraordinary activity and heroic overwork on the part of Evangelicals and ritualists alike. The surveyors had their own explanations however for the small impact of so much devotion, money and effort.

'Partly it was put down to the cultural gap and lack of communication: either the mysterious evangelical language of Canaan or the even more mysterious and frigid Anglican ritual. The disunity of the churches was also to blame, and their moral failures, for example, the failure to give the working men positions of status and responsibility, the constant dispensation of a flood of charity instead of social justice, the "people be good" attitude of Anglicanism and the indifferent business Christians of the suburbs. On the other side there was the sheer apathy of the poor and the embarrassment which their poverty brought them on entering church.

'But the weight of explanation lay most heavily on the problem of uprooting from the countryside, the breaking of old attachments and assimilation to a pre-existing majority pattern. In any case the working-class Sunday needed to be the one moment of respite from the grind: a nap, a newspaper, a saunter, an early supper and a pipe. And Sunday was also the great day for visiting by shop assistants, clerks and warehousemen, who settled down to play games and give concerts in their tiny parlours. Moreover visiting equally affected the rich, and amongst them a new important source of infidelity had made its appearance: the weekend habit.'[40]

What of the twentieth century? Are there new lessons to learn or was the rift between the church and the working classes all but complete? Wickham observes that, 'The First World War put religion, as much else, into the crucible; it terminated one era and introduced another, and mightily consolidated forces and trends already at work.'[41] Following this, 'a culture pattern emerged in the inter-war years that progressively excluded the habit of worship, even in social groups to whom the custom had been traditional. At the same time the long hard depression further defined and solidified the working class, with its traditional lack of adult participation in the churches.'[42]

Concrete jungles and crumbling communities

We turn now from our historical survey to consider a number of aspects of life in working-class areas today. Over the last three decades many inner-city and industrial areas have experienced massive upheaval and change. Slum clearance and redevelopment have transformed the external features of these areas beyond all recognition. Families who moved out to the suburbs some years ago return on a visit, only to find themselves strangers in a place which once was home. How do working-class folk cope with these upheavals? What does a complete change of environment do to the people and the communities in which they live? What things do we need to understand so that we may be better equipped to present the gospel to these people? We shall examine seven features of working-class life today.

Streets and roots

'It's not like it used to be round here. I wish I was still in my old house in Trafalgar Street. I still miss it. I think I always will. We didn't have a bathroom or an inside toilet or central heating and all that, but we were happier then. I know the walls were damp. The paper was peeling off. The windows didn't fit, and the floor was a bit rickety. Hitler's bombs had knocked it about a bit. But it was home. I lived there for sixty years and my parents lived there before me. We didn't have much money in those days, but they were good old days. Neighbours cared more about you than they do today. The front door was always open. The kettle was always on. I wish we could have those days back again.'

Those words have been said a thousand times. They are the typical comment of an older 'nan' who has lived in the inner-city all her life. Nostalgically, she thinks back to the days of hardship and comradeship in two world wars. She views the passing of the old streets with sadness. She continues to try to readjust to living in a tower block of flats. But it is not at all easy. 'Something' is missing and it seems that it will never come back.

When slum dwellings are demolished and new homes take their place there are both gains and losses. Of course, it is convenient to have the bathroom, the indoor toilet and the central heating. It is nice to have a larger and well-equipped kitchen instead of that poky scullery with its stone sink and one cold tap. But what of the losses? They are less tangible but, in fact, more valuable. When the bulldozer tears down the substandard dwellings of an old slum area, it also tears up the roots of a community. That imperceptible asset of a whole network of human relationships, which has taken generations to establish and maintain, is suddenly destroyed beyond repair. Life on the new estate is different. Now the doors are always closed, and the kettle is not always on. There is a sense of lostness and loneliness. All the folk around are new neighbours. A whole new network of relationships has to be 'grown'. But the seeds take so long to come up! Because it is impossible to create 'instant community', the sense of 'not belonging' is something that just has to be accepted and endured. When they pulled down the houses they pulled up the roots of a community. And there is no way of reversing the process.

Changing values

Together with the coming of the new flat or maisonette on the sixteenth floor of the tower block, there also comes, largely unnoticed, a big change in values.

In the street where the houses used to be, what used to mean most to the folk who lived there was, not their material possessions, but the fact that they had 'good neighbours you can trust,' and who will always 'help you out if you're in trouble'. This was the best thing about living in that old tumbledown street. 'People matter more than things!'

But now that has all gone. The move to the new flat is the signal for the big spend. Now is the chance to have the kind of furnishings you always wanted. The delivery vans make their succession of calls — new carpets, new suite, new table and chairs, new fridge, new stereo and the rest. But who is going to pay for all these acquisitions? That does not matter. The fact that you have not got the money is the least of worries. That can be produced 'somehow'. And so the flat-dweller relaxes in the castle for which he has waited. After working hours, the working man retreats behind his flat door to idle away his hours surrounded by his creature comforts. Neighbours no longer seem to matter so much. And besides you do not really know very much about that person living next door. So why bother? Almost unnoticed, values have now changed. Things now matter more than people. The new flat-dweller is less human and less happy because of the change, but he is unlikely to discover how it has happened.

The grey desert

Is 'concrete jungle' a misnomer? If we probe the expression we discover it contains a virtual contradiction. Concrete is dead. It is lifeless and inanimate. But the jungle is living. It throbs with life and variety and colour. A more appropriate term to describe a tower-block estate would be a 'grey desert' rather than a concrete jungle. God is a God of variety and colour. His seven-coloured rainbow in the sky is both a symbol of His power and a token of His grace. The jungle with its varieties of shape in bush and tree, flower and grass, and its refreshing and relaxing shades of green, serves to remind us that 'God has made everything beautiful in its time' (Eccles. 3:11). But the desert is not like that

In darkest England

at all. The desert suggests to our minds an absence of colour, an absence of life. The desert is uninviting. The monotony of its featureless landscape sparks no appreciation or wonder in the soul.

Tower-block estates are not really concrete jungles; they are grey deserts. The homes of the people have no character or individuality about them. They are like a mound of boxes piled high in the sky. Slabs of dull grey concrete reach high and heavenwards. Down at ground level people scuttle to and fro as though surrounded by some 'technological Stonehenge'. But the visible symbols of the 'concrete age' kindle no spark within the soul. They crowd the skyline and hem us in. They restrict our ration of God's blue sky. One thing is certain: the architects who designed them would never live in them!

Dimensions of deprivation

The term 'deprivation' is frequently used in connection with inner-city areas. In what ways are working-class folk at a disadvantage? We have already touched on *housing*. Slum clearance and redevelopment will continue for many years yet. The experience of being rehoused often proves traumatic, particularly for the elderly. When slum clearance is scheduled, routine care of the old houses abruptly halts. Apathy and vandalism increase. Everybody must move. No one can choose to stay. And so the community crumbles.

Education is a matter of high importance to children and their parents. But inner-city schools generally have old buildings, limited facilities, a high turnover of staff and low academic levels. Where classroom discipline problems increase, the rate of learning must be slowed. 'In the good and typical local comprehensive school that served the area [North Southwark] less than one child in six got one or more 'O' level passes. Out of the whole school with an annual intake of 240 children a year there were only five 'A' level passes one year. No single child went on to university or any form of higher education.'[43]

The inner city is *noisy* for a variety of reasons. There is a high volume of road traffic through these areas. Rush-hour traffic clogs our roads and pollutes our air. On warm summer evenings windows are opened. Television and stereo churn out the top of the pops with maximum decibels! A gang of youths sit astride their motor cycles joking and arguing until they all decide it is time for another 'burn up'. As the throttles roar, the 'trapped sound' reverberates around the walls of our concrete desert.

Young children have little or no safe place to play. A young mother's choice is a difficult one. Should she keep her energetic child cooped up in their flat on the fourteenth floor, or should she let him play at ground level where she has no way of seeing what he is doing or where he is going? A garden is a luxury in the inner city. Most families have to do without one. Many more aspects of urban deprivation could be considered. At this stage in our study it will be sufficient that we just note that they exist.

Racial problems and tensions are most evident in working-class areas. Immigrants are largely settled in these areas rather than in suburban situations. Clashes of culture and temperament easily spark hostility and prejudice. Immigrants are also the convenient scapegoats for all kinds of problems which seem to mushroom in racially mixed communities.

Unemployment hits urban working-class areas more than suburban 'professional' districts. Immigrants, too, find that levels of unemployment in their communities are higher than for the 'whites'. Immigrant youths who feel that society does not want them because it can provide no jobs for them will inevitably give vent to their feelings of being frustrated and the victims of injustice. Relations between disaffected immigrant youths and local police are often at flash-point level in inner-city areas.

Vandalism and crime are now 'accepted' features of city life. Their occurrence fails to shock any more. An East London youth club run by Christians claims, 'Most of our members have problems — it is estimated that at least 80% have been before the courts or are committing "successful" burglaries or T.D.A. offences regularly.' [T.D.A. = take and drive away cars.] One of their members commented, 'You're considered a freak if you ain't been nicked for nothin' round here.'

Power and the professionals

Another aspect of inner-city working-class life, which has a great bearing on attitudes to 'authority', is the nature of the decision-making machinery which has the power to affect the 'quality of life' in the local community. How are these decisions taken? By whom are they taken? Who has the power to bring about the provision of safe play areas for young children? Who decides whether the construction of tower blocks should be discontinued? Who has the power to encourage the development of local industries in order to provide more jobs locally?

Inner-city areas are usually one-class areas. This means that the 'professionals' who work in and for the benefit of the working-class area are commuters 'from outside' and not local residents. This would apply to doctors, dentists, surveyors, architects, solicitors, accountants, bank managers, school teachers, social workers, local government officers, magistrates, town planners, company directors and managers. All these are involved in decision-making which, in a small way or large, will affect the quality of life in the local community. But none of these people will be directly affected by their decisions because they are not resident in the community they serve. Is this a fair distribution of power? Should 'the professionals' from outside have the weight of power that they do in the decision-making process? Should not local people have more of a say? How can the weight of their preferences be indicated?

People who live in suburban areas or small towns find this much less of a problem than do inner-city dwellers. If they are in one of the professions which exercise the power of decision-making, then they are more likely to be regularly in touch with similar decison-making bodies in the routine work of their particular profession. Consequently, when, in their own private and domestic situation, they need to get action on some matter, they at least know how 'the system' works and possibly may already know 'the right people' to secure prompt action. Whether the issue is the need for the provision of further social amenities or a small personal grievance, the majority of local residents in an urban area would not know where and how to penetrate the 'power structure' to secure the necessary action. It is understandable if attitudes of apathy or hostility or non-co-operation colour the outlook of working-class people when they are frustrated in their attempts to make their voices heard and their grievances known.

Glimpse of a ghetto

What is life like for residents in tower blocks? In my judgement there is no person better qualified to answer that question than Miss Elizabeth Braund, who is serving the Lord in connection with the work of Providence House in Battersea, South West

London. Her work among inner-city youth in an area with a large immigrant population has gone on for nearly twenty years. Apart from the courage and compassion which has taken her into what is, by any standards, 'a tough assignment', Miss Braund has a most penetrating grasp of what is really happening to the people in these concrete jungles. What does the grey desert of concrete slabs do to the people who are compelled to live their lives within its boundaries? Some years ago, Miss Braund, who was then Managing Editor of the *Evangelical Magazine,* contributed an article to that journal which she entitled 'Doomwatch in the Ghettoes'. We select one paragraph from her long and discerning article to give us a glimpse of a ghetto.

'Can you, in your conventional background, or you with the Rock of the Christian faith to build upon — can you even imagine the confusion of mind, the tensions, anxieties, pressures and even the upsurge of violence and hate that results from a population herded close together and each behaving according to the dictates of their own wills and moods? There are old people who live in a nightmare of fear — largely justified. Neighbours break into their flats and open their gas-meters, their windows are broken; fireworks and bangers put through their letter-boxes — and the parents of those responsible shrug their shoulders. There are families who are violent and noisy so that the rest of the flats are kept awake. There are some who make no attempt to look after their children, and others are led astray with them. There are some who are dirty and others have to bear the consequence of fouled lifts and smelly corridors. There are people who damage the lifts and the tired young mum has eighteen floors to walk up with baby and the shopping. There are parents who go away on holiday and leave teenagers at home, to indulge in wild parties that go on all night and turn into sexual or drug orgies. There are cars smashed up as they are parked in their owners' bays, others are stolen. So what? You may judge the miscreants, but if there is no absolute right or wrong, by what standards are you to judge anyway? And without moral absolutes and restraints, the outward hand of the law will fight a losing battle.'[44]

Spiritual darkness

When William Booth published his book *In Darkest England and the Way Out* about ninety years ago, he did so in order to draw attention to the massive and urgent social needs of working-class areas, besides the spiritual needs which had been his primary concern in the earlier years of the Salvation Army. Since that time the material progress and prosperity of our nation has advanced far beyond anything our forefathers might have dreamed. But for all that, our nation, and particularly in working-class areas, sinks ever deeper into the mire and misery of pagan darkness. It is difficult to portray adequately and concisely the nature of the heathen darkness in which the people live. Is it ever possible to describe darkness?

The writer of Proverbs tells us, 'There is a way that seems right to a man, but in the end it leads to death' (Prov. 14:12). This is the road on which the working classes are travelling. It is a 'broad' road, but that seems to be the right one because nearly everybody else is going that way, too (Matt. 7:13:14).

There are other reasons, too, why this road seems right. The adversary of souls has played havoc with the signposts and signals ahead of the unsuspecting traveller. Gone are the traffic lights at red, the warning signs and danger signals. God's moral and spiritual signposts have been torn down. His wise instructions on family life have been set aside. The Bible's teaching on sin and salvation, heaven and hell, the present life and the life hereafter are almost totally ignored. God's 'red signals' are swiftly challenged. Who has the right to restrict us? Is not this an intrusion into man's personal freedom? The signposts that appeal are easy to follow: 'Man shall live by bread alone.' 'Things matter more than people.' 'It is better to gain the whole world even if you do have to forfeit your soul.' After all, what is a soul anyway? Deceived by the invisible Satan and dehumanized by our industrial society, the working man motors on, into the darkness and on to destruction.

Where have all the Christians gone?

The exodus of Christians from inner-city areas to the more desirable residential areas of suburbia has seriously undermined the life and witness of churches in working-class areas. A selection of observations from various writers clearly confirms that from the earliest days of the Industrial Revolution down to the present time the trend has continued unabated.

An observer of eighteenth-century Wesleyan Methodism in the city of Sheffield comments, 'Of course all places of worship suffer from the westward tendency of wealthy people. It is the ambition of a tradesman to have his house at Ranmoor and he naturally seeks a church or chapel not far from his own vine and fig tree.'[45]

In the opinion of Bishop Wickham, 'This was a trend that could have the most serious consequences for the most stable and vigorous chapel communities when the group that literally possessed them moved away to better areas, leaving them near derelict in a sea of poorer people who had never felt any sense of belonging. It could entail the complete pulling out by a chapel from a poor district with the loss of all the hitherto exerted influence.'[46]

What was true of the industrial city of Sheffield was no less true of the capital city, London. Wickham says, 'One further feature of London should be noted — the movement of population, first of the better-class people into the growing suburbs of Greater London leaving the solid masses of the poorer and less enterprising of the population, duly followed by the outward moving of the working classes into the suburbs, and the further emigration of the better classes.'[47]

Wickham goes on to cite George Haw, a man passionately concerned about the working classes and the church. He wrote, 'All the strong and prosperous people are running away from the inner belt of London as fast as they can; forgetting it, owning no responsibility for it, leaving it to the weaker, poorer, more weary ones.'[48]

Another historian writes, 'The movement of population from the centre of the cities to the suburbs, which accelerated momentously after 1850, was observed by Nonconformists as a force damaging to their churches.'[49]

A contemporary Christian sociologist observes, 'Movements of population are not simply individually motivated, but occur in response to market factors and government policy. The flight to the suburbs remains also a flight of the churches. Generally this means full suburban churches (partly) because these are few enough to meet demand whereas the churches in the older areas are like beautiful hulks resting on mud banks from which the main channels of life have long since flowed elsewhere...'[50]

Miss Braund of Battersea also raises a pertinent question: 'Why is it that within a nation whose society is predominantly conurban, living in massed densities and concrete jungles, the great majority of Christian people and churches are outside such areas, and even those with buildings situated in them draw members from outside their locality rather than from those living nearby? In other words, do we interpret the Scriptures to serve our own generation, by ignoring the greater part of it?'[51]

All that we have discovered concerning population movements in British cities since the time of the Industrial Revolution finds a very close parallel in the cities of the United States of America. In his book, *Calling our Cities to Christ*, Roger Greenway observes the present position: 'Today, in the closing decades of the twentieth century, we are witnessing the steady exit of city Christians to the suburbs. They leave behind them the bewildered remnants of once mighty churches, and the empty edifices which no one wants to buy. There is nothing new about this kind of movement. The abandonment of old neighbourhoods for more socially congenial locations elsewhere was happening already at the time of the Civil War. As American cities began to grow and working-class people — not blacks in particular, but whites from southern Europe and America's own rural areas — old stock Americans, moved away, they took their churches with them to the "great avenues up town". Running away from changing neighbourhoods has been occurring for a long time in America, and the lower classes have not failed to get the message. By their locations, their architecture, their liturgy, their sermons, and their entire programme, urban Protestant churches have conveyed the message to the masses that these churches are not for them.'[52]

As the trends continue today many small church fellowships in working-class areas are getting perilously near the point of extinction. The plain facts are these. Where the populations are greatest, there the Protestant Christian church is weakest.

The doors are closing

As we have just noted, many small churches in urban areas are on the point of closing. The gospel light in dark pagan areas is almost out. The church of which I am pastor is in a street where there used to be four churches. Now we are the sole survivor of the four. 'Other small streets in the area bring you to the ghosts of churches which once catered for the spiritual needs of this populous area. These great 19th century shells, like deserted Greek temples, now rise almost frighteningly above the smaller houses and are used today usually for various commercial purposes.'[53]

We may think that it is probably those churches who did not preach a fully biblical gospel that have seen their causes extinguished. But that is not the complete picture. Many evangelical causes have a lifeline that seems to hang by a thread. If church-going in many working-class areas is now less than 1% of the community, it only requires a marginal drop in church-going and the witness of the church will be terminated.

'According the latest [1975] estimate of church attendance in East London, only one person in every 200 attends a place of worship on Sunday ... Drop into an average Sunday Service in all but a few of the churches in Stepney or Bethnal Green, and you will find a dozen — or maybe 20 — people huddled together in a building designed for 500.'[54]

'In the East End of London more than half of all the churches that existed in 1945 have now closed and if the present closure rate is maintained there will be no churches left at all by 1988.'[55]

If the gospel light goes out, how easily could it be rekindled? With the continuing redevelopment of large urban areas and the long waiting lists for rehousing because of slum clearance, doors for the gospel may prove very hard to reopen.

We began this chapter by referring to the prophet Ezekiel and the way he pondered the true condition of the Jewish exiles in Babylonia. It moved him deeply. The dimensions of their distress crushed his sensitive soul. If Ezekiel were with us today what would he do and say? 'I came to the multitudes of working-class folk who lived by the River Thames and by the River Mersey. And there, in darkest England, where they were living, I sat among them for seven days — overwhelmed.'

3.
Battle for the mind

The battle to win the working man to Jesus Christ must be fought out 'in the kingdoms of the mind'. In fact, this applies to all people, irrespective of so-called 'class'. The gospel is the Word of life to be declared to all people. God reasons with sinners (Isa. 1:18). The response required is that of repentance: God demands a change of mind. Nor does it end there. Growing in the Christian life is vitally bound up with the activity of the mind. The believer is to set his mind on 'things above' and to be transformed progressively by the renewing of his mind. But here is the crux. To identify the mind as the strategic citadel within the being of a man is one thing: to capture that apparently impregnable fortress within the working man is something else altogether. A proper understanding of a person's thinking not only involves us in an attempt to discover the substance of his thoughts — *what* he believes — it also demands an understanding of the 'mental mechanisms' of his thought processes —*how* his mind works. Before we can change *what* a person thinks, we have to understand *how* he thinks so that the mind-changing process can effectively be set in motion.

Language forms — 'concrete' and 'conceptual': the distinction explained

What style of language is most suitable for communicating with working-class people? The answer is *concrete* language, rather than *conceptual* language. By this we mean that it is most natural for the working man to think visually. When he hears words his mental mechanisms translate the sounds into visual pictures thrown on to the screen of his mind. His mind is like a camera which turns words into pictures. He sees life situations which he has observed before and into which he can project his own participation. That is concrete language. By contrast, conceptual language operates in abstract ideas and propositional terms which cannot readily be translated into visual mental images. Some biblical examples should help us understand the distinction between these two language forms.

Our Lord's parables are a good example of concrete thought. They present life-situation events with which the hearers can identify and which are designed to convey basic principles of Christian living. What is the meaning of 'repentance' in the Bible? It is the Lord's parable of the 'lost son' which explains this teaching in *concrete* terms (Luke 15:11-24). A young rebel left home and family to 'live it up' in a distant country. At first things went well, but as soon as the money ran out all his 'friends' disappeared. He was reduced to ruin. He had learnt the hard way. When he 'came to his senses' he returned home to confess his sinful ways and to plead for his father's forgiveness. The waiting father eagerly welcomed and freely forgave his boy. He was restored to the family and reinstated as a son. This returning rebel had by the nature of his home-coming displayed genuine repentance.

God now calls 'all people everywhere to repent' (Acts 17:30). Therefore, we should expect to find many other instances of repentance in the pages of Scripture. But this time we shall look at an example which presents its teaching on repentance in *conceptual* terms. In his second letter to the Christians at Corinth, Paul wrote to express his joy at the news of the repentance of a church member who had been guilty of a serious sin. He said, 'Yet now I am happy, not because you were made sorry, but because your sorrow led you to repentance. For you became sorrowful as God intended and were not harmed in any way by us. Godly sorrow brings repentance that leads to salvation and leaves no regret, but worldly sorrow brings death. See what this godly sorrow has produced in you: what earnestness, what eagerness to clear yourselves, what indignation, what alarm, what longing, what concern, what readiness to see justice done' (2 Cor. 7:9-11). The words 'sorrow', 'salvation', 'earnestness', 'eagerness', 'alarm', 'longing', 'concern' and 'justice' are all conceptual terms. They present abstract ideas, conveying with them no automatic association with particular visual life-situation imagery.

The distinction between concrete and conceptual language is an important one to preserve. It has a significant bearing on our concern to reach the working man with the gospel and to see him established in the faith. The average working man normally thinks in concrete terms. He finds it difficult to grapple with conceptual thinking. His school career is unlikely to have given much, if any attention to this aspect of intellectual development. It is also unlikely that this capability will have been among the qualifications for the job he now does. Richard Hoggart draws to our attention this feature of the 'working-class mind' in connection with the type of newspapers which are preferred by working-class people. He says, 'The quite unusual degree of 'personalization' in the newspapers designed particularly for working-class people is derived, one can see immediately, not only from common human interest in the detail of other people's lives, but also from the peculiarly strong working-class attachment to the concrete, the emotionally bold and understandable, the local and particular.'[1]

In the 'academic world', largely unknown to the working man, the ability to think in conceptual, as well as in concrete terms, is essential. How necessary is it for Christians in working-class communities to be able to think in conceptual terms? Is conceptual thought necessarily superior to concrete thought?

'Various aspects of ... research have been questioned, in particular the notion that operational thinking in concrete, matter-of-fact, here-and-now terms is at a lower level than conceptual, abstract, generalized, ideational thought. There is, nowadays, more willingness to see that operational and conceptual thinking are different in kind. Value judgements about higher and lower are inappropriate. Nevertheless, it remains true that the majority think, many highly intelligently, in concrete, matter-of-fact terms, while academic training still puts high value on the ability to conceptualize. Propositional revelation is more easily handled in conceptual terms. Reformed theology and the academic attitude go very well together.'[2]

Our observations on the operation of what we might call 'the working-class mind' should influence the kind of language we employ in evangelism, whether it be in formal preaching or in informal personal witness. It is probable that few sermons are either wholly concrete or wholly conceptual in the language they employ, although there will be some exceptions. We have referred to the parables of our Lord. Their language appears to be wholly concrete. On the other hand, the subject matter of some sermons may demand language which is almost entirely conceptual — for example, sermons on some of the attributes of God may fall into this category.

Generally, we may expect some sermons to have a predominance of concrete language, and others to major on the conceptual. This we can illustrate by reference to two particular New Testament evangelistic sermons. It is instructive to contrast the form of language used by Paul in the sermon he preached to the chiefly Gentile audience at Lystra (Acts 14:8-18) with that which he used when he preached to another mainly Gentile audience at Athens (Acts 17:16-31). In the sermon at Lystra, where his hearers were manual workers — agricultural labourers — his language was predominantly *concrete*. By contrast, in the sermon he preached at Athens, where his hearers were largely 'intellectuals' — Epicurean and Stoic philosophers — his language was predominantly *conceptual*.

Both sermons commenced with reference to the doctrine of creation. Thereafter, in the sermon at Lystra Paul focused attention on the 'concrete' items of heaven, rain, crops and food. These 'gifts' came to the people solely due to the kindness of God. The sermon at Athens covered a wider range of 'ideas'. And 'ideas' were the staple intellectual diet of those who frequented 'Speakers' Corner' on Mars Hill. These folk spent their time doing nothing but 'talking about and listening to the latest new ideas' (Acts 17:21). Beginning with the doctrine of the Creator, Paul went on to touch upon such subjects as the nature of true worship, the purpose of creation and the necessity for redemption. He also referred to the two very important theological concepts of the transcendence of God (Acts 17:24) and the immanence of God (Acts 17:27,28).

From these two addresses we see that the *content* of the language Paul used was determined by *Scripture;* the form of the language used was governed by *local culture*.

Biblical languages: Hebrew (concrete) and Greek (conceptual)

A general but valid contrast of the Hebrew language of the Old Testament with the Greek of the New Testament confronts us again with the two forms of thought which we have just examined. Hebrew is marked by *concrete* thought; Greek is marked by *conceptual* thought. This is far from being an absolute distinction. We find examples of conceptual thought in the Old Testament, and we find plenty of concrete thought in the New Testament. Why was Hebrew selected by God to be the language through which He conveyed the body of revealed truth which we know as the Old Testament? What features of the Hebrew language demonstrate its suitability for the purpose that God had in mind?

Original revelation

There are three particular features of the Hebrew language which suggest answers to the questions we have raised.

1. Hebrew thought is 'dynamic' whereas Greek thought is 'static'. 'The Greeks were ultimately interested in contemplation, the Hebrew in action. Movement could not be ultimate reality for the Greeks, to whom being must be distinguished from becoming, and the ultimate must be changeless. For the Israelite the true reality was action and movement, and the inactive and motionless was no reality at all.'[3]

It is not surprising, therefore, for us to find that the characteristic expression of Hebrew thinking is the *verb*, while that of the Greek thinking is the *noun*. For the Greek 'God is', but for the Hebrew 'God does'.

2. Hebrew thought is characterized by a great interest in history whereas Greek thought is not. 'The dynamic approach of the Hebrews to reality is expressed in their interest in history. Their God is characteristically one who acts in history, and these actions in history are the core of the religious tradition of Israel ... The highest philosophical developments of the Greeks were interested in an unchanging reality and paid no attention to action in history.'[4]

The God who revealed Himself to Moses was the God of history, the God of 'Abraham, Isaac and Jacob' (Exod. 3:6,15). Many of the psalms contain references to Israel's history (Ps. 66;68; 77;78;81; 99; 105; 106; 108; 114; 126; 135; 136; 137). God's spokesmen, the prophets, frequently reminded God's people of their history (e.g. Isa. 1; Hos. 13:4-9; Amos 3:2). Some of the earliest preaching in the book of Acts provoked the Jews to reflect upon their national history (Acts 2:25-36; 3:20-26; 7:1-53).

3. Concrete thought is characteristic of the Hebrew language whereas conceptual thought is characteristic of Greek. The Hebrew did not think in terms of abstract thought but the Greeks did. The Greeks could think of goodness, strength and beauty as descriptions of certain properties. The Greek was at ease with these concepts. The Hebrew would only comprehend the reality of these ideas when they were applied to specific objects or situations, such as, a good boy, a strong man, a beautiful woman.

As a general observation on the Old Testament Hebrew, we can say that its imagery is largely drawn from the objects and activities of everyday life. In this sense it has a universal quality and lends itself without difficulty to translation. Hebrew makes a wide use of figures of speech, parables, similes and metaphors. In particular, there is a considerable use of anthropomorphism, that is, the operation of various organs of the body is used to describe the activity of God, for example, 'the eyes of the Lord' (Gen. 6:8; Deut. 11:12; Ps. 34:15); 'the hand of the Lord' (Exod. 9:3; 16:3; Deut 2.15; Josh. 4:24); 'the ears of the Lord' (Ps. 34:15; James 5:4); 'the face of the Lord' (Ps. 34:16; 67:1; 1 Peter 3:12); 'the arm of the Lord' (Isa. 51:9; 52:10; 53:1).

The Hebrew of the Old Testament could be described as the language of God's *original revelation*. The Old Testament is a record of God's saving activity in the history of a particular people, Israel. These 'wonderful works of God' point forwards to the climax of God's saving activity through the birth, life, death, resurrection and ascension of His only Son Jesus Christ. But why, for the New Testament, was there a change of language? What was it that made Greek particularly suitable for the divine revelation in the New Testament? That is our next enquiry.

Universal transmission

There are several reasons why Greek was the appropriate language for the New Testament. We will mention three of them.

1. Prompt obedience to the Great Commission (Matt. 28:19,20) to carry the Christian gospel to the uttermost parts of the earth ideally required a language which was *in universal use*. Greek was such a language. The international character of Greek is perhaps its most obvious contrast with the Hebrew of the Old Testament.

2. The New Testament required a language which was *capable of embodying and confirming all that God had revealed* in the Old Testament, and also of conveying the climax and completion of all that God purposed to reveal in the New Testament.

3. The New Testament required a language which was *capable of expressing precise formulations of Christian doctrine*. The Christian gospel had to win its way through many pagan nations. The infiltration of alien ideas was a constant threat to the churches of the New Testament (Acts 20: 29,30).

Michael Green makes an illuminating comment on the suitability of the Greek language for the New Testament revelation. He says, 'The advantages for the Christian mission of having a common language can hardly be over-estimated. It did away with the necessity for missionary language schools. Missionaries using it would incur none of the odium that English-speaking missionaries might find in some of the under-developed countries; for Greek, the language of captive people, could not be associated with imperialism. Moreover, it was a sensitive, adaptable language, ideally suited for propagation of a theological message, because for centuries it had been used to express the reflections of some of the world's greatest thinkers, and thus had a ready-made philosophical and theological library. The lack of this specialist vocabulary in Latin led to difficulties some 250 years later, when Latin replaced Greek as the common language of the Western Empire.'[5]

Concrete and conceptual: New Testament analysis

Our brief look at the biblical languages and their contrasting characteristics has pin-pointed the likely areas of difficulty for those who find that their mental apparatus has not been developed to cope with conceptual thought. We shall now attempt a further analysis which we hope will give us more clues to help us in this vital matter of communication.

How Jesus taught

So far we have made only a broad and general contrast between the form of language which we find in the Old Testament and that which we find in the New Testament. Strictly speaking, we should take the Old Testament books plus the four Gospels and the book of Acts, and contrast them with virtually all the remainder of the New Testament.

Some commentators might want to modify that division by removing the Gospel of John from the former category and transferring it to the latter. Why should this be so? It was Clement of Alexandria who said that 'John, perceiving that the external facts had been made plain in the Gospels, being urged by his friends and inspired by the Spirit, composed a *spiritual* Gospel.' But what exactly does Clement mean by his use of the word '*spiritual*' in this context? If, as seems probable, he means that John's Gospel concentrates less on historical fact and more on doctrinal instruction than do the Synoptic Gospels, then we can understand the point he is making. But there is a danger here. We may create a false antithesis between 'history' and 'doctrine' which is not in accord with accepted principles of biblical interpretation.

R.V. Tasker gives necessary instruction and warning when he says, 'Recent study of the Gospels has made it abundantly clear that to separate doctrine and history in *any* of the four Gospels is to draw a false distinction; though it is obvious that in John doctrine is much more in evidence. The words of Westcott on this subject could scarcely be bettered. "If we compare", he wrote, "the avowed purpose of St John with that of St Luke (1: 1-4), it may be said with partial truth that the inspiring impulse was in the one case doctrinal, and in the other case historical. But care must be taken not to exaggerate or misinterpret this contrast. Christian doctrine is history, and this is above all things the lesson of the Fourth Gospel. The Synoptic narratives are implicit dogmas no less truly than St John's dogmas are concrete facts. The real difference is that the earliest Gospel contained the fundamental facts and words which experience afterwards interpreted, while the latest Gospel reviews the facts in the light of their interpretation. But in both cases the exactness of historical truth is paramount".'[6]

What, then, can we say of the way in which Jesus taught? What lessons may we learn to equip us better for the task of spreading the gospel? How did our teaching Master, the Master Teacher, present His message to those who heard Him? By far the largest part of Jesus' teaching was presented in concrete thought, making wide use of the objects and events of daily life. A close examination of the sermon on the mount, for example, provides clear evidence of the extent to which 'visual imagery' was a prominent feature of His teaching method. The list of words in the sermon on the mount conveying visual imagery is considerable. Jesus spoke of salt, light, city, lamp, bowl, house, eye, hand, body, cloak, tunic, sun, rain, trumpets, face, treasure, moth, rust, thieves, darkness, money, food, birds, barns, lilies, grass, plank, dogs, pigs, door, stone, fish, snake, gate, road, wolves, sheep, figs, thistles, trees, fruit, rock, fire, sand, winds and streams. The teaching of Jesus was clear and memorable, not only because of the authority with which He spoke (Matt. 7:28,29), but also because He presented it in concrete thought forms. His hearers could both hear *and see* what He was talking about.

Not only was Jesus wise in the language forms which He employed to present His message, He was also the Master Tactician in the way He dealt with individuals in personal counselling. When John tells us that Jesus 'knew what was in a man' (John 2:25), this is never more skilfully demonstrated than in the personal interviews he conducted. The writer of the Book of Proverbs says that 'He who wins souls is wise' (Prov. 11:30).

A study of Jesus' dealings with the Samaritan woman (John 4: 4-42) reveals unique spiritual wisdom in the conduct of the interview. Commenting on Jesus' request to the Samaritan woman, 'Will you give me a drink?' J.C. Ryle makes the following observations: 'In this simple request of our Lord there are four things deserving notice.

   a. It was a gracious act of spiritual aggression on a sinner. He did not wait for the woman to speak to Him, but was the first to begin conversation.

   b. It was an act of marvellous condescension. He by whom all

things were made, the Creator of fountains, brooks and rivers, is not ashamed to ask a draught of water from the hand of one of His sinful creatures.
c. It was an act full of wisdom and prudence, He does not at once force religion on the attention of the woman, and rebuke her for her sins. He begins with a subject apparently indifferent, and yet one of which the woman's mind was doubtless full. He asks her for water.
d. It was an act full of the nicest tact, and exhibiting perfect knowledge of the human mind. He asks a favour, and puts Himself under an obligation. No line of proceeding, it is well known to all wise people, would be more likely to conciliate the woman's feelings towards Him, to make her willing to hear His teaching. Simple as the request was, it contains principles which deserve the closest attention of all who desire to do good to ignorant and thoughtless sinners.'[7]

In the tenth verse of the same chapter Jesus introduced the topic of 'living water'. Although the woman's response to His offer showed that she had not understood what Jesus was saying, nevertheless, we can see the direction in which Jesus was skilfully guiding her thinking. Ryle says, 'The first step to take with a careless sinner, after his attention has been arrested, is to produce in his mind the impression that we can tell him of something to his advantage within his reach. There is a certain vagueness in our Lord's words which exhibits His consummate wisdom. A systematic statement of doctrinal truth would have been thrown away at this stage of the woman's feeling. The general and figurative language which our Lord employed was exactly calculated to arouse her imagination, and to lead her on to further enquiry.'[8]

How Paul taught

'Therefore, since we have been justified through faith, we have peace with God through our Lord Jesus Christ, through whom we have gained access by faith into this grace in which we now stand. And we rejoice in the hope of the glory of God. Not only so, but we also rejoice in our sufferings, because we know that suffering produces perseverance; perseverance, character; and character, hope' (Romans 5: 1-4). At the beginning of the fifth chapter of his letter to the Romans Paul sets before us a dazzling

Battle for the mind

array of basic truths of God's 'so great' salvation. Into the space of just four verses Paul crams no fewer than *ten* aspects of truth which all hinge upon the acquittal which Christ has secured for the believer. Justified, faith, peace, access, grace, hope, glory of God, sufferings, perseverance, character — all these are vital salvation truths, but all expressed in conceptual rather than concrete terms.

How should we respond to this presentation of Christian truth? Is conceptual thought necessarily an advance on concrete thought? Certainly there is progress in the *content* of the revelation contained in the conceptual portions of the New Testament. The New Testament letters contain the climax of God's revelation through His Son Jesus Christ. The doctrines of the person and work of Christ are very carefully formulated in the New Testament letters. In that sense, at least, there is progress of thought from the concrete to the conceptual. But we must be careful, in the New Testament letters, to distinguish between the thought *form* of God's revelation and the *content*.

It is at this point that our earlier contrast between Hebrew and Greek thought may shed further light on this issue. We have seen that Hebrew thought was concerned with 'God in action', what God has done in history. The Gospels of the New Testament demonstrate the same interest. They record what God has done in history through the saving events of the incarnation and the atoning work of Jesus Christ. The *form* of truth in the Gospels is chiefly *historical*. In that sense it displays the characteristic Hebrew interest. When we turn to the letters, and particularly those of the apostle Paul, we meet a different *form* of God's truth. Although the letters were written for specific historical situations, their structure and style of thought are very different from those of the Gospels.

Generally, the letters of Paul are in two parts. In the first part, following a greeting and introduction, various aspects of Christian doctrine are expounded. It is here that we are put through our 'conceptual gymnastics' and may find the intellectual exercise not a little taxing! Ephesians 1 is a good example of this. The second part of each letter details the appropriate Christian behaviour which is consistent with the doctrines that have been expounded. It is the formulation of these doctrinal statements that is characteristic of Greek thought. Now that Christ's saving work has been accomplished, the truths of God are viewed in a static rather than a dynamic way, from an eternal and unchanging point of view, rather than at a specific point in the ongoing history of the human race. It is probably fair comment to say that whereas the *form* of truth in the Gospels is *historical*, that in the letters is *eternal*.

Knowledge and experience

It is every Christian's duty to be 'increasing in the knowledge of God'. We are called to understand God's truth; we are called to defend it as well (Jude 3). But the essence and heart of our Christian faith is not just receiving and retaining doctrinal facts, *learning about God*, we are to be enjoying and deepening a daily living *experience of God*. Doctrine and experience are not synonymous. Our adversary, the devil, has more doctrinal knowledge about God than either the reader or the writer of these words. He has been around a long time! But Satan has had no experience of God. We cannot have an 'experience' of doctrine, but our Creator has so designed man that he needs a continuing personal encounter with the living God (1 Thess. 1:9). It is part of the plan of creation that 'men would seek him and perhaps reach out for him and find him' (Acts 17:27). 'He has also set eternity in the hearts of men' (Eccles. 3:11). An encounter with God is an experience of God. It is an event, a happening, and thus we need to think of it in a Hebrew rather than a Greek way.

The two men who were responsible, under the inspiration of the Spirit of God, for the major part of the content of the New Testament letters, were the apostles Paul and John. If conceptual and abstract thought were the pinnacle of Christian thinking then there would be a need only for God to make a *verbal* revelation to them. Concrete thought would have been transcended and relegated to the area of 'beginner's basics' in the scheme of God's revelation. But we discover that what were undoubtedly among their most memorable *experiences* of God involved *visual* appreciation as well as *verbal*. Paul experienced 'visions and revelations from the Lord' (2 Cor. 12:1), 'surpassingly great revelations' (2 Cor. 12:7), which could have led to pride in the apostle's heart. His 'thorn in the flesh' was given to check any such tendency. In the last book of the Bible, Revelation, John the apostle tells of what he *saw* when God unveiled to him the contents of the 'Revelation'. This apocalyptic revelation began with an overpowering *visual* encounter with the Son of Man in all His dazzling majesty. This unique experience of John was so memorable because it was visual (Rev. 1:9-18).

To what conclusions does our discussion of concrete and conceptual thought lead us? Looking at the two Testaments in chronological sequence, we can say that there is progress in the content of the revelation. But we must not overrate conceptual thought, which is suitable and necessary for the precise preservation of 'sound doctrine', but does not of itself automatically guarantee an experiential encounter with God. It may be that Christians who find themselves competent to cope with the 'intellectual gymnastics' of conceptual thought find that this leads them towards these experiences of God that they so much desire. On the other hand, there are those who find that God's truth expressed in concrete terms provides them with the spiritual understanding and nourishment they need.

One example may suffice to clarify the point we are making here. Paul speaks of his prayer-answering God as the One 'who is able to do immeasurably more than all we ask or think' (Eph. 3:20). That is conceptual truth. When Jesus taught us about prayer and His heavenly Father, He used more simple and memorable terms: 'Which of you, if his son asks for bread, will give him a stone? Or if he asks for a fish, will give him a snake? If you, then, though you are evil, know how to give good gifts to to your children, how much more will your Father in heaven give good gifts to those who ask him!' (Matt. 7:9-11.) Jesus used the 'how much more' process of reasoning from the human to the divine (Matt. 6:30), in order to teach us about our prayer-answering heavenly Father. He *started* with the familiar concrete idea and then used that as a *stepping-stone* towards a conceptual understanding of an aspect of God's character.

There is no need to regard concrete thought as inferior to the conceptual, but neither must a Christian believer be mentally lazy. We are to love God with '*all* our mind'. Every believer should be committed to the development and discipline of the Christian mind. '*All* Scripture is God-breathed' (2 Tim. 3:16), and 'Man does not live on bread alone, but on *every word* that comes from the mouth of God' (Matt. 4:4). No Scripture can be neglected, without spiritual loss, whether the form be concrete or conceptual. Paul was just as much guided to pen Christian truth in conceptual terms as Jesus was guided to employ mainly concrete forms of language. Although there may be a more direct and theologically accurate apprehension of the nature of God in conceptual terms, the impact of that truth may be more powerfully felt where the concrete thought has been used as a convenient stepping-stone towards the appropriate concept. An example of this is the 'I AM's' of Jesus — Vine, Door, Good Shepherd, etc.

Language and learning

So far our discussion on language has focused on ideas or images, conceptual or concrete, as the input to our minds which our mental mechanisms are to process. Knowledge and understanding are not to be equated solely with the volume of material our minds contain, but rather with the way in which we relate and connect the individual facts that have been stored in the mind. Two of the problems encountered in processing this mental material we are now to examine.

The limitations of logic

Information fed to the mind, particularly through books, is so arranged that there is a linear absorption of the material, a process of reasoning that leads to a conclusion. We are familiar with the steps of an argument where a number of facts are presented to the mind, and the concluding statement begins, 'Therefore...' That kind of learning largely depends on linear thinking, but that is not the way many people do think. Modern media tend to present information which is not readily arranged in logical sequence.

Instead of step-by-step logical reasoning built upon conceptual thought, society is now powerfully influenced by concrete thought presented in an 'instant-tell' manner. We must explain the term 'instant tell'. Nearly a quarter of a century ago, Richard Hoggart viewed with disquiet the trends among popular newspapers and magazines in their style of communication. Although 'instant tell' is a term of current journalistic jargon, what Hoggart describes is, in fact, the developing process of 'instant tell'. What he wrote then is almost certainly even more true now. He says, 'The popular press has to become ever more bitty in its presentation ... What is to be read is gradually ousted by what is only to be seen. The 'strips' spread like a rash ... There has to be some verbal guidance to the action, but descriptive comment is kept to a minimum ... All premasticate their material so that it shall neither bore nor tax anyone, shall not prompt any effort at correlation ... Everything is interesting, as interesting as the next thing, if only it is short, unconnected and pepped-up.'[9]

If the popular newspapers encourage their readers' powers of reason to atrophy, television only serves to reinforce what is already happening. Speaking of television's effect on the 'average man' and the way he absorbs his information, Gavin Reid says, 'The immediacy of the medium coupled with the need to participate in what is being experienced by the viewer leads to a mode of apprehension very different to that of the book reader. Television man is inclined to be intuitive in his grasp of what is being presented, either he *sees* it, or no amount of explanation will make it clearer.'[10]

If these observations concerning language and learning are correct, then all preachers need to give very careful thought to the ways in which these findings should affect the style of their preaching. Reid observes, 'Much, though not all, preaching assumes that people think in linear, sequential, patterns of logic. The sermon usually — and especially from the more intellectual preachers — builds up its case in a logical flow with one point following another. This is a typical product of a literary subculture. The majority of people have their thinking patterns conditioned by television, conversation and instant-tell newspapers and just cannot cope with sustained logical argument. The result is that at best they manage to grasp *moments* within the sermon when what was said and implied "struck a chord" and at worst there is little they can remember afterwards.'[11]

Reason and impression

Closely allied to the previous linguistic phenomenon is the matter of the way the working man forms his opinions. This is in some ways an extension of what we have already noted. We have looked at the way the media develop techniques of communication whereby a change of mind is secured with little or no reference to logical thought. We know that the media are particular instruments of communication with a view to persuasion. But 'impression' is an unplanned mental process which is going on all the time, and we are probably little aware of the influence that it is making upon us.

Roger Lloyd detects for us this very important feature of the working man's thinking. He says that the working man 'forms his opinions by responding to his sense impressions and not by the use of his reason'. 'The general impressions that he gets of an employer, a trade union, or a church are hard to change. People, experiences and things are for him exactly what they seem at first sight. They carry the values they once conveyed to him as a result of a single chance and fleeting glimpse; and what these sense impressions have taught him reason cannot easily correct nor logical refutation disturb.'[12]

Roger Lloyd is not claiming here that these thought processes are unique to the working man. It is rather that this characteristic is much more true of the working classes than of any other social group. If the working man has the impression that 'The church is a money-making racket', that church is not really for 'his sort', that 'People who go to church are a lot of hypocrites', that 'Parsons are on to a cushy number', and that 'You don't need to go to church to be a good Christian', then a reasoned demonstration of the error of these views may do little or nothing to change his mind.

It is Roger Lloyd's belief that we have failed to grasp the significance of the way the working man thinks. He says, 'This is a fact which advertisers and propagandists know perfectly well, and the church either does not know it, or if it does, it takes far too little notice of it.' Here again his words (written in 1952) have a prophetic ring about them. For since the dawn and development of television as a powerful medium of communication and persuasion, the divide between reason and impression has become further accentuated.

How are we to respond to this situation? Clearly we cannot ignore reason, for it is a faculty with which man has been endowed by his Creator. It must not be disregarded or abused. The way in which we present the gospel should exhibit sound biblical reason. But neither must we ignore the matter of impression. In fact, if we were to understand more fully what

Battle for the mind

impressions working people have about the Christian gospel and the church, and why, we might find the information disturbing, humbling, but helpful. If in the witness of the Christian church, what we say in our *verbal reasoning* is contradicted by what we show in our *visual impression*, the work of the gospel will be seriously hindered.

How are we to change the impressions that working-class people have about the Christian church and faith? We need to think carefully about the working man's mental mechanisms, through which a change of mind must be secured. Roger Lloyd analyses the process in more detail. The contrast he draws between the 'artisan' (working man) and the 'trained thinker' is certainly real but by no means absolute.

'If we are honest about the way our convictions mostly come to us we shall not at this point have any difficulty understanding the artisan's perception. The difference between him and the trained thinker is not that he responds to his sense impressions while the trained thinker does not, but that the thinker knows he responds to sense impressions while the artisan does not. To put that more exactly, the thinker, knowing something of how his opinions and convictions come to him, checks them by reflection and reason. The artisan rarely knows how his opinions are formed, and so does not check them by reason. Thus his opinions once formed, are generally quite impervious to rational demonstrations of their mistakenness. They can only be changed by his coming under the influence of a contrary set of sense impressions from those which gave rise to his original opinions.'[13]

Intelligence

One other factor which ought to be included in the present discussion is what we refer to as 'intelligence'. It has a bearing on the way a person's 'mental mechanisms' operate. But what is it? How is it measured? How does it affect the way a person thinks? A thermometer is an instrument which measures accurately the temperature of any human body — male or female, child or adult, weak or strong, black or white. A thermometer provides us with an accurate measure of temperature which is universally valid. An I.Q. test is supposed to provide us with a measurement of a person's intelligence. But does it do that? What exactly is intelligence? Who is to say how it shall be measured? Do I.Q. tests provide accurate and meaningful levels of intelligence? Or are there different types of intelligence which cannot be measured properly by the current design of tests of intelligence? The importance of this issue is easily demonstrable.

A young man who lives a few streets away from me has had links with the life and work of our church over a number of years. At one time he professed conversion but his progress has been extremely erratic. This does not surprise me. His home background has not helped this. His introduction to the Christian faith came through the counsel and friendship of a Christian probation officer. How intelligent or unintelligent is this young man? He can drive a London bus; I cannot. He has the ability to service my car; I have not. He has some remarkable gifts as an artist; I have not. There is a sad irony here. Such is his difficulty with 'words' that he would have more confidence doing the *work* of a motor mechanic than he would have in filling in the right *words* of a job application for a post as motor mechanic. This gifted young man has a number of aptitudes that I do not possess. But, it is certain, he would do badly in a standard I.Q. test. So, how intelligent or unintelligent is this young man?

'It is important to note that we must not equate the ideas of being non-literary and being unintelligent. The two have no relationship. The factory worker may well be extremely intelligent and shrewd. He may even be able to grasp fairly complex ideas quickly without having to go through a logical sequence in his mind. He may well "just see" what you are getting at. To write him off as simple because he is non-bookish is only to show the ignorance and short-sightedness of the literary type of person.'[14]

There is evidence to indicate that where there has been a quickening of interest in the Christian faith it has not infrequently been accompanied by a growing incentive to become competent in reading the Scriptures. The fact that the Holy Spirit imparts and sustains the incentive and aids the progress in reading and understanding Scripture does not release us from our responsibility to care for the spiritual progress of every individual believer. The Good Shepherd 'calls his own sheep *by name* and leads them out' (John 10:3). He cares for us individually.

Day schools for children give particular attention to pupils who need the special individual care that can be offered through a 'remedial group'. I see no spiritual reason why in the church's teaching the same remedial principles should not be adopted, provided that the 'remedial' label is avoided. This approach could be of immense help to those who have 'problems with words' as they begin or continue in the Christian life.

The Holy Spirit has not been given so that we can take 'short cuts' to the development of a person's mental powers. Christian biography records the achievements of those who have gone from near illiteracy to become omniverous readers of the Puritans in a comparatively short space of time. Praise God for all such! But we must be careful how we use these historical examples. It can be most depressing to learn what someone else has attained if your own achievements of an elementary ability and fragile habit of Christian reading have only been gained by a plodding perseverance.

How should these observations of mental processes affect the way we think and preach — particularly in the matter of persuasion? It may well be that we regard the processes of linear reasoning and logical deduction as the best method of intellectual persuasion because we can demonstrate their use from Scripture. However, we may have an understanding on this matter which is too inflexible and narrow. We refer back to the contrast between Hebrew and Greek thought. Greek thought operates in 'abstract' terms, whereas, says James Barr, 'Hebrew thought on the other hand does not work with abstractions; its terms are always related to the actual object or situation and not to an abstraction from it. Similarly the Israelite argues not by making one premise and then showing what must follow from it but by presenting *a series of related situation-images.*'[15]

Why should Christians not 'store up treasure on earth'? The apostle Paul instructs Timothy what he is to teach: 'Command those who are rich in this present world not to be arrogant nor put their hope in wealth, which is so uncertain ...' (1 Tim. 6:17). Paul's answer is expressed in conceptual language. Christians are to recognize the basic *insecurity* of this world's wealth: it is 'so uncertain'. How did Jesus answer the same question? He said, 'Do not store up for yourselves treasures on earth, where moth and rust destroy, and where thieves break in and steal' (Matt. 6:19). Our Lord presented His answer in concrete language with a 'series of related situation-images'. It is the threat of moth, rust and thieves that make this world's wealth 'so uncertain'.

Why should Christians not worry about the things which they need? Paul tells Timothy what he should teach: God's children are not to put their hope in this world's wealth which is so insecure, but they are to 'put their hope in God, who richly provides us with everything for our enjoyment' (1 Tim. 6:17 b). 'My God will meet all your needs ...' (Phil. 4:19). Jesus answers the same question by saying that we should not worry about what we are to eat, drink or wear.

Like Paul, Jesus assures us that 'your heavenly Father knows that you need them' (Matt. 6:32). But Jesus argues His case by presenting a series of related situation-images. Because the birds of the air 'do not sow or reap or store away in barns', they are utterly dependent on circumstances beyond their control for their necessary food for survival. Worrying about the need cannot extend the duration of life even by one hour for either bird or man. God their Creator is also God their Sustainer. If our heavenly Father provides for the needs of the birds without any active co-operation on their part, He is bound to meet our needs as well. Not only are God's children of more value than the birds, but they have been endowed with skills for sowing, reaping and storing in order to make provision for their necessary food. Nevertheless, bumper crops and full barns must not mislead us into thinking we can be independent of God's daily provision (Prov. 30: 7-9). Jesus said that we should pray, 'Give us today our daily bread' (Matt. 6:11). God 'clothes the grass of the field', even though its life could be measured in hours rather than days. God has made us for eternity. It is unthinkable that our heavenly Father should neglect His children (Matt. 6:30).

James, our Lord's brother, teaches that the careless use of the human tongue can have an impact far beyond its comparatively small size. James explains and enforces this teaching by reference to a series of related situation-images. A small bit placed in the mouth of a horse enables the rider to keep control over a large, strong animal. Large ships are steered by the operation of a 'very small rudder'. The size of the ship is out of all proportion to the rudder by which its steering is achieved. One small spark can set a forest ablaze (James 3:3-6).

It may seem that our concentration on mental processes is placing too much emphasis on the form and delivery of the message, rather than on its content. Surely, *what* we have to say matters more than the *way* we say it. Are not sincerity and intensity more important than a clinically correct structure and manner of appeal? I would agree. But we ought also to remember that though we cannot improve on the message, we ought to want to improve on its form and delivery so that it might be of the greatest blessing to the greatest number. We have been looking briefly at the mental mechanisms of persuasion. And we are in the 'persuasion business'! We reject all cunning and craftiness (2 Cor. 4:2; Eph. 4:14) in pursuit of this goal. But 'since ... we know what it is to fear the Lord, we try to persuade men' (2 Cor. 5:11). 'We are ... Christ's ambassadors, as though God were making his appeal through us — we implore you on Christ's behalf: be reconciled to God' (2 Cor. 5:20). There are variations in the manner and method of persuasion, as we have seen. We must suit our approach to bring the maximum understanding to the mind, coupled with the maximum impact on the heart and conscience. Biblical persuasion requires that our presentation of the gospel should be clear, credible and compelling.

The mind and the media

Smoking can seriously damage the lungs. When a God-given faculty is abused, then there must be adverse consequences. Sometimes the damage is irreversible and even fatal. Can the human mind be similarly affected? Can the mind 'inhale' certain mental material which will leave it seriously impaired and unable to perform the function for which God designed it? Such an occurrence is not only possible, but very probable in our twentieth-century society. The danger is a very real one. In this instance we are not thinking of the actions of those who engage in brainwashing in order to 're-educate' a person's political or religious views, nor of any kind of mind-bending techniques deliberately carried out in order to secure a radical change of thought. These are known to exist, but because the methods and aims are known there is a sense in which we can defend ourselves when we know that we are likely to be attacked. Much less obvious, and in that sense much more sinister, is the abuse of the mind through a process which is occurring without deliberate intent and over a long period of time. This form of abuse of the thinking faculty happens with the apparent consent of the victim because there is no obvious threat and, therefore, no need of defence. We must now be specific.

Television viewing on a large scale over a period of time is a real threat to the health of the human mind. Also, the greatest threat is to working-class people because they, as a social category within our society, are the most avid viewers of television. We must first support that claim and then go on to explain the nature of the threat to the health of the mind. *Tomorrow's Television* by Andrew Quicke is the source from which we have drawn the material for our assessment.

'According to BBC audience research the working class spend on average twenty hours per week watching television. At the time of the survey (1974/75) 41 per cent of the working class watched BBC, and 59 per cent watched ITV. The lower middle class on average watched slightly less, and slightly preferred the BBC. They watched sixteen hours per week, divided into 57 per per cent to BBC and 43 per cent to ITV.'[16]

What kind of impact does television have compared with the other forms of media? 'Research has shown that one of the main effects of the media is their tendency to reinforce each other and to emphasize the same values. Television seems to have an increasingly powerful influence over public thought and action. Whereas formerly newspapers were the main force influencing public attitudes, with radio and television reinforcing them, now the pattern is reversed and television is the most important influence.'[17]

Granted that there is much in television programmes which is good and wholesome and is of benefit for educational advancement, cultural enrichment and recreational enjoyment, we must set over against these positive benefits two particular dangers to which we must draw attention. One is the matter of 'unreality'; the other is that of 'insensitivity'.

As long ago as 1961, Ferdynand Zweig (*The Worker in an Affluent Society*) expressed his concern about the influence of television on the working classes. He said, 'The working man

Battle for the mind

used to be known for his great sense of reality and large fund of common sense. I believe that these qualities, although they are still there, are being somewhat weakened by his constant dwelling in the world of illusion and make-believe. He is too often exposed to the world of personal fantasies and the world of artificialities.'[18]

'Television has created a fantasy world of visual dreams, and invested it with a greater authority of "reality" than the world a person experiences away from the television screen. And this fantasy world is one where no moral order obtains, where such words as "good" and "evil" have no meaning.'[19]

If this is the impact on adults, it is even more marked among children and young people: 'Television enters powerfully into the learning process of children and teaches them a set of moral and social values about violence which are inconsistent with the standards of a civilized society. Younger children and a large proportion of *teenagers from low income families* believe that people behave in the real world the way that they do in the fictional world of television.'[20]

Patterns of programming involving massive distortion of human values are not helpful for the growth of the just society. We are given programmes where heroes and villains alike only triumph by being better at violence; where commercial materialism and the life of the very rich is held out to be the right goal for citizens; where "personalities" and their views are held to be more important than people and their opinions.'[21]

Too much television viewing blunts the mental faculty. Part of the function of the mind is to distinguish between fact and fiction, the real and the unreal. Where this faculty is damaged and distorted it has repercussions for our work of evangelism among such people. It is all too easy for the sceptic or the critic of the Christian faith to dismiss it as a lot of fairy tales written a long time ago. Even if he does not dismiss it altogether he may claim that the Bible is a mixture of historical fact and mythological fiction. Perhaps such a reaction is not surprising and this accounts for the way in which some New Testament writers are careful to establish the historicity of what they are saying. Consider, for example, Luke's introduction to his Gospel. He says, 'Many have undertaken to draw up an account of the things that have been fulfilled among us, just as they were handed down to us by those who from the first were eyewitnesses and servants of the word. Therefore, since I myself have carefully investigated everything from the beginning, it seemed good also to me to write an orderly account for you, most excellent Theophilus, so that you may know the certainty of the things you have been taught' (Luke 1:1-4).

The apostle Peter also defends what he says because he was an eyewitness of the events of which he speaks: 'We did not follow cleverly invented stories when we told you about the power and coming of our Lord Jesus Christ, but we were eyewitnesses of his majesty ... We ourselves heard this voice that came from heaven when we were with him on the sacred mountain' (2 Peter 1:16,18).

How are we to convince people of the reality of their sin and of their need of salvation, if their ability to distinguish between fact and fiction, reality and unreality, morality and immorality, has been badly distorted?

The other matter to which we referred was that of 'insensitivity'. It has to do with our feelings. God has so designed us that we are capable of experiencing a wide range of feelings which are appropriate to the various circumstances and events we encounter in everyday life. Peace, joy, excitement, satisfaction, fear, guilt, shame, grief — these are all normal emotional responses to the varied events of daily life. But where there has been too much television viewing these responses will be blunted. The world of television is 'a fantasy world coarsened by the camera's insensitive eye prying into scenes of cruelty, violence and death from which our human sensitivities otherwise shrink. Thus we have the filming of public assassinations and executions, as well as of the very last moments of a human being's life in, for instance, films about hospitals or about Bangladesh. Also of accidents and shootings, when the lens is pushed as close as possible to the victim's dead face, if necessary tearing away the covering which others, with a natural feeling of respect, have placed over it.'[22]

If a sense of shame, guilt and unworthiness are all part of the godly sorrow which is a proper accompaniment of true repentance, can we expect to see these emotional responses in people who have had their capacity for right feeling distorted? If a person's capacity for right feeling is over-exposed, then the proper sensitivity of response to the varied events of life is blunted. The right responses will no longer occur naturally.

Over-exposure of this faculty will produce a swing towards apathy — no feeling.

In this context it is appropriate to ask whether frequent viewing of 'horror films' has a detrimental effect on the proper functioning of the mind. Presumably the viewer obtains some twisted pleasure in having strange shudders and shivers triggered through the nervous system. When the viewing stops, there is probably an attempt to erase the impact of the film so that sleep will not be disturbed. Stories of mysterious powers and beings and a general assortment of 'occult dabblings' may be dismissed as nothing but a lot of fictitious make-believe. If that is a fairly standard reaction to viewing horror films, how does that practice affect the functioning of the mind in a serious attempt to consider the Bible's teaching on hell? Jesus warns us, 'Do not be afraid of those who kill the body but cannot kill the soul. Rather, be afraid of the one who can destroy both soul and body in hell' (Matt. 10:28). The sick substance of a horror film may prove to be useful ammunition in the hands of the devil. A regular mental diet of the horrible and the hideous may help effectively to anaesthetize the mind against feeling and fearing the awesome horror and terrifying reality of the place called 'hell'. It is worth noting that it is not only Christians who are disturbed by these trends. In an article entitled 'Why Satan is taking over the box' (*Daily Mail*, 6 December 1980), Martin Jackson voiced the concern being felt: 'It is not all as harmless as it may appear. The retreat from reason into a new age of superstition and credulity is worrying both scientists and religious authorities.'

Thankfully, these distortions of human faculties present no insuperable barriers to the grace of God. But this does not relieve us of the responsibility to understand how our hearers think and feel, how their mental and emotional mechanisms are conditioned by the environment in which they live. Like the prodigal son in our Lord's parable, the working man has taken himself off to a far country to seek satisfaction in the fleeting fantasies of our entertainment-orientated society. Our task is to bring him back to face reality: the reality of sin and salvation, the reality of spiritual and eternal values and, above all, the reality of a forgiving Father who will bestow upon returning sinners all the riches of His grace.

Decision-making

Our Lord's parable of the talents (Matt. 25: 14-30) aims to demonstrate certain spiritual principles in relation to the responsibilities and rewards of Christian service. The 'five-talent' servant and the 'two-talent' servant traded conscientiously with their master's property and received their due commendation and rewards when the master returned. The 'one-talent' servant did not follow the policy of his colleagues but pursued a course of action (or rather inaction) which earned his master's stern anger and solemn judgement.

An essential requirement in profitable trading is the proper exercise of the human faculty of decision-making. The 'five-talent' and the 'two-talent' servants no doubt faced a number of opportunities for business enterprise. As each opportunity was assessed, a decision necessarily followed. Their skill in decision-making inevitably proved a major factor in their successful stewardship. However, the 'one-talent' man, for the reasons or excuses he concocted, buried his talent in the ground. He made the decision to avoid all decision-making, its responsibilities and risks. He acted as though he had no talent at all. The reward for this gross neglect of duty was severe in the extreme.

God, our Creator, has endowed all people with the capability, or faculty, of decision-making. It is an aspect of the normal activity of the human mind. This activity occurs at the point where the mental process of assessment leads to a particular course of action. In our work of the gospel it is important for us to understand how this faculty operates in the people we are seeking to evangelize. Can we identify particular intellectual skills within the overall decision-making process which it is possible to define and develop? Can we identify particular influences which affect the function of decision-making in working-class people?

The basic input to our decision-making faculty must be *facts*. We make our decisions on the basis of the information available to us. Every Christian is expected to be 'growing in the knowledge of God' (Col. 1:10). A basic skill in our thinking process is that of *reason*. All Christians are to be ready to give a 'reason' or 'logical defence' for the 'hope' that they have (1 Peter 3:15). But no one will become savingly convinced of the truth of the gospel solely because it has been presented in a reasoned way. Otherwise, we would all be lawyers! Nevertheless, we have plenty of biblical example for presenting the gospel in a clear, convincing and reasoned way (Acts 17:2,3; 18:4,5; 19:8). We are to be God's 'persuaders' (2 Cor. 5:11). We are also to cultivate the faculty of *discernment* (Phil. 1:9,10). We are to develop a *sense of proportion* (2 Cor. 4:16,17). (For the opposite see Matt. 23:23.) We need to formulate a *scale of values* (Matt. 5:30; Mark 8:36; Rom. 14:17; 1 Tim. 4:8). *Experience is* also a necessary factor contributing to the decision-making process. We learn by our failures as well as by our successes (Heb. 5:14). Decisions themselves may be influenced by impulse or intuition, but should not be governed by these factors. Decision-making should involve a co-ordination of the various aspects of the process of assessment. When a conclusion is reached the mind then signals to the will to set in motion a particular course of action.

The apostle Paul's response to the vision of the man from Macedonia provides us with a useful example of Christian decision-making. The vision which Paul received was not regarded as a divine directive bypassing the need for any intellectual evaluation of that experience. It is plain from Scripture that both Paul and his colleagues subjected the vision to serious and sober analysis. 'After Paul had seen the vision, we got ready at once to leave for Macedonia, *concluding* that God had called us to preach the gospel to them' (Acts 16:10).

The word translated 'concluding' (confidently inferring — Amplified Bible) also appears in Acts 9:22. When in Damascus Paul (then Saul) defended his new allegiance to Jesus by 'proving (comparing and examining evidence and proving — Amplified Bible) that 'Jesus is the Christ'. The normal and regular use of our decision-making faculty promotes a growing maturity, and often leads to increasing responsibility (Matt. 25: 21,23).

All the faculties with which we have been endowed by God are to be exercised and developed for the glory of God and the good of our neighbour. But, regrettably, there are often barriers which block the way to our pursuit of the ideal. People suffering from severe emotional problems often find that uncontrolled feelings lead to irrational decisions and actions (1 Sam. 19:9,10).

People with moral problems may also be at a serious disadvantage here. I well recall the time several years ago when

I came into contact with a man who had just been released from prison. When he returned to his home and family he was not welcome. His wife openly despised him in front of the children. It was tragic to observe. Within a short while he expressed the longing to be back in prison. This apparently strange wish was not solely related to the hostile reception by his family. His major problem was decision-making. When he was released from prison he came out into a society where people have the right and duty to think for themselves and make their own decisions. But prison life had not equipped him to face the normal decisions of everyday life. Earning and spending, coping with work and caring for the family — these and other everyday responsibilities were too much for him. In prison other people has made his decisions for him. He had been shielded from the normal human activity of decision-making. Consequently, in this area of his mental development he was seriously retarded.

A more common, and in some ways more serious problem, concerning decision-making is the reverse of the one we have just considered. The ex-prisoner was only too ready to surrender to someone else his responsibility for decision-making. By contrast, many working-class people who ought to have the opportunity for decision-making are denied this right because of the nature of certain industrial and residential 'structures' of our urban society. In our earlier survey of features of urban life we drew attention to what we called 'power and the professionals'. We claimed that positions of power and influence in local government are often concentrated in the hands of people who do not live within the urban community over which their authority is exercised. Local residents should have a bigger share in the decision-making which directly affects the 'quality of life' in their neighbourhoods. Where a just sharing in decision-making is denied to local people, it is very easy for suspicion, prejudice and antagonism to fester in relationships with 'the authorities'.

On the work scene there is a similar problem. Power and decision-making are often concentrated in the hands of a few senior officers who may be remote from the many employees affected by their decisions. Roger Lloyd speaks of 'the industrial psychologist, the efficiency expert, the productivity planner' as officials who do the working man's thinking for him and devise the necessary incentives. In a large business enterprise the average worker may feel that he is being treated as a bit of the machinery rather than a person. He is not there to *think;* he is there to *do.* This feature of industrial society's depersonalizing influence is probably more serious than we at first realize. No fat wage-packet can ever be a compensation for the dehumanizing effects of his work environment.

Bishop David Sheppard has expressed his concern on this matter. He says, 'The change from school to work is often the period when flickering hopes and ambitions are snuffed out. At a good school a boy has been expected to learn to use increasing freedom, to think for himself, to question the way things are, to make choices which will effect change. When he starts his first job, unless he is a management trainee or apprentice, the emphasis will be on conformity, on fitting in, on doing what he is told. That way he will come to be regarded as a good worker.'[23]

Bishop Sheppard also says, 'I believe as a Christian that man is made in the image of God. Part of what I understand by this is that men should not be just creatures who react to the forces of the universe. They should be able to make decisions which alter their own (and other people's) destiny. We have allowed urban conditions to make people despair — and with good reason — of making significant decisions about anything. We mustn't be surprised that they have turned away from the Christian challenge to make decisions about the whole of life and about eternity. It is highly relevant for Christians to try to understand the pressures which limit people's development of ability and to search after ways of removing such barriers.'[24]

The use of the word 'decision' in the present context has no association with a suspect 'easy-believism' which is often linked with certain forms of evangelism. The whole range of the demands of Christian discipleship face the believer with the continuing responsibility for decision-making. If we are to see working-class Christians grow in maturity then we must be sensitive and sympathetic to their particular limitations and potential for making decisions.

Mental discipline

As we conclude this investigation into the way the working

man's thought processes operate, we may be wondering whether this careful analysis of language forms is not taking things a little too far. Are we making a mountain out of a molehill?

This query of the value of studying mental processes and language forms would not arise if our work was on the overseas mission field. The overseas missionary expects to engage in language study. He would not expect to make progress without it. But *we are* in a mission field situation in our urban areas. Missionary principles ought to be applied to the situation. We have already noted that a common view of working-class people is that, 'Churches are cold, dark and dull, with people singing dull hymns, saying dull prayers and listening to *unintelligible sermons. The language of Christianity is foreign* — so are its practices, and its people.'

We have already learned of John Wesley's profound impact upon the working-class people of the eighteenth century. Not only was he greatly used in his preaching to bring men and women into an experience of the new birth, he was also highly skilled in establishing these converts in their faith, and overseeing their Christian growth. Was this just the natural gift of an exceptional communicator, or was it more the mental discipline of a dedicated and discerning servant of God? John Wesley lets us into the secret, and leaves us in no doubt. His preaching policy is published in the preface of a book of *Forty-Four Sermons*. He says, 'I design plain truth for plain people: therefore, of set purpose, I abstain from all nice and philosophical speculations; from all perplexed and intricate reasonings; and, as far as possible, from even the show of learning, unless in sometimes citing the original Scripture. I labour to avoid all words which are not easy to be understood, all which are not used in common life; and, in particular, those kinds of technical terms that so frequently occur in Bodies of Divinity; those modes of speaking which men of reading are intimately acquainted with, but which to common people are an unknown tongue. Yet, I am not assured, that I do not sometimes slide into them unawares; it is so extremely natural to imagine that a word which is familiar to ourselves is so to all the world.'[25]

These principles, no doubt hammered out by Wesley over a period of time, may take some digesting, particularly if we have given little thought to them before. We may conveniently

Battle for the mind

summarize his policy under five headings.
1. He had a constant awareness of the mental capacities of the people to whom he was speaking: '*I design plain truth for plain people.*'
2. He avoided the use of abstract and intricate reasoning: '*I abstain ...from all ...philosophical speculations ...intricate reasonings...*' Wesley was aware of the normal mental mechanisms of his hearers.
3. He deliberately used a simple and restricted vocabulary: '*I ...avoid all words which are not easy to be understood ...technical terms that ...occur in Bodies of Divinity.*'
4. He made a cautious use of 'learning' and only used it as it served to make clearer the meaning of Scripture: '*...unless in sometimes citing the original Scripture.*'
5. He cultivated this manner of preaching through a strong mental discipline: '*Of set purpose, I abstain ...I labour to avoid...*'

If the thought of grappling with the mental mechanisms of the working-class mind is an exercise we do not relish, then perhaps the example of the saintly David Brainerd (1718-1747) will inspire us to persevere. The language barrier he had to overcome, in the work of the gospel among the Red Indians of North America, makes our linguistic problems look small in comparison.

'Brainerd said, "There are no words in the Indian language to answer our English words, 'Lord, Saviour, salvation, sinner, justice, condemnation, faith, repentance, justification, adoption, sanctification, grace, glory, heaven', with scores of the like importance." He had to call regeneration "the heart's being made good", and entering into glory was described as "being made more happy". He also complained, "What renders it more difficult to convey divine truths to the understandings of these Indians, is that there seems to be no foundation in their minds to begin upon; I mean no truths which may be taken for granted, as being already known while I am attempting to instil others." He goes on to explain how he set about teaching the Indians the perfections of God, the difference between the soul and the body, the reality and nature of sin, and the necessity of Christ's work for salvation. It is clear that he showed considerable skill in adapting his presentation of the truths of Scripture to the mental capacities of the Indians.'[26]

We are in a Holy War. We must fight if we would win. Our

great objective is to conquer the mind and to capture the soul. Like David Brainerd, we must persevere with devotion and discipline so that we, too, may show 'considerable skill in adapting the presentation of the truths of Scripture to the mental capacities' of our hearers. 'For though we live in the world, we do not wage war as the world does. The weapons we fight with are not weapons of the world. On the contrary, they have divine power to demolish strongholds. We demolish arguments and every pretension that sets itself up against the knowledge of God, and we take captive every thought to make it obedient to Christ' (2 Cor. 10:3-5).

4.
A message for the millions

'Evangelism' is not a Bible word. Does that surprise us? It does not appear in our English versions. Nor is there its equivalent in the original language. So why do we use it? It has to do with spreading the gospel — the 'evangel'. But why is it a word in common usage among evangelical churches today, even though the word does not appear in Scripture?

It is possible to detect a marked contrast between the New Testament Christians and those of today in relation to the spreading of the gospel. Put simply, it is this: they did it; we talk about it! Evangelism for the early Christians was not something they isolated from other aspects of Christian living in order to specialize, analyse, theorize and organize. They just did it! Of course, the New Testament contains teaching on the subject of the 'evangel' — what it is; and how to 'evangelize' — how we are to spread the good news. But there was never any intention to prepare an 'elite' of keen believers who were 'specially trained' for this Christian activity. In one sense, none of the New Testament believers was a 'specialist' in evangelism; in another sense they all were! It was a part of everyday life for every believer. What is striking about the spreading of the gospel in the New Testament era is the natural way in which this took place.

When the Samaritan woman had received the living water which Jesus offered to her she could not go back to her townsfolk fast enough to tell what had happened to her (John 4:28,29). Jesus did not have to urge her to pluck up courage, to be brave and bold, in order to tell others about the Lord. Without any prompting or persuasion from Jesus, she hurried back to the town and immediately engaged in gospel witness. The Lord did not suggest that she should attend a series of seminars on personal evangelism before she embarked on this task of telling others about her new-found Saviour. She just did it. It came naturally.

When persecution broke out against the early Christians in Jerusalem they were scattered to other areas. Then what happened? 'Those who had been scattered preached the word wherever they went' (Acts 8:4). They did not sit down and lick their wounds and lament that persecution had disrupted their plans and spoiled their future. How could they be expected to spread the gospel now? After all, they were in new and unfamiliar situations. Their spiritual leaders, the apostles, had remained in Jerusalem. Who was going to take the lead? Rather than rush in with the good news, would it not be wiser to set up a 'working party' to investigate in depth this matter of spreading the gospel? Nothing of the sort! They just went everywhere announcing the gospel — no special training, no special techniques, no committees, no conferences, no international congress. They just did it. For those early Christians, spreading the gospel was (in the words of an old song) 'doing what comes naturally'! Amazing, but true. And so it should be for any and every Bible-taught and Spirit-directed Christian.

Why is the situation so different among evangelical Christians today? I would not want to disparage the conferences we plan, the commissions we set up or even the articles and books we write! If it is 'unnatural' for believers to gossip the gospel nowadays, then there must be reasons for it. Much as I wish there were some short cuts whereby we could discover and regain the naturalness of the Samaritan woman and those 'scattered believers' in their bold and instinctive witness, I believe we must do some hard and patient thinking. There is no way round it. Transformed lives stem from renewed minds.

It is interesting to note that certain functions of our physical bodies happen 'naturally' when we are in good health. Normally, I breathe naturally without thinking about it. But should a virus or infection attack my lungs, I then become aware of difficulties in my breathing. I am forced to think about it. It may require conscious effort. Diagnosis of the trouble is required. A remedy is needed in order to restore the lungs to their normal functioning again. When I am breathing normally again the sign of recovery will be that I do not need to think about it. It will happen naturally.

For many believers, their 'evangelistic lungs' are in a poor state of health. Witnessing to our faith in Jesus Christ is such an effort — just like laboured breathing! We cannot go on like this. We must carry out some biblical tests on our patient to diagnose the problems and propose the remedies.

Thinking scripturally

'I am of Apollos.' No, do not misunderstand me. I fully accept the apostle's warning to the Corinthian Christians about the dangers of parties and cliques within a local church (1 Cor. 1:10-12; 3: 1-9). But when it comes to 'thinking scripturally', then Apollos is a man of God whom I would want to emulate. 'He was a learned man, with a thorough knowledge of the Scriptures' or, as another version puts it, he was 'well versed and mighty in the Scriptures' (Acts 18: 24-28).

This man who had applied himself with great diligence to taking in the Word of God was equally competent in giving out the Word of God. 'He had been instructed in the way of the Lord, and he spoke with great fervour and taught about Jesus accurately...' Even so, although Apollos was already a powerful teacher, he also retained the spirit of a humble learner. As yet 'he knew only the baptism of John'. Aware of this deficiency, Aquila and Priscilla took it upon themselves to invite Apollos to their home where, from the Scriptures, they 'expounded to him the way of God more definitely and accurately' (Acts 18: 26, Amplified Bible). His passion for ever-increasing competence in the knowledge of God equipped him for ever-increasing usefulness in the service of God. In subsequent ministry he 'vigorously refuted the Jews in public debate, proving from the Scriptures that Jesus was the Christ'.

What has the example of Apollos to teach us about evangelism? In this servant of God we find that the attribute of 'zeal' is happily married to that of 'knowledge'. But where there is a breakdown of the marriage between 'knowledge' and 'zeal' there is trouble ahead. The apostle Paul lamented the conditon of his fellow Jews. He says, 'For I can testify about them that they are zealous for God, but their zeal is not based on knowledge' (Rom 10:2).

How often have the apostle's words, 'by all means save some' (1 Cor. 9:22), been used to justify anything and everything done in the name of evangelism? Red hot zeal coupled with any kind of novelty or innovation designed to gain a hearing for the gospel can bring disgrace on the gospel of grace and does disservice to the cause of Christ. What Paul wrote about evangelism in his first letter to the Corinthian church ought never to be detached from what he said to them in his second letter. He claimed, 'We have renounced secret and shameful ways; we do not use deception, nor do we distort the word of God. On the contrary, by *setting forth the truth plainly* we commend ourselves to every man's conscience in the sight of God' (2 Cor. 4:2).

A balanced exposition and application of the words, 'by all means save some', must be qualified and limited by the Scripture to which we have just referred. It follows that biblical evangelism necessarily involves a renunciation of all carnal or cunning methods of evangelism. Anything which employs gimmick, fosters an atmosphere of entertainment, exploits the emotions or trivializes the message stands condemned by Scripture. Biblical evangelism must honour God, exalt Christ and abase the sinner. Every aspect of our evangelism should derive from thinking that is saturated in Scripture.

Our chief concern at this stage of our study is an examination of biblical principles of evangelism with particular reference to our desire to reach the working classes with the gospel. I want to make my conscience captive to the Word of God. If other Christians wish me to amend or modify my views on evangelism then they must persuade me from Scripture. The lessons from church history and Christian experience are valuable and should not be ignored. But ultimately even those lessons, however impressive in themselves, must be brought to the bar of Scripture. We must be satisfied that they are in accord with biblical precept or practice. This is how I want to be persuaded. This is how I want to persuade others. Hence my admiration for Apollos. As a pastor, I believe I can best lead the flock in which the Lord has placed me by striving to be 'well-versed and (dare I say it?) mighty in the Scriptures'.

The message we are called to proclaim

A gospel for the working classes?

Before we get down to examining the manner and methods of our evangelism among the working classes, we must first of all give some attention to the message of the gospel that we are called to declare. There is little point in bringing our methods into line with Scripture if the message we convey is other than that taught by Scripture.

Is there really a problem here? Surely, there is only one message, one gospel. 'Christ Jesus came into the world to save sinners' (1 Tim. 1:15). That is how I understand it. Apparently, however, not all find it as simple and clear-cut as that.

Inner urban areas and industrial working-class communities are receiving increasing attention from government departments, sociologists, theologians and the like. They all acknowledge responsibility to face up to the problems and deprivation which are the particular features of these areas. Out of this great volume of thinking that is taking place, the 'urban theologians' are coming up with their policies for the renewal of these inner-city areas. But some of the terminology used by these 'experts' triggers off alarm bells in my mind. When I hear a person speaking about 'the gospel for the working classes' or talking about 'a gospel for the city' my suspicions are aroused. Is the message we preach in our urban churches to be different from that proclaimed elsewhere?

If some of these 'experts' are using their terms in an imprecise way, then perhaps my fears are unfounded. It may be that they are trying to draw our attention to the fact that we do need to present the gospel to working-class folk in ways that differ from that which might be appropriate in suburbia. If, behind their unwise terminology, they still hold to 'one gospel', then I am happy. The Bible makes it abundantly plain that there is only one gospel, one message. The apostle Paul was very firm on this matter when he wrote to the Galatian Christians: 'If anybody is preaching to you a gospel other than what you accepted, let him be eternally condemned' (Gal. 1:9).

Confusion and its causes

Is there then, in reality, a departure in evangelism today from the one gospel taught in Scripture? Regrettably, I believe there is. It goes deeper than methods and affects the message we are charged to declare. What is the gospel? That is the matter above all else on which we must be clear in our evangelism. But there is plenty of evidence that there is a large measure of confusion among the churches on this particular issue. There are unmistakable signs that the primary concern of the gospel, which seeks to bring about a restoration of a sinner's relationship with his Maker, is now being replaced by concern for his physical and social welfare.

Roger Greenway, an American writer with much experience of urban work in a number of countries, pin-points this disturbing change of emphasis. He says, 'Major changes are occurring in churches' conceptions of their mission and message to the world. There is a shift from personal and experiential understanding of the gospel to communal and social concerns. There is a change from the vertical emphasis in the Christian message to the horizontal. Whereas in the past the horizontal was neglected, today the vertical is increasingly ignored. We are told that in response to the question, "Are you saved?" we should not answer by talking about heaven, but about this world and the changes we want to bring about here and now.'[1]

Another American author, David Moberg, more than confirms the fears of his fellow-countryman. He claims, 'There is a wide-spread confusion about the definition of evangelism among all except fundamentalist and "conservative evangelical" Christians. A wide variety of activities is included by various religious groups under the heading of evangelism. These range all the way from traditional revivalistic efforts to social ministries, administration and reception of the sacraments, fellowship, the church school, worship, recreational activities, church-sponsored bowling leagues, small-group discussions, studying the community social action and casual contacts and friendships of church members. What one group identifies as evangelism is totally excluded from evangelism by another.

Some argue that everything done by a Christian person or by a church congregation has evangelistic implications. But does this make all of their activities evangelism?'[2]

This is very disturbing. Whether or not these emphases, evident in the United States, are more or less advanced there than in our own country is something I do not know. What is plain is that the gathering trends are moving in the same direction.

Before we attempt to unravel some very tangled thinking, let us first examine some of the reasons why urban churches are in this position today.

1. Urban deprivation. We have already drawn attention to 'urban deprivation' in an earlier part of our study. The problems of living in the inner city have received a fair amount of publicity through the media, and have attracted the help of the government in financial terms, the help of voluntary welfare organizations and also, as we would expect, the help of the churches. But how can the churches maintain a biblical balance of spiritual priorities when they are surrounded by urgent and escalating social needs? Were the churches to use all their resources of personnel and finance in meeting social needs alone, this would barely scratch the surface of all that needs to be done.

As we have already discovered, historically these areas are thoroughly pagan. It is not surprising that churches who do have a gospel to declare find that indifference and apathy towards the church and what it stands for swiftly chill the keenest evangelistic zeal and dim the spiritual vision. Is it not more rewarding to offer to the needy that social help, which they know they desperately need, rather than slog on wearily from door to door with a spiritual message that nobody appears to want? These factors determine the climate of church thinking in these working-class areas.

A true gospel church will need strong faith and firm resolve if it is to battle on with its God-given task in evangelism without compromise or capitulation to prevailing trends. It is all too easy for a church in an urban working-class community to become a church without a message. When that happens the end result is inevitable. In the course of time that situation will become a community without a church!

2. Marxism. Marxist thinking is most likely to take root in the urban areas. Up to the present time this factor has probably made only a minor contribution to those influences of thought and practice affecting urban churches. But there is good reason to believe that its influence is bound to increase.

If Marxist ideology offers to the working man a shorter route to the social utopia to which he believes he is entitled, then the Christian church is an unequal competitor for his allegiance. The message of the church will have to be directed to the working man's need for patience and his need to eschew materialism. 'We are with you. Things will get better. We are not here for ever. Although you may be among the "have-nots" in this life, never mind. You will be among the "haves" in the next life.' The Marxist offer is far more immediate and attractive: 'You deserve to be, and you can be among the "haves" in this life. It is the only life you are going to get!'

How can the church respond to this challenge? The church will need to demonstrate to the working man that what it offers is a more than comparable 'quality of life' with that offered by its rival. But inevitably this contest for the allegiance of the working man is going to pressurize the churches into majoring on the social, rather than spiritual, benefits which the Christian faith offers.

3. *Reaction to 'social gospel'*. Earlier this century the 'social gospel' made its inroads into the preaching and practice of the churches. Rightly, evangelicals saw this as a betrayal of the true gospel and consequently swung away from it. But swings can go too far. Now the pendulum is going the other way. It is moving in the direction of increasing social concern. For some the pendulum is still moving towards the point of biblical balance. But for others the swing has already gone too far. There will be pressure on evangelicals to go too far because of the other influences in that direction which we have already considered.

4. *The ministry of Jesus.* A fourth factor which has some bearing on the current uncertainty surrounding the question, 'What is the gospel?' stems from Scripture itself. This is surprising. Normally we expect that when the Word of God is brought to bear on any issue then clarification and not confusion should be the result. However, there appear to be exceptions. There is at the present time (and not for the first time) a tendency to set the message and ministry of Jesus over against that of the apostle Paul. There is the suggestion that, whereas Paul's gospel was an exclusively spiritual message which dealt with the sinner's

relationship to God, the message preached by Jesus was not so narrowly drawn. It had something to offer men and women in their external social conditions rather than being directed solely to their inward spiritual condition.

One of the chief Scriptures used to support this contention is Jesus' reference to the prophecy of Isaiah at the beginning of His ministry. He went into the synagogue at Nazareth. The scroll of Isaiah's prophecy was handed to Him and He read the following words: 'The Spirit of the Lord is on me, because he has anointed me to preach good news to the poor. He has sent me to proclaim freedom for the prisoners and recovery of sight for the blind, to release the oppressed, to proclaim the year of the Lord's favour' (Luke 4: 18,19). After He had finished that reading from Isaiah, Jesus went on to claim, 'Today this scripture is fulfilled in your hearing' (Luke 4:21).

The crucial question is this: 'What is the correct interpretation of Jesus' application of Isaiah's words to His own message and ministry?' Evangelical commentators are not of one mind on this. Some interpret this wholly in 'spiritual' terms by applying the words to the sinner's inward and 'vertical' needs of a new relationship with God — release from the bondage of sin, recovery of spiritual sight and release from inward oppression. Others interpret these verses in the 'horizontal' dimension applying them to social needs. Their claim is that this was the intended interpretation when applied to the situation in which Isaiah spoke these words originally. It is argued that the same rule of interpretation must be applied in Jesus' use of these words. It does appear indefensible to interpret this Messianic prophecy solely in spiritual terms, and particularly in view of the message that Jesus sent back to John the Baptist when he was passing through a period of doubt as to whether or not Jesus was the Messiah for whom they had been waiting (Matt. 11:1-6).

Whatever the correct interpretation is, we must say that the gospel we are called to preach and spread cannot be precisely defined by two verses which have a specific application to Jesus as the Messiah. The gospel we are to proclaim must be one which takes account of a much wider range of Scripture, chiefly in the New Testament, in which we see from the book of Acts and the letters the gospel both defined and declared (1 Cor. 15:1-4; Gal. 1:11,12).[3]

One gospel

1. A definition. What is the gospel? The New Testament word 'gospel' comes from the Greek word 'evangel' which means 'good news'. The word is used over seventy times in the New Testament. It is 'the glorious gospel of the blessed God' (1 Tim. 1:11). It is 'the gospel of God's grace' (Acts 20:24). It is 'the gospel of the glory of Christ' (2 Cor. 4:4).

Stuart Olyott has attempted a definition of evangelism in the following terms: 'Evangelism is the relating of the Evangel, by means of the spoken word, and in the power of the Holy Spirit — in order that men may seek God, repent of their sins, and believe on the Lord Jesus Christ and be saved; and then order the whole of their lives by his Word.'[4]

The essential content of the gospel is the news of the provision, by a gracious God, of the way whereby the alienated sinner may come into a restored and permanent relationship with his holy Creator. Its concern is with the inward condition and eternal need of the sinner. The gospel in itself is not primarily concerned with outward conditions and the temporal needs of the sinner. The gospel should have immediate and inevitable social consequences, but these blessings are not the essence of the gospel. They flow from it. The gospel is directed to the 'root' of our problem — the need for a changed heart. When this objective has been achieved, then the 'changed root' will produce 'changed fruit'.

2. Jesus and the gospel. Jesus began His public ministry by preaching the gospel. 'After John was put in prison, Jesus went into Galilee, proclaiming the good news of God. "The time has come," he said. "The kingdom of God is near. Repent and believe the good news!" ' (Mark 1:14,15.) Towards the end of His ministry, two of His followers described him as 'a prophet, powerful in word and deed before God and all the people' (Luke 24:19). The principal role of a prophet is to speak God's Word to man.

3. Body and soul. God made man's body and his soul. They were both created very good. Man has been wonderfully made by his Creator; he is also utterly dependent upon his Creator. Because man has been designed by God with physical, social and spiritual needs, these are all important. None is unimportant; but the spiritual need is more important than the physical and social needs.

A number of Scriptures support this differentiation and evaluation. We will mention just two. Jesus said, 'Do not be afraid of those who kill the body but cannot kill the soul. Rather, be afraid of the one who can destroy both soul and body in hell' (Matt. 10:28). Paul wrote to Timothy, 'Train yourself to be godly. For physical training is of some value, but godliness has value for all things, holding promise for both the present life and the life to come' (1 Tim. 4:7,8).

4. A matter of life and death. There is a good measure of logic in the claim that in fulfilling our duty towards our unbelieving neighbour our first task should be to prepare him to die; then we can prepare him to live. This may sound back-to-front and a little morbid, but a strong case for it can be argued from the Scriptures. This seems to be the main thrust of the Lord's teaching in the parable of the 'rich fool' (Luke 12:13-21).

The greatest certainty of life is death! Before our Lord's return no one will avoid it; none may cheat it. It is certain, whereas life on this earth is uncertain. We may live another fifty years; we may not live another day. We may face years of peace and plenty; we may face years of strife and sorrow. It is all uncertain. At the point of death a person's social condition is irrelevant. 'For we brought nothing into the world, and we can take nothing out of it' (1 Tim. 6:7, Eccles. 5:15). Death is the great leveller. The king and the beggar die as equals. Their respective social conditions have no necessary bearing on the way they die. Can we claim to have combined wisdom with compassion, if we work to improve a person's social condition in this life while we repeatedly postpone preparation for death and the next life until, without warning, the event overtakes us? Death may cheat us and may make us look a fool. The road to hell is paved with good intentions.

This is not to say that we must react against the emphasis of which we have just warned. To be wholly concerned, in the first place, about a person's spiritual needs and, at that stage, to be wholly unconcerned about his social needs may also be biblically indefensible. If a man is illiterate, there is little point in leaving him a booklet on *The Way of Salvation*, if there is no one to read and explain it to him. If a young widow with a large family works herself to the bone, it is cruel and not kind, at the end of a long day, to expect her to listen to your exposition of John 3, when she can barely force her eyelids open. The wasted vagrant is hardly going to welcome your gospel tract if he has not had a square meal for some time. So we could go on. A man's soul is more important than his body, but until his elementary needs are met (e.g. food, clothing, shelter, attention to health etc.), it is unlikely that he will be ready to consider seriously his spiritual condition and eternal destiny. There will be occasions where a man's social need will take precedence, from a time point of view, over the meeting of his spiritual needs.

5. *Words and deeds.* The Scripture makes it abundantly plain that God's people *must* be concerned about the social needs of their neighbours. Like our Master, our earthly Christian service must be 'in word and deed' and not in word alone. We are not saved *by* our good works, but we are saved *for* good works.

'For we are God's workmanship, created in Christ Jesus to do good works, which God prepared in advance for us to do' (Eph. 2:10).

Jesus Christ 'gave himself for us to redeem us from all wickedness and to purify for himself a people that are his very own, eager to do what is good' (Titus 2:14).

Religion that God our Father accepts as pure and faultless is this: to look after orphans and widows in their distress and to keep oneself from being polluted by the world' (James 1:27).

'What good is it, my brothers, if a man claims to have faith but has no deeds? Can such faith save him? Suppose a brother or sister is without clothes and daily food. If one of you says to him, "Go, I wish you well; keep warm and well fed," but does nothing about his physical needs, what good is it? In the same way, faith by itself, if it is not accompanied by action, is dead' (James 2:14-17).

Neglect of the Christian's duty of social concern will bring some shocks and tears at the judgement day (Matt. 25:31-46).

The people we are concerned to reach

Do we practise unfair discrimination?

'My brothers, as believers in our glorious Lord Jesus Christ, don't show favouritism. Suppose a man comes into your meeting wearing a gold ring and fine clothes, and a poor man in shabby clothes also comes in. If you show special attention to the man wearing fine clothes and say, "Here's a good seat for you," but say to the poor man, "You stand there," or, "Sit on the floor by my feet," have you not discriminated among yourselves and become judges with evil thoughts?' (James 2:1-4.)

There is no problem in understanding the principle James is dealing with here. But in what context is it being applied? Surely it must be evangelism. The two men who come into the Christian assembly are not spoken of as Christian brothers: they are strangers perhaps attending a Christian meeting for the first time. The response of the believers is the beginning of their evangelistic responsibility to these two men. But, because of the way they are dressed, one man receives special attention and the other man is neglected. That is the sin of favouritism. It is unfair discrimination. The warning of James has the ring of reality about it. It does happen.

How does this apply to reaching the working classes with the gospel? We have already seen that, generally speaking, the working man is not willing to go to church — it is outside his circle; he does not belong to that 'class'. But if we make the main focus of our evangelism the preaching of the gospel from the pulpit we are discriminating unfairly against the working man. It is the church-goer who is able to hear and understand the gospel. He receives 'special attention', but the person who does not attend church is neglected. This is not to say that there are no attempts to take the gospel to him, but because the main focus of evangelism centres on the pulpit, the person who is not willing to come to church is unlikely to have the same level of attention as the church-goer.

We should remember that the rejection of an invitation to attend church is not the rejection of the gospel itself. We must clearly distinguish between these two. Nowhere does the New Testament *demand* that the unbeliever should come within the gathered congregation in order to hear the gospel preached. In fact, there are some good logical and theological reasons why we should *not* expect people to come to church to hear the gospel. How can a person who is still spiritually 'dead in transgressions and sins' be expected to appreciate what 'church' is for? When we set the gospel preaching within the context of a service of Christian worship are we not in some way expecting the visitor to do something which we know (theologically) he is not able to do? We worship 'by the Spirit of God' (Phil. 3:3). Until the unbeliever is born again by the Spirit of God he cannot worship in the way that God requires (John 4:21-24). Should we be surprised at all that so few working-class folk are prepared to attend church?

If there are large cultural and theological barriers to overcome before the working man can expect to hear the gospel, we ought to ask who has the responsibility for seeing that he hears it? Is it the responsibility of the unbeliever to 'come and be evangelized'? Or, is it the responsibility of the believer to 'go and evangelize'? Clearly the New Testament places the responsibility firmly on the believer to spread the gospel. Does the person who is prepared to come to church to hear the gospel have any more right to hear the gospel than the person who is not prepared to come to church?

In this connection it is interesting to contrast the apostle Paul's method of evangelism among the Jews with that which he used among the Gentiles. Among the Jews he had an obvious base from which to begin. He shared in common with his hearers an orthodox religious heritage, attendance at a place of worship and familiarity with the Holy Scriptures. All these contributed to provide Paul with a suitable opportunity in which to explain from the Scriptures that Jesus was the Christ (Acts 17:2,3; 18:4,5; 19:8). Among the Gentiles it was very different. There was no 'standard religious situation', comparable to the synagogue, within which he could make known the gospel to these people. Whereas his evangelism among the Jews shows a certain uniformity, his labours among the Gentiles were characterized by an inevitable variety. There was no one 'best opportunity' which could provide the focus of his evangelism among the Gentiles. The only way Paul could fulfil his commission to 'carry God's name before the Gentiles' was to be a spiritual opportunist and strategist under the constraint and restraint of the Holy Spirit (Acts 16:6-10).

Our evangelical heritage makes us much more favourably disposed towards what we might call 'Jewish evangelism' than we are to the pattern of Paul's 'Gentile evangelism'. We most naturally evangelize those people who are prepared to come into a religious building, attempt to participate in a service of Christian worship, and in that context to listen to reasoning from the Scriptures. Thus in our day the gospel is, in most cases, 'to the church-goer first', and also, if we can make the time, if

A message for the millions

we can find a way, 'to the non-church-goer'.

There are some important questions which every local church ought to ask in relation to its outreach: 'Is our church membership and congregation socially representative of the community we are called to serve? If not, why not?' Is the church in practice (if not in theory) mainly interested in a fairly select minority group within its local community?

New Testament 'God-fearers' and working-class church-goers

Before we explore further how we may reach those working-class people who will not come into a church building to hear the gospel, it may help us in our enquiry if we are able to say something about the very small minority of working-class folk who *do* come to church. Can we give any reasons why they are prepared to be different from the majority of their social group?

A comparison between New Testament 'God-fearers' and working-class church-goers may help us to shed light on this matter. We will ask and attempt to answer four questions in relation to these two particular groups: (i) What kind of people were they *spiritually*? (ii) What kind of people were they *socially*? (iii) Is there any link between the 'spiritual' and the 'social' factors? (iv) What conclusions can we draw?

1. New Testament 'God-fearers': what kind of people were they spiritually? The God-fearers were Gentiles who were 'attracted by the simple monotheism of the Jewish synagogue worship and by the ethical standards of the Jewish way of life. Some of them attended synagogues and were tolerably conversant with the prayers and Scripture lessons which they heard read in Greek.'[5] The people who belonged to this minority group among the Gentiles clearly had sufficient independence of thought and courage of conviction to enable them to break through their inherited social and religious traditions in order to identify themselves with another group. Within that new group they shared in attendance at a place of worship. In that context they were able to hear the Scriptures expounded and the gospel preached.

2. What kind of people were they socially? Does the New Testament give us any clues as to their status in society? A survey of the book of Acts does provide us with some evidence concerning the social standing of the God-fearers. But the evidence is not really sufficient to form a firm conclusion.

Sometimes Luke makes no mention of the social status of the God-fearers or 'devout persons' as they are often called. But wherever social status is indicated, it shows the God-fearers to be more associated with the 'ruling' or 'employer' class than with the 'average Gentile'. Where God-fearers are referred to by name they are among the ruling class, as for example, the Ethiopian treasurer (Acts 8:27,28), Cornelius the Roman centurion (Acts 10:1,2), Lydia the business woman from Thyatira (Acts 16:14).

Also, Luke seems concerned to stress that women of some social standing were among the God-fearers. There are three references to this in which he speaks of women of 'high standing' or 'the leading women' (Acts 13:50; 17:4,12). 'An interest in Judaism was not at all uncommon among the Roman aristocracy, and within the leisured classes generally, particularly the women, whose idleness called for a decent attention to religion. Judaism was presumably felt to offer the respectability of antiquity and a certain austerity of manners which appealed to the Roman mentality.'[6]

A further factor which accentuated the link between the 'ruling class' and the God-fearers was the nature of the Roman household. 'The household, like the republic, expressed its solidarity in a common religion.'[7] In the matter of a change of religion, the conversion of the husband or other head of the household (e.g. Lydia) would commit the rest of his dependent group. On this basis it could be argued that, since a household would have one head and a number of the servant or slave class, then a God-fearing head of household would lead to a number of God-fearing slaves. In the case of Cornelius, 'he and all his family were devout and God-fearing' (Acts 10:2). Although this observation may indicate that the 'God-fearers' were by no means confined to the 'ruling' (rather than 'ruled') class, it does not invalidate the link between social and spiritual factors which we can now demonstrate.

3. Is there any link between the spiritual and the social factors? If not in every case, there seems to be sufficient evidence to say that in many instances there was some link between the spiritual and social factors. The Gentile of social standing would find that his calling in life would involve him in making important decisions, giving commands, exercising independence of thought and judgement. This inherited social factor proved to be an asset in

the matter of considering religious issues. He would be less influenced by the pressures to conform to the thinking of the rest of his group. He was prepared to make up his own mind and act upon it. By the action of the head, the rest of the household had their minds made up for them!
4. *What conclusion can we draw?* In His gracious work of drawing men and women to God, the Holy Spirit is able to work through social factors which may prove helpful, or He can override social factors which would prove harmful, in the process of His work within the soul. In the case of the New Testament God-fearers, it would seem that often the Holy Spirit was able to use the social asset of independence of thought and conviction to work for that person's spiritual good.

Now we come to put the same four questions concerning working-class church-goers.
1. *What kind of people are they spiritually?* They are people who have sufficient strength of conviction to break through the inherited traditions and prejudices of their natural group in order to be identified with another group generally outside their class and circle. As with the God-fearers, they are willing to attend a place of worship. In that context they can hear the Scriptures expounded and the gospel preached.
2. *What kind of people are they socially?* There are sub-divisions within the general category of the working classes as we noted earlier. Working-class church-goers are most likely to be found among the 'privatized' group. They are the kind of people who aspire to leave a working-class area and culture behind them. They want to 'get on' in order to 'get out'. They swim against the tide. They do not conform to their native group. Also, this kind of person will be relatively more numerous in the socially mixed communities (working-class and middle-class) than in the larger urban and industrial areas which have become one-class areas and exhibit a much stronger resistance to church-going.
3. *Is there any link between the spiritual and the social factors?* It would appear, as with the God-fearers, that in many cases there is a link between the two. The aspiring and independent-minded working-class person will be able to bring this social asset into use in considering religious issues. He would be less influenced by the pressure to conform than would others in that same social group.

4. What conclusion can we draw? We may repeat what we said in conclusion about the God-fearers. In His gracious work of drawing men and women to God, the Holy Spirit is able to work through 'social factors' which may prove helpful, or He can override social factors which prove harmful, in the process of His work within the soul. In the case of the working-class churchgoers, it would seem that often the Holy Spirit is able to use the social asset of independence of thought and conviction to work for that person's spiritual good.

In our conclusion about the work of the Holy Spirit in the instances we have cited, we ought to stress that the Holy Spirit normally works through and with those social factors which prove to be an asset for the spiritual welfare of the person concerned. We should *not* expect the Holy Spirit to override those distinctions — educational, cultural, social — which it is normally the responsibility of a missionary-minded church to overcome.

In the foregoing social analysis I do not want to give the impression that I am seeking to intrude into the mystery of God's gracious and sovereign election of His people. There are bound to be Christians in our churches who do not line up with the categories and descriptions we have attempted. Thank God for such people. But we should understand what kind of people we are able to reach with gospel preaching in church, and also what kind of people are not generally reached by this form of evangelism. By all means let us preach the gospel to those people who will come into our church buildings. But that is only a beginning, and no more.

The apostle Paul was specially commissioned by God to bear the gospel to the Gentiles. If Paul had *confined* his gospel labours to those God-fearing Gentiles he met in the Jewish synagogues, he would have been disobedient to his heavenly calling. He would also have been guilty of unfair discrimination. If those churches located in working-class areas confine their gospel labours to the exceptional 'God-fearing' type of working-class person, then that is disobedience and discrimination. Also, if a church in a working-class area is composed of people who are largely unrepresentative of the local community, there will be great difficulty in integrating working-class Christians into the life of that church.

Preachers or witnesses?

The logic of what we have been arguing is that pagan (and I do not use this word in any derogatory sense) working-class folk, as opposed to those we might call God-fearing working-class, are not going to be evangelized primarily through gospel preaching within the gathered congregation in a church building. Outreach that will bring the gospel to these people will have to be what the word says — 'reaching out'. But as soon as we begin to shift the focus of evangelism away from the pulpit we may begin to feel that this inevitably means a diminished emphasis on preaching. If that is so, then for some preachers, almost instinctively, alarm bells ring in our consciences! They did so for John Wesley! (See p.154.) If we detract from the centrality of gospel preaching from the pulpit, will we become unbiblical, unsound and suspect among our colleagues? But what light or advice can we find concerning the place of gospel preaching within the gathered congregation?

The Puritan pastor Richard Baxter (1615-1691) was firm in his denunciation of any attitudes which regarded evangelistic obligations as fulfilled, provided there was regular public preaching of the gospel. Baxter says, 'It is easy to separate from the multitude and to gather distinct churches, and to let the rest sink or swim; and if they will not be saved by public preaching, to let them be damned: but whether this be the most charitable and Christian course, one would think should be no hard question.'[8]

C.H. Spurgeon said, 'I rejoice that God *allows* us to preach in churches and chapels, but I do not pretend that we have any apostolical precedent for it, certainly none for confining our ministry to such places.'[9]

A few years back, Iain Murray, Editor of the *Banner of Truth* magazine, contributed an article to that journal which he entitled: 'Three Proven Principles in Evangelism'. He began the discussion on the second of these principles by saying, 'If it is true that vital evangelism is the consequence of vital Christianity then it follows that the progress of evangelism depends more upon the state of Christians as such than it does upon the work of those who occupy the ministerial office. The exercise of spiritual gifts by preaching elders in the meetings of the church is *not* the primary means by which the gospel spreads. That exercise is limited both by time and by place, but the witness of Christians in the midst of the world is not thus limited.'[10] It is his next remark which should challenge us to re-examine our thinking on this matter. He says, 'It seems to me that this point demands our special attention because I am afraid that the tendency of our tradition has been *away from the New Testament*.'[11] He is openly admitting that our 'Reformed tradition' is in need of reformation at this point!

What we have just discussed in principle was amply demonstrated in the experience of the early church. Michael Green in his book *Evangelism in the Early Church* says, 'The break with the synagogue, the rise of persecution and the absence of Christian buildings for worship all hindered formal proclamation of the gospel. It was not easy to gather a large assembly without inviting police action, and Latourette is undoubtedly right in his judgement that: "The chief agents in the expansion of Christianity appear not to have been those who made it a profession or made it a major part of their occupation, but men and women who carried on their livelihood in some purely secular manner and spoke of their faith to those they met in this natural fashion".'[12]

Our concern to preserve the right content and accurate transmission of the gospel may lead us to overrate the competence of preachers to do this, and also underrate the ability of 'many witnesses' to perform this task with adequate competence but on a much wider scale. We have already drawn attention to the way the gospel spread widely and rapidly in the early church as a result of persecution. The apostles (the professionals) remained with the church at Jerusalem but many ordinary believers (the amateurs) were uprooted and scattered. 'Those who had been scattered preached the word wherever they went' (Acts 8:4).

One has only to recall the conversion of John Bunyan to be reminded that God is well able to work through 'the weak things of the world' to achieve His purposes. Overhearing some women literally 'gossiping the gospel', John Bunyan was deeply convicted by their knowledge and experience in matters of religion. ' "Upon a day," says Bunyan, "the good providence of God did cast me to Bedford, to work on my calling; and in one of the streets of that town, I came where there were three or four poor women sitting at a door in the sun, and talking about the things of God." With eye and ear alert he "drew near to hear what they said". Not curiosity alone prompted him to do so: he had another motive, "for", he explains, "I was now a brisk talker also myself in the matters of religion". But his head drooped and his heart fell as he listened to the women. "I heard, but I understood not," he acknowledges with a humility he had not previously known; "for", he continues, "*they were far above, out of my reach*".

'Hitherto, Bunyan had only measured himself by himself, not even by the father whom his wife has so often put before him; and now he discovered the significance of his own religious life. The women were talking of a new birth, "the work of God in their hearts", and "how they were convinced of their own miserable state by nature". They talked too, of God visiting "their souls with his love in the Lord Jesus". They told also of words and promises, which had refreshed, comforted and supported them 'against the temptations of the devil".'[13]

These comments should help us towards a more biblical and less traditional view of gospel preaching. It has a very important place, and we shall examine it more thoroughly later on. Preaching, however, does have its limitations, and we must be realistic about this. We can now, with an easier conscience, examine why it is that 'Gentile evangelism' is the New Testament model for our gospel work among the working classes today.

Features of New Testament evangelism among the Gentiles

It is important for us to develop a framework of thinking about Gentile evangelism so that our approach to our task is biblical. Now that we have had to say that preaching the gospel from the pulpit is not the way we are going to be able to *introduce* average working-class folk to the gospel, we must be careful that we do not look around for just *one* alternative as the complete answer whereby we can take the gospel to these people.

This is probably the place at which to begin our examination of the features of evangelism among the Gentiles.
1. *A variety of opportunities.* We noticed earlier that Paul's evangelism among the Jews showed a certain uniformity. But his gospel work among the Gentiles exhibited great variety. There was no 'standard religious situation' comparable to the synagogue. So Paul preached and witnessed in the open air

(Acts 17:22-31); in the market-place (Acts 17:17); in a hired hall (Acts 19:9); in private homes (Acts 18:7); in prison (Phil. 1:12,13); by the riverside (Acts 16:13); before Roman authorities (Acts 26:1-29), and on board ship (Acts 27:23-25).

Some Christians may view a variety of opportunities as undesirable because this may suggest that the church lacks decisive convictions about the nature of biblical evangelism. Is the use of many forms and methods just a pragmatic approach which involves experimenting to see what works best? That could be the case, but it need not be so.

In fact, the use of a variety of opportunities may stem from a very firm biblical principle which others have failed to think through. It brings us back again to the issue of unfair discrimination in evangelism. We need to recognize that practically all forms of evangelism discriminate against some people to a greater or lesser extent. A few examples will explain what we mean. Some people in our locality work permanent nights and most weekends. They work through the night and sleep through the day. So daytime evangelism discriminates against them. Like most churches, we have a women's meeting. But there is nothing like that for men. A church which may seek to cater for the particular needs of 'students' in its youth evangelism may unknowingly discriminate against young people whose educational attainments are not nearly so good. A church which directs its evangelistic visiting to the 'owner-occupied' residences in its neighbourhood may be discriminating against the council tenants on the estate where the response is noticeably less.

Obviously this kind of reasoning could be continued to extremes. But this principle of Gentile evangelism is clear. A local church ought to have a variety of forms of evangelism. Every local community has a variety of types of people. Writing of the forms of evangelism employed by the servants of God in the eighteenth-century Evangelical Awakening, Bishop J.C. Ryle writes, 'No place came amiss to them. In field or by the roadside, on the village green or in a market-place, in lanes or in alleys, in cellars or in garrets, on a tub or on a table, on a bench or on a horse-block, wherever hearers could be gathered, the spiritual reformers of the eighteenth century were ready to speak to them about their souls. They were instant in season, and out of season in doing the fisherman's work, and compassed sea and land in carrying forward their Father's business.'[14]

2. *Flexibility.* Preaching the gospel in a place of Christian worship takes place usually at a time and a place which *suit the believers.* Gentile evangelism will inevitably involve us in reaching the unbelievers at a time and place which suit *them.* Is Sunday necessarily the best day for evangelizing the working classes?

John Wesley regularly preached at *five o'clock in the morning*! He did this in order to reach the 'labouring-class' people before they went off at daybreak to commence work in a factory or a mine.

On the matter of the *best day* for reaching the working classes with the gospel, C.H. Spurgeon records an incident which provoked him to further thought: 'A curious circumstance came under my own notice lately; it seems that men may come to hear a preacher on a week-evening with less suspicion than on the Sunday. One who had attended a week-night service was asked to come on the Sabbath, but he replied, "Oh, no; I have not gone so far as that yet!" Attendance at a place of worship on the Sunday has in London become to many people a profession of religion. Merely to hear Spurgeon on a Thursday is a different matter.'[15]

3. *Many witnesses.* One of the reasons why churches continue to have a gospel service is because it does give the opportunity to reach a good number of people at one time and one place. To reach the same number or more with outreach away from the church building will require many witnesses and not just one preacher. Commenting on the event of the scattering of the believers from Jerusalem, Michael Green provides some detail as to what their bold witness would have involved: 'This must often have been not formal preaching, but the informal chattering to friends and chance acquaintances, in homes and wine shops, on walks, and around market stalls. They went everywhere gossiping the gospel; they did it naturally, enthusiastically, and with the conviction of those who are not paid to say that sort of thing. *Consequently, they were taken seriously, and the movement spread, notably among the lower classes.*'[16]

I was once challenged by a man who lived in a dilapidated old tenement block. He was prepared to listen to what the gospel was about. He did not reject what I said. But he made it plain that he did not believe it would work for him. 'It's all right for you,' he retorted, 'you are a professional Christian!' That was his impression and no amount of reason could modify his opinion. In his view, I had it easy. He did not have my job, so he could not have my faith. In that situation, what I could say was very limited. I was at a disadvantage. What was needed was an ordinary working-class Christian who could say simply, 'It works for me, too.'

4. Response and risks. When we preach the gospel in our church buildings that activity has certain similarities with a football team playing a home match! We are on familiar territory. We are surrounded by our supporters. At worst we may encounter apathy, but rarely hostility. But when we take the gospel to the unbeliever, we are 'playing away' and not at home. We may not have any of our supporters with us. We may well run the risk of hostility. It could lead to verbal or physical assault. Remember Paul's fears at Corinth and God's reassurance (Acts 18:9-11).

5. Message. So far we have drawn attention only to differences in form and method in evangelism, we have not yet said anything about the differences in approach and structure of the message. A study of Peter's sermons in the early chapters of the book of Acts compared with some of Paul's sermons will bring out the contrast (Acts 2:14-36; 3:12-26; 4:8-12, compared with Acts 14:15-18, 17:22-31. See also table on pp. 160-161). The sermons of Peter were preached to Jews. The sermons of Paul preached at Lystra and Athens were preached to Gentiles. In the preaching to the Jews, the preacher *began* by reasoning from the Scriptures that Jesus was the Christ. In the preaching to the Gentiles the preacher *began* by reasoning from the world about us that God is Creator and Sustainer of life. We owe Him honour and gratitude and we are totally dependent upon Him.

These five features provide for us a framework of thought within which we should be able to work out what forms of evangelism are most suitable among the working classes today.

We shall go on to examine further principles of biblical evangelism in the next part of our study.

5.
Winning them wisely

We have thought about what the gospel is. We have considered how we are going to find and meet the people we want to hear the gospel. We shall now examine some rules about the way we should carry out our task of spreading the good news.

Plain speaking

The gospel is dynamite! It is nothing less than the '*dunamis* of God'. For this reason every Christian should handle it carefully and use it wisely. A preacher of the gospel has particular responsibility in this direction. That is why the apostle Paul urged Timothy to 'do your best to present yourself to God as one approved, a workman who does not need to be ashamed and who correctly handles the word of truth' (2 Tim. 2:15). Only a fool would toy or play with dynamite! Careless handling of the Scriptures can lead to disaster and even destruction (2 Peter 3:16).

As we have already noticed, zeal without knowledge in the work of evangelism can lead to unworthy methods and a misguided use of Scripture. These things can bring dishonour to God and damage to the cause of Christ.

There are some very sincere Christian believers who seem to have such a high veneration of the Word of God that they view the gospel not as a spiritual message to be communicated to the human mind, but rather as a spiritual explosive to be detonated in the human soul. The general idea is that, in the fight for souls, if only we hit the target with sufficient well-directed scriptural dynamite, then the defences are bound to crumble in time and Satan's captives will be released.

A colleague in the ministry drew my attention several years ago to a Christian brother who engaged in his own very novel style of evangelism. A regular traveller on the London underground trains, he would make his bold witness the moment he stepped off the ascending escalator. Looking down upon a stream of people steadily approaching him, he would let fly what he called his 'gospel shots'. He would bombard the ears of the temporarily captive tube travellers with a fervent volley of gospel texts — John 3:16; Romans 3:23; Romans 6:23 and the rest. Now this good brother obviously had a high regard for the Word of God. The fact that there was no opportunity to explain the Scripture he was quoting did not deter his enthusiasm for this form of witness. From what he was doing, it would appear that he regarded the gospel texts as 'spiritual hand-grenades' which could, if aimed well, explode in the consciences of the hearers and produce conviction of sin and a turning to God. The need for an explanation and understanding of the Word of God was not regarded as vitally necessary. The power of the Word would somehow make its impact on the conscience even though the God-given faculty of thought and reason had largely been bypassed.

Now we must acknowledge that the Word of God does have its own unique power (Heb. 3:12). It is dynamite — in the right sense. Christian history would also bear testimony to those believers who were drawn to the Lord solely through reading the Holy Scriptures and without the intervention of any human instrument to guide or explain.[1] But this is not the scriptural norm. It is exceptional. If it were the norm then there would have been no need for Paul to speak to Timothy in the way that he did. The Amplified Bible renders Paul's exhortation to Timothy in these words: 'Study and be eager and do your utmost to present yourself to God approved (tested by trial), a workman who has no cause to be ashamed, correctly analysing and accurately dividing — rightly handling and skilfully teaching — the Word of Truth' (2 Tim. 2:15, Amplified Bible). If

Winning them wisely

Scripture did have some in-built 'self-explaining', 'auto-expounding' ingredient then it would have saved Timothy a lot of time and toil...and many others, too! Normally, God entrusts human instruments with the task of *explaining* His Word. We shall refer to two examples from Scripture which demonstrate this principle.

When Nehemiah returned from exile (about 444 B.C.) to lead and inspire the work of rebuilding the walls of Jerusalem, there also had to be a rebuilding of the lives of God's people according to the Word of God. As with the rebuilding of the walls, this work, too, was undertaken with diligence and determination by leaders and people. On a particular day, Ezra the scribe was summoned to 'bring out the Book of the Law of Moses, which the Lord had commanded for Israel' (Neh. 8:1). Ezra duly complied and came before the assembly of the people which was comprised of 'men and women and all who were able to understand' (Neh. 8:2). Then came the marathon sermon! 'He read it aloud from daybreak till noon as he faced the square before the Water Gate in the presence of the men, women and others who could understand. And all the people listened attentively to the Book of the Law '(Neh. 8:3). Ezra stood on a high wooden platform built for the occasion and he led the worship in which the people praised the Lord and bowed before Him. Ezra was then assisted by the Levites whose duty was to instruct the people in the Law while they were standing there. The object of this important exercise is stated plainly. 'They read from the Book of the Law of God, making it clear and giving the meaning so that the people could understand what was being read' (Neh. 8:8). Their reaction to hearing the words of the Law brought both tears and joy. Their tears came as they realized their departure from God's law, but eventually their tears gave way to joy. 'Then all the people went away to eat and drink, to send portions of food and to celebrate with great joy, *because they now understood the words that had been made known to them*' (Neh. 8:12).

In His parable of the Sower our Lord warns us that where the seed of God's Word is sown, but there has been a failure to achieve *understanding* in the mind of the hearer, the seed will be swiftly snatched away by the devices of our adversary. 'When anyone hears the message about the kingdom and *does not understand* it, the evil one comes and snatches away what was sown in his heart' (Matt. 13:19).

When God sent Philip the evangelist to meet the treasurer of Ethiopia he found him reading from the prophecy of Isaiah. 'Do you understand what you are reading?' Philip asked. 'How can I,' he said, 'unless someone explains it to me?' Whereupon Philip joined the treasurer in his chariot and began to explain the meaning of the prophecy he had been reading. Philip began with that very portion of Scripture and told him the good news about Jesus (Acts 8:30-35). If all Scripture was 'self-explanatory' then it could have saved Philip an unnecessary interruption in a very fruitful ministry in Samaria.

Any Christian, whether preacher or witness, must be concerned to present the good news of Jesus Christ plainly and simply. Understanding is a faculty given to us by God. It is something that is not possessed by other creatures in God's creation. It is not to be bypassed or neglected in our endeavours to convey the gospel to others. 'Setting forth the truth plainly' (2 Cor. 4:2) — this was the overriding principle which determined the manner in which the apostle Paul communicated the gospel. It must be 'the truth'. There can be no deviation. It must be made plain. It is the preacher's responsibility to speak in words that are intelligible to his hearers. But what does plain speaking demand of us? Surely it is just a case of talking naturally as we might speak about any other topic of everyday life. This may sound to us a simple assignment, but there may well be more to it than we first realize.

Bishop J.C. Ryle draws our attention to one of the great virtues of the gospel preaching which took place in the eighteenth-century Evangelical Awakening. He says, 'They preached simply. They rightly concluded that the very first qualification to be aimed at in a sermon is to be understood. They saw clearly that thousands of able and well-composed sermons are utterly useless, because they are above the heads of the hearers. They strove to come down to the level of the people, and to speak what the poor could understand. To attain this they were not ashamed to crucify their style, and to sacrifice their reputation for learning. To attain this they used illustrations and anecdotes in abundance, and, like their Divine Master, borrowed lessons from every object in nature. They carried out the maxim of Augustine — A wooden key is not so beautiful as a golden one, but if it can open the door when the golden one cannot, it is far more useful.'[2]

It is John Newton who tells us how William Grimshaw of Haworth adapted the vocabulary and manner of his preaching in order to reach the 'labouring-class' folk for whom he was particularly concerned. Newton says of Grimshaw, 'The desire of usefulness to persons of the weakest capacity, or most destitute of the advantages of education, influenced his phraseology in preaching. Though his abilities as a speaker, and his fund of general knowledge, rendered him very competent to stand before great men, yet, as his stated hearers were chiefly the poorer and more unlettered classes, he condescended to accommodate himself, in the most familiar manner, to their ideas, and to their modes of expression. Like the apostles, he disdained the elegance and excellence of speech which is admired by those who seek entertainment perhaps not less than instruction from the pulpit. He rather chose to deliver his sentiments in what he used to term "market language" '.[3]

It may seem that our case for the need of plain speaking in presenting the gospel is conclusively proved. But that is not so. Not all will be convinced. There are those evangelical Christians who sincerely believe that this concentration on the need for simplicity of expression — 'trying to solve the problems of communication' — is a diversion from a scriptural truth which has been overlooked. It is this: 'The man without the Spirit does not accept the things that come from the Spirit of God, for they are foolishness to him and he cannot understand them, because they are spiritually discerned' (1 Cor. 2:14). It is argued by some that no amount of attention to vocabulary and style of speech can ever overcome the unregenerate nature of a darkened mind and a deceitful heart. So why all this talk about simplicity? Is not Holy Spirit power all that we need? I firmly believe that the answer to that question must be 'No!' It is not as simple as that. There is confusion of thought at this point, and we need to do some straightening out. We will answer this objection with four points for consideration.

1. There is a failure to draw a distinction between 'intellectual understanding' and 'saving knowledge'. This distinction is valid, in accord with Scripture, and most necessary to preserve. It is possible for a person to possess an intellectual understanding of the gospel and yet not to have a saving knowledge of that truth. Felix, the Roman governor, of whom we read in the book

of Acts, is a good example of this. We are told that he 'was well acquainted with the Way ...'(that is, the Christian faith). Another version puts it like this: '...having a rather accurate understanding of the Way' (Acts 24:22). Felix already had a good measure of intellectual understanding of the gospel and sought for more. He summoned Paul to speak further 'about faith in Christ Jesus', but there is no later evidence that his intellectual understanding ever became saving knowledge.

Perhaps the best-known of Christians who possessed intellectual understanding some time before it became a saving knowledge was John Wesley. He confessed, 'It is now two years and almost four months since I left my native country, in order to teach the Georgian Indians the nature of Christianity: but what have I learned myself in the meantime? Why (what I the least of all suspected), that I, who went to America to convert others, was never myself converted to God.'[4]

Wesley's restless search continued until a 'quarter before nine' on the evening of 24 May 1738, in a society meeting in Aldersgate Street, London, when he himself experienced that 'change which God works in the heart through faith in Christ'. For John Wesley, 'missionary', the distinction between intellectual understanding and saving knowledge was all too real. That warm assurance that his own sins had been taken away came none too soon.

2. In presenting the gospel to others we must do our part and God will do His. With God's help, it is our responsibility to present the gospel simply and clearly. We should aim to bring about an intellectual understanding in the minds of our hearers — just as did the Levites who helped Ezra the scribe in Jerusalem, and just as Philip helped the Ethiopian treasurer. This is our work. But it is the work of the Holy Spirit so to operate in the minds and hearts of our hearers that, by His illuminating and life-giving power, intellectual understanding then becomes saving knowledge. This is the work of the Holy Spirit alone (John 1:12,13; 3:5; 1 Cor. 2:10-14). We cannot do this for Him, but neither will He do our work for us. It is our task — and it may prove a very demanding one — to speak plainly.

3. If we reject the need for careful attention to vocabulary and style of preaching we are then claiming that the men whom God used so mightily in the religious revival of the eighteenth century were toiling needlessly in making adjustments in their manner of

preaching in order to bring the gospel to the ordinary working people of those days. Do we really know better than John Wesley and William Grimshaw in this particular matter?

4. If a person is regarded as having *rejected* the gospel when, in fact, he has not yet *understood* the gospel, then the consequences can be serious and eternal. Wrong diagnosis is bound to lead to wrong treatment. Personal interest and prayerful concern may be withdrawn and redirected away from a person who needs, and possibly even still desires to understand the gospel more adequately.

We shall conclude our discussion on the importance of plain speaking with the observations of two men of God who are well qualified to speak on this subject.

In his book *The Soul Winner*, C.H. Spurgeon confesses that he is not surprised that so many people have an aversion to attending a place of worship where the gospel is preached. He says, 'I think, in many instances, the common people do not attend such services because they do not understand the theological "lingo" that is used in the pulpit; it is neither English, nor Greek, but Double-dutch; and when a working-man goes once and listens to these fine words, he says to his wife, "I do not go there again, Sal; there is nothing there for me, nor yet for you; there may be a good deal for a gentleman that's been to college, but there is nothing for the likes of us." No, brethren, we must preach in what Whitefield used to call "market language" if we would have all classes of the community listening to our message.'[5]

In words of power and clarity, Richard Baxter reminds us of the manner and the goal of good gospel preaching. In doing so, he draws to our attention the solemn obligation laid upon God's ambassadors (1 Cor. 9:16). 'What skill doth every part of our work require! And of how much moment is every part! To preach a sermon, I think, is not the hardest part; and yet what skill is necessary to make the truth plain; to convince the hearers, to let irresistible light in to their consciences, and to keep it there, and drive all home; to screw the truth into their minds, and work Christ into their affections; to meet every objection, clearly to resolve it; to drive sinners to a stand, and make them see that there is no hope, but that they must unavoidably either be converted or condemned — and to do all this, as regards language and manner, as beseems our work, and yet as is most suitable to the capacities of our hearers.'[6]

Instruction and persuasion

How much of the gospel does a person need to know and understand in order to become a Christian? That is not an easy question to answer. Certainly there are instances in the New Testament which suggest that comparatively little knowledge is absolutely necessary for conversion to take place. Think of the Samaritan woman of whom we read in the fourth chapter of John's Gospel. Her receiving of that living water that Jesus offered became a conversion experience at a time when she understood little of what He was talking about. Think of the dying and repentant thief. He knew he was guilty; he knew Jesus was not guilty. So he asked Jesus, 'Jesus, remember me when you come into your kingdom' (Luke 23:42). He received the assurance he wanted. How little or much did he know about Jesus? As he hung on his cross and listened to the things that Jesus said, was his first 'Bible study' also his last, before he departed this world to meet his Saviour in paradise? And there are more. This is all very encouraging, especially for people who find learning and understanding things from a book not very easy at all.

But there is another side to what we are discussing. It would seem from the Scriptures that the all-important issue concerning understanding of the gospel is not the quantity or amount of our Bible knowledge but rather the *depth* at which it has been implanted in our lives. The apostle Paul explained to his friends in the church at Rome why he was so thrilled at what had actually happened to them now that they had become Christians. 'But thanks be to God that, though you used to be slaves to sin, you wholeheartedly *obeyed* the form of teaching to which you were entrusted' (Rom. 6:17). It is in this connection that we need to examine a particular aspect of Jesus' teaching in the parable of the sower.

In the parable of 'the sower' Jesus indicated that one of the categories of 'soil' which we can expect to encounter is one which produces only a temporary response. It is the soil Jesus describes as the 'rocky ground'. 'What was sown on rocky places is the man who hears the word and at once receives it with joy. But since he has no root, he lasts only a short time. When trouble or persecution comes because of the word, he quickly falls away' (Matt. 13:20,21). We have been warned. It will happen. It will bring sadness and shock. But we should not really be surprised.

The parable of the sower has a limited purpose. It is to prepare us for the types of response we can expect in our preaching or sowing of the Word of God. It would be pressing the detail of the parable too far to ask how much, if any, blame can be attached to the sower. Did he prepare the soil properly? Did he plant the seed carefully? The parable is not intended to give an answer to these questions. But certain details of the 'rocky places' do suggest reasons why, in that case, there was only a temporary response. This kind of person 'hears the word and at once receives it' but it only lasts for a short while because 'he has no root'. The external evidence of the response to the Word of God suggests a more encouraging reception of the Word than has actually been the case. The response has been too shallow. Early optimism eventually fades into disappointment.

How does this condition arise? Can we identify the causes and prescribe the remedies? Ideally, prevention is better than cure. Much of the cause may be traced to a faulty link between 'instruction' and 'persuasion'. Where there is ignorance of the facts of the gospel there must first be instruction. The opening words of Paul's sermon on Mars Hill provide a suitable example: 'I found an altar with this inscription: To an unknown God. Now what you worship as something unknown I am going to proclaim to you' (Acts 17:23). Instruction comes first. But preaching must do more than inform the mind. It must aim to move the will. Persuasion is required. The 'free offer' of the gospel must be made, but we cannot say when that offer will be withdrawn. There is only one gospel. There is only one life. The day of grace is not unlimited. There is urgency. We must preach for a verdict. Balanced biblical evangelism requires a carefully considered relationship between instruction and persuasion. Spiritual problems arise where inadequate instruction has been too hastily followed by impatient persuasion.

What kind of factors are involved where there is merely a temporary response to the gospel? An *impetuous* response to the gospel can cause this. In this soil the seed 'sprang up quickly' but when trouble or persecution occurs they quickly fall away. Jesus warns against a hasty unthinking commitment to the life of Christian discipleship. We are to weigh carefully what it will demand of us. An *emotional* response to the gospel can also cause the same problem. These are people who upon hearing the Word 'at once receive it with joy'. The crucial question is this, 'What is the source and substance of that joy?' Is it primarily determined by the content of the gospel they have heard? Or is it largely conditioned by the atmosphere of the occasion in which the gospel is presented? If the gospel has been presented to people within the context of an evening of Christian entertainment, and the mood of the music rather than the truth of the gospel has been the major factor conditioning the response to the message, we should not be surprised if the result is a number of temporary believers.

The two categories of temporary believer we have just considered can occur in any local church situation — urban or suburban, rural or coastal. But there is a further category of temporary believer and this is one where the response to the gospel is *superficial*. There is no rejection of the Word. There is no indifference to the Word. But the reception of the Word is not deep enough. The good seed lies too near the surface. There is no real root. An immediate flowering of the seed excites and deceives at the same time. The fragile plant has no depth or strength. When the scorching sun beats down, the seedling withers and dies. This kind of hearer, our Lord explains, is one whose response to the preaching of the gospel is perilously shallow. It lasts for a while but does not survive the heat of opposition.

It is surely significant that the point of attack, which is the devil's target, is opposition 'because of the word'. The very Word which has the potential to save him and keep him has not been received deep enough to effect a transformation of heart and life. Such response as there is proves to be deceptive and short-lived. Jesus made it plain that those who follow Him must expect opposition. In His sermon on the mount Jesus warned what might happen: 'Blessed are you when people insult you, persecute you and falsely say all kinds of evil against you *because of me*' (Matt. 5:11). A loud mouth on the factory floor makes sure that you know, and others know too, that you are suffering from religious mania! A group of your former mates may have a little giggle at your expense as you turn aside from their conversation when the jokes turn blue. Your best friend may give you an occasional 'dig' when, for instance, you turn down a chance to share in the Grand National sweepstake. If you stand up for someone who is being blamed unfairly and often has his good nature exploited you may be told in no uncertain terms what you can do with your Christianity! These hostile actions should not surprise us. We are in good company. 'Rejoice and be glad because great is your reward in heaven, for in the same way they persecuted the prophets who were before you' (Matt. 5:12).

When the predicted opposition comes, what effect is it likely to have? Those whose roots are deeply in God's Word will find that the opposition cannot damage them or detach them from Jesus Christ. But where the seed has lodged in shallow soil, the heat of opposition will expose its frailty. The flower of a superficial faith will wither away. The teaching of Jesus at this point is a solemn warning. The 'fine-weather' disciple with shallow beliefs and without adequate roots is dangerously vulnerable. When trouble and persecution come 'because of the word' the hour of testing will bring to light whether the apparent faith is genuine or false.

In what way does this particular category have a special application to the preaching of the gospel among working-class communities? It relates to their level of understanding of the gospel. It has to do with their grasp of scriptural truth. Do those who preach the gospel take too much for granted? Do they give credit to their hearers for a minimum level of Bible knowledge which is foolishly optimistic? At the beginning of this section on 'instruction' and 'persuasion' we made some encouraging observations that a person may become a Christian even with a very small grasp of biblical knowledge. That much is true and is obviously good to know. But, and the 'but' is a big one — unless that small amount of knowledge is dwelling at depth in the heart, then a day of trouble and eventual disillusionment will surely come. We must look into this further to see why this may have particular reference to evangelism among the working classes.

We will know by now that working-class people generally show, and have shown the least interest in the gospel. Because of this it follows that these are the situations where there is most ignorance of the content of the gospel. While that is true it would be wrong to think that the situation has remained static for as long as we can remember. In the earlier years of this century many working-class parents sent their children to Sunday School. They appreciated that it did some good for their children — an elementary moral education and a bit of discipline. The fact that it gave Mum and Dad a chance for a Sunday afternoon nap was a bonus not to be ignored! Now, however, the large working-class Sunday Schools of the earlier years of the century have gone. The trickle of Bible knowledge which found its way into many working-class homes has virtually dried up. Added to this, the teaching of religious education in schools and the conduct of morning assemblies in schools may do more harm than good. We now live in a multi-racial society, consequently, it is argued, religious education must take account of this and take a multi-faith approach. What little Bible knowledge a child may gain is likely to become diluted and distorted as it is presented within the overall panorama of modern religions and their respective holy books.

Gospel preachers in the first half of the twentieth century, consciously or unconsciously, took an elementary level of Bible knowledge for granted. But that would not be appropriate today. In the major working-class areas, with the exception of a very small minority, virtually the entire community, parents and children, are thoroughly pagan. We have to face facts and suit our evangelism accordingly. We must assume nothing. It is only safe and sensible to start at 'square one'.

In his book, *God-centred Evangelism*, R.B. Kuiper contrasts the situation which prevails today with what it was like at earlier times in working-class history. He says, 'Historically the appeal of mass evangelism has been largely to the will and the emotions. That holds of the evangelistic preaching of both Wesley and Whitefield, to a limited extent to that of Jonathan Edwards, and most certainly to that of Dwight L. Moody, Charles G. Finney, Billy Sunday, and the Gipsy Smiths of more recent times. There was some justification for the nature of that appeal. All the aforementioned evangelists had good reason to assume on the part of their audiences a measure of knowledge of the basic teachings of Christianity. Today that assumption is no longer valid, not even in such supposedly Christian lands as England and the United States of America. The general populace is well-nigh absymally ignorant of Bible history, and

Bible doctrine, as well as Bible ethics. In consequence, evangelistic preaching must today be first of all instructive. People need to be taught the Word of God.'[7]

Instruction and persuasion must both have their proper place if we are to achieve a wise biblical balance in the content and manner of our evangelistic preaching. If we press on to persuasion in undue haste we may create problems for ourselves. If the gospel content has been either inadequate, or incomprehensible to the hearers, ill-judged persuasion may produce a suspect response. It is right to yearn to see souls won for the Lord. There must be urgency in our preaching. But we must guard against the temptation to play the role of a spiritual midwife in order to induce an early new birth. Let the Holy Spirit determine the time of 'delivery'. That is His work, not ours!

'Publicly and from house to house'

In his address to the elders of the church at Ephesus (Acts 20:17-35) the apostle Paul described the twin foci of his gospel preaching strategy. Paul claimed to have discharged his responsibility fully when he said, 'You know that I have not hesitated to preach anything that would be helpful to you but have taught you *publicly and from house to house*' (Acts 20:20). The locations in which he explored the opportunities for gospel preaching provide us with an example which we should follow.

The nature of the *public* opportunity at Ephesus is described for us in the preceding chapter: 'Paul entered the synagogue and spoke boldly there for three months, arguing persuasively about the kingdom of God. But some of them became obstinate; they refused to believe and publicly maligned the Way. So Paul left them. He took the disciples with him and had discussions daily in the lecture hall of Tyrannus. This went on for two years, so that all the Jews and Greeks who lived in the province of Asia heard the word of the Lord' (Acts 19:8-10).

As was his custom, Paul began his gospel preaching work in the synagogue. After three months opponents stirred up trouble. Paul was compelled to abandon that particular opportunity for gospel preaching. But Paul had learned to be flexible in his evangelism. As one door closed so another opened. Paul was able to secure the use of the 'lecture hall of Tyrannus'. The nature of this opportunity permitted a less formal declaration of the gospel. This work was able to continue, in spite of hindrances, for a period of two years. Although the city was infected by idolatrous and occult practices, 'the word of the Lord spread widely and grew in power' (Acts 19:20).

Concerning the *private* opportunity for evangelism at Ephesus little is recorded. What did the 'house-to-house' work involve? Is Acts 20:31 a clue to this? Paul solemnly charged the Ephesian elders: 'So be on your guard! Remember that for three years I never stopped warning each of you night and day with tears.' It would seem reasonable to assume that private gospel exposition and personal pastoral counsel are included within this reference to Paul's ministry in the homes of the people. Acts 19:10 also has a bearing on this.

How far did the impact of Paul's work at Ephesus produce 'gospel ripples' in the region surrounding where he was working? We are told that Paul held 'discussions daily in the lecture hall of Tyrannus'. At the end of his two-year stay in Ephesus how far had the gospel spread? At the close of that period, '*all* the Jews and Greeks who lived in the province of Asia heard the word of the Lord' (Acts 19:10). But what does that mean in precise terms? Surely this cannot mean that the entire population of that region visited the hall of Tyrannus during that period. How then was the province of Asia evangelized? We know that some of Paul's colleagues carried out missionary work in the neighbouring cities of Colossae, Hierapolis and Laodicea. But added to their influence there will have been the gospel work set in motion by the 'disciples' (Acts 19:9) whom Paul had instructed at Ephesus and who returned to their native towns and regions to establish a gospel witness 'publicly and from house to house'.

Although we do not read of a 'gospel service' in the pages of the New Testament, there are good reasons why a regular opportunity for a public declaration of the gospel should be sought. This gospel preaching ought to have in mind the needs of those who are believers already and those who have not yet responded to the gospel message. But why preach the gospel to Christians? It is essential that the plan of redemption — its breadth and length and height and depth be unfolded and expounded to the people of God. A God-centred gospel declaring the majesty of God's law and the miracle of God's grace is the only gospel that will produce an ongoing transformation in the lives of believers. As the Christian's understanding of the greatness and grace of God is progressively enlarged, the utter unworthiness of the sinner will progressively be exposed. Through careful exposition of this 'so great salvation', the believer's worship will be stimulated, gratitude increased, assurance deepened, understanding enlarged, faith strengthened and zeal inspired. There is surely no more effective way to promote in the saints a sustained hunger for holiness and concern for evangelism.

In saying that the gospel must be preached to believers we may assume that this will take place from the pulpit within the context of Christian worship. Though the pastor may have in mind chiefly the aim 'to prepare God's people for works of service, so that the body of Christ may be built up' (Eph. 4:12), such gospel preaching will always be with the prayer and possibility that the seeker and 'outsider' present in the congregation may be blessed and brought to the Lord. The New Testament clearly recognizes the evangelistic potential within the congregation of God's people gathered for worship (1 Cor.14:24,25).

The gospel must be preached to unbelievers. As long as we have church buildings, there will be an essential place for preaching the gospel within the gathered congregation. But the evangelistic opportunities afforded within this context will vary considerably.

A realistic assessment of the actual opportunity provided by pulpit evangelism must be made by individual churches and their leaders and kept under constant review. Being faithful in gospel preaching means much more than refusing to quit, or to change our ways, or to compromise our message. Faithfulness also demands spiritual sense and practical industry, without which neither a man nor a church is truly faithful (Matt. 25:14-30). A number of factors will determine how the opportunity of pulpit evangelism will be measured: the quality of the preaching, its content and power; the personal zeal and holiness of the church members in their evangelistic witness and endeavours to encourage unbelievers to hear the gospel; the geographical and sociological situation in which the church is set, and also the general spiritual apathy or spiritual concern of the age. Yet beyond these things there is another factor which cannot be *measured* in the same way. 'The wind blows where it wills.' God in His sovereign mercy and wisdom does choose to send seasons of refreshing upon a local congregation during which time the experience of blessing and the evidence of opportunity go far beyond any merely human explanation.

If God should grant His blessing in an exceptional manner upon the preaching of the gospel from the pulpit to the saving of many souls, this token of His favour in no way absolves the pastor from the duty of teaching and training all church members to be effective witnesses in whatever local situation God has placed them. The evangelistic responsibility resting on all believers must go well beyond that of just inviting a friend to church. No matter how good the gospel preaching in church, all believers are to be taught and encouraged to 'hold out the word' in a 'crooked and depraved generation' in which they should 'shine like stars' (Phil. 2:15,16). All believers are to be equipped to give a reason for the hope that they have (1 Peter 3:15). All are to be shown how to live a life that is 'worthy of the gospel of Christ' (Phil. 1:27).

It is the Puritan pastor Richard Baxter (1615-1691) whose ministry is remembered particularly for its emphasis on the *private* opportunities for spreading the gospel. Baxter was vicar of Kidderminster for the period 1647-1661. With phenomenal discipline and devotion he pursued a policy of systematic instruction in the homes of the people. The character of the town was entirely transformed by his ministry. The town contained about 800 homes and 2,000 people. They were 'an ignorant, rude and revelling people' when Baxter arrived. Baxter says, 'When I came thither first there was about one family in a street that worshipped God and called on his name, and when I came away there were some streets where there was not past one family in the side of a street that did not do so; and that did not by professing serious godliness, give us hope of their sincerity.'[8]

Baxter, who was a sick man for almost all his ministry, and felt himself to be constantly walking close to 'neighbour death', did not spare himself in his gospel labours. With holy zeal he applied himself to visiting the homes of the people of Kidderminster. His purpose was twofold. He aimed to evangelize the sinners and to edify the saints. In particular, he was greatly persuaded of the need for believers to learn a catechism. It is for his diligent catechizing ministry that Baxter is chiefly remembered. He set out his approach in his book *The Reformed Pastor*, which Philip Doddridge later described as 'that incomparable treatise'. Many later men of God frequently turned to *The Reformed Pastor* for spiritual inspiration and challenge — John Angell James and C.H. Spurgeon, to name but two.

We shall refer later to the example and purpose of Baxter's catechizing ministry. Our concern now is to understand his views on evangelizing in 'private': 'I know that preaching the gospel publicly is the most excellent means because we speak to many at once. But it is usually far more effectual to preach it privately to a particular sinner, as to himself: for the plainest man that is, can scarcely speak plain enough in public for them to understand; but in private we may do it much more. In public we may not use such homely expressions, or repetitions, as their dulness requires, but in private we may. In public our speeches are long, and we quite overrun their understandings and memories, and they are confounded and at a loss, and not able to follow us, and one thing drives out another, and so they know not what we said. But in private we can take our work gradually, and take our hearers along with us; and, by our questions and their answers, we can see how far they understand us, and what we have next to do. In public, by length and speaking alone we lose their attention; but when they are interlocutors [when they take part in the conversation], we can easily cause them to attend. Besides, we can better answer their objections, and engage them by promises before we leave them, which in public we cannot do. I conclude, therefore, that public preaching will not be sufficient: for though it may be an effectual means to convert many, yet not so many as experience, and God's appointment of further means may assure us. Long may you study and preach to little purpose, if you neglect this duty.'[9]

Was Baxter's policy in any way dictated by the success he saw in the means he used? Ultimately we must say that his methods were scriptural and that is what determined the pattern of his ministry. But we can also say that we would expect God to own and bless any work which is built firmly upon the principles contained in His Word. Baxter's public preaching was greatly blessed. As the number of converts grew steadily over the years, he could claim that 'The congregation was usually full, so that we were fain to build five galleries'! The church held up to 1,000 people.

How did Baxter view God's rich blessing on his 'private' gospel labours? He says, 'I wonder at myself, how I was so long kept off from so clear and excellent a duty ...Whereas, upon trial, I find the difficulties almost nothing (save only through my extraordinary bodily weakness) to which I imagined; and I find the benefits and comforts of the work to be such, that I would not wish I had forborne it, for all the riches in the world. We spend Monday and Tuesday, from morning almost to night, in the work, taking about fifteen or sixteen families in a week, that we may go through the parish, in which there are upwards of eight hundred families, in a year; and I cannot say yet that one family hath refused to come to me, and but few persons excused themselves, and shifted it off. And I find more outward signs of success with most that do come, than from all my public preaching to them.'[10] 'I have found by experience, that some ignorant persons, who have been so long unprofitable hearers, have got more knowledge and remorse of conscience in half an hour's close discourse, than they did from ten years' public preaching.'[11]

During the following century the advance of the gospel gained a new impetus with the advent of the Evangelical Awakening. Writing of the conditions which prevailed as the century drew to a close, a leading Particular Baptist, John Rippon, drew attention to the way in which *public* proclamation of the gospel was being suitably complemented by the *private* opportunities for further biblical instruction. After Sunday *afternoon* services in their own chapels, multitudes of men were dispersed among the villages. In the gospel witness that took place, some would lead the singing and others would preach or read specially written 'village sermons'. When a village community showed signs of response, prayer meetings and 'village readings' were arranged. These were often held on mid-week evenings in the cottage of some person who had displayed special interest. These cottage meetings formed the basis of numerous Nonconformist congregations. John Rippon reckoned that 'the whole country was open for village preaching in the 1790's.

How do we respond to the examples of the apostle Paul, Richard Baxter and our more recent Evangelical forefathers? The tireless devotion of Baxter — always abounding in the work of the Lord — is both an inspiration and a challenge. It is all too easy to contrast the circumstances under which we minister today with conditions in Baxter's day. True, he ministered before the industrial age, and in a community which was no larger than a village today, but the people of Kidderminster, 'ignorant, rude and revelling', sound little different from those we meet in urban areas today.

Even though we have no comparable public opportunity with that which Baxter had, at least we can pray and persevere for private opportunities of bringing the gospel into the homes of the people. Even though we may not have Baxter's particular gifts and ministry, at least we have his sympathy for the urban areas as he knew them in his day. He was under no illusions concerning the strenuous demands of God's work in the cities in the seventeenth century. He observed, 'It is a lamentable impediment to the reformation of the Church, and the saving of souls, that, in most populous towns, there are but one or two men to oversee many thousand souls; and so there are not labourers in any degree equal to the work; but it becomes an impossible thing for them to do any considerable measure of that personal duty which should be done by faithful pastors to all the flock. I have often said it, and still must say it, that *this is a great part of England's misery, that a great degree of spiritual famine reigns in most cities and large towns throughout the land*, even where they are insensible of it, and think themselves well provided. Alas! we see multitudes of ignorant, carnal, sensual sinners around us — here a family, and there a family, and there almost a whole street or village of them — and our hearts pity them, and we see that their necessities cry aloud for our speedy and diligent relief, so that 'he that hath ears to hear' must needs hear.'[12]

If Baxter could say that three hundred years ago, what would he say now? The present national population is more than *ten times* what it was in Baxter's day!

Salvation and solidarity: the influence of the 'group'

In the book of Acts and in 1 Corinthians we have several accounts of what we know as 'household baptisms'. There is the household of Cornelius, the Roman centurion (Acts 10:47,48);

the household of Lydia, the business woman residing in Philippi (Acts 16:14,15); the household of the Philippian jailor (Acts 16:33); the household of Crispus, the ruler of the synagogue at Corinth (Acts 18:8) and the household of Stephanas (1 Cor. 16:15; 1:16). If we ask the question, What do Baptists make of these references in support of 'infant baptism'? the answer is, usually, 'Nothing!' There are no explicit references to infants. It is an argument from silence. We tend to pass over these references to 'household baptisms' fairly quickly.

If we make nothing particular of these references in relation to 'infant baptism', then we *ought* to make something of them in relation to conversion. What really happened to these households? What exactly was the Holy Spirit doing in these situations? Another reason why we may skip over these passages is that what the Scripture appears to be teaching here does not accord with what we have come to experience as the norm today. We normally see individual conversions; occasionally we may see 'double' conversions, perhaps two members of the same family — a husband and wife, or a brother and sister. Rarely do we see all the members of one family, father, mother and children of an age of understanding, converted on the same occasion. Where whole families are brought to the Lord it would be more usual to see some sort of 'chain-reaction' series of conversions rather than a simultaneous conversion of all the members of one family.

A closer look at these household conversions appears to teach multiple simultaneous conversions on an even larger scale. The household of New Testament days comprised blood relations, slaves, clients and friends. This is obviously a much greater number than our 'nuclear' family today with father, mother and two or three children. How are we to interpret these household conversions? What do they have to say to us today?

If we attempt to interpret these occurrences from a purely sociological point of view, we would get one answer. The household was the fundamental unit of society and had a long history both in Israelite and Roman culture. The household, like the republic, expressed its solidarity in a common religion. Thus when a change of religion was considered, the action of the head of the household committed the rest of his dependent group. That to me seems a fairly simple and valid interpretation, sociologically.

But when we turn to the Scripture to interpret this phenomenon spiritually, we have no grounds for concluding anything less than that there were multiple simultaneous conversions. In the case of Cornelius and his household, there is explicit reference to the activity of the Holy Spirit on that occasion: 'The Holy Spirit came on *all* who heard the message' (Acts 10:44).

In order to arrive at what we might call a balanced interpretation of these occurrences, we need to see if it is fair to regard the interpretations given so far as complementary, and not unrelated nor contradictory. The link between the two interpretations seems to be in the 'solidarity' factor present in each situation. Simultaneous multiple conversions can take place today. They must have been common in days of revival. But such simultaneous conversions may have nothing to do with the links that the hearers had to each other. There is no 'solidarity' factor involved. But where all the members of one close-knit group respond to the gospel at the same time, it would seem reasonable to suppose that the solidarity factor has some bearing on the course of events. It seems fruitless to speculate about the exact nature of the spiritual response of the members of those households mentioned in the book of Acts. The Scripture implies true belief; the subsequent baptisms support true belief. I believe that the balanced and accurate interpretation of these household conversions does require us to take into account the solidarity factor. I would want to explain it in these terms: in the household conversions, the Holy Spirit did not work apart from the cultural phenomenon of solidarity; He worked with and through that factor to the spiritual blessing of the persons involved. In other words, the Holy Spirit did not override or obliterate the factor of solidarity, but turned it to good spiritual account.

As we have already seen, solidarity is an important feature of working-class culture. In his solidarity with others of his class the working man finds his security and his ability to defend his rights against those who might want to exploit him. Apart from his mates, he feels exposed and vulnerable, but within his class and group, he is ready to take on anybody ...even a prime minister!'Class exists for all, but for most it exists consciously and matters deeply. For the urban industrial wage-earner — the proletarian of Marxist terminology — his class solidarity and his consequent separation from other classes is something of which he is very conscious. In one mood he will repudiate it in the spirit of a man trying to live in the classless society before it has been born. In another socially militant mood he will strongly assert it. Either way it is a deeply felt element in his consciousness.'[13]

It would be quite wrong to view working-class solidarity as a static concept — a form of working-class birthright handed down from generation to generation. The character and course of working-class solidarity are always undergoing some measure of change as they are affected by decisions and events — political, social, industrial, economic and moral. In 1961 Ferdynand Zweig foresaw some major social changes in working-class life and outlook. The subsequent decades have proved his predictions correct. Twenty years ago it was Zweig's opinion that 'Social changes among the working classes in the last decade or two have been far-reaching and cannot be measured only in quantative terms. There are deep changes not only in the mode of living but also in the code and ethos of the class as a whole. Large sections of the working classes are on the move, not only to higher standards of living, but also to new standards of values and conduct and new social consciousness. The impact of these changes on social, political and economic life can hardly be foreseen. They are the augury of a new age, a new social horizon which is unfolding before our very eyes.'[14]

Some erosion there may be, some change of social direction, but the cultural phenomenon of 'solidarity' is still a deeply felt element of working-class consciousness. In no other category of British society today is this cultural feature so evident and active.

The Christian gospel requires the working man to leave 'the world's side' and to step over to 'the Lord's side'. Now that is a hard thing for the working man to do. Apart from the gracious work of the Holy Spirit, it is a harder thing for a working-class person to do, than it is for the middle-class person. The middle-class man will have a more individualistic outlook than will his working-class brother. If this issue of 'solidarity' does play a large part in keeping the working man from the church and the gospel, how are we to tackle the problem spiritually and practically? Do we necessarily have to emphasize from the start that 'following involves forsaking'; that we are to be separate from others? Do we have to pray that the Holy Spirit will override this matter of solidarity, or can we ask that He will work through it and with it as He has done before? I think we can say something positive on this.

Over more recent years it has been our experience in Walworth, South London, that a weekly home Bible study group has provided a situation in which the solidarity factor can be turned to good spiritual advantage. After a handful of conversions a few years ago, some of the young converts asked for something more than our weekly church Bible study. So we started a weekly beginners and enquirers group. To start with, there was a mixture of young believers and enquirers. The style of the study was very informal. We stayed on gospel basics. I tried to encourage and provoke as much participation as possible. Numbers grew and so did enthusiasm, and also the bonds of friendship between the members of the group. Best of all, we saw folk coming to the Lord through the work of the group. It is only on reflection that I have seen why the group structure can be so helpful to the working man in this inner-city community. The new contact or enquirer starts coming along to the weekly group meetings; he becomes known and accepted. He can ask questions. He has something to contribute. He is missed if he is away. In the security and sense of belonging that the group provides, the Holy Spirit can draw a person 'from the world's side' over to 'the Lord's side', without requiring that he should abandon all previous ties in order to move into another group. He is not asked to 'stand alone', to become isolated from others. Within the activity of the group, the Lord brings him into an experience of conversion.

The spiritual activity and experience we have just described is not the same *expression* of solidarity that we see in the household conversions in the book of Acts. But it is, in essence, an aspect of the same cultural phenomenon: the need to feel safe in 'belonging'. Also, we must not think of solidarity as something peculiar to the New Testament society of the first century and British working-class life in the twentieth century. There are examples of solidarity in the Old Testament and also in the overseas mission-field today.

In the Old Testament the book of Jonah contains an astonishing example of solidarity. It occurred in response to the preaching of Jonah to the people of the great pagan city of

Nineveh. Commissioned to preach a message of doom, Jonah delivered the message he was given and, remarkably, Nineveh repented. Both the 'extent' and the 'depth' of this repentance exhibit exceptional solidarity (Jonah 3:1-10).

We may speak of a particular group or class of people within our society demonstrating its solidarity. When Jonah preached to Nineveh *the entire population* of over 120,000 people repented. 'The Ninevites believed God. They declared a fast, and *all of them, from the greatest to the least*, put on sackcloth' (Jonah 3:5). This repentance and belief seem to have been entirely spontaneous and genuine and not organized, since the king issued his proclamation concerning national repentance *after* the people had repented, and not before.

We sometimes speak of a group of people putting on a 'show' of solidarity. There is the suggestion in the word 'show' that, at times, demonstrations of solidarity may be merely to create an impression, but such exercises may be largely superficial and lacking in depth and reality. The people of Nineveh in no sense put on a display of solidarity in repentance to impress God or His servant Jonah. The wearing of sackcloth by both king and people was an outward sign. But this was accompanied by genuine heart response. The king insisted that all the people *and* their cattle should share in the fast of repentance. The king also decreed that everyone was to 'call urgently on God' and to 'give up their evil ways and their violence'. This solidarity 'in depth' brought forth the tender forgiving mercy of a compassionate God.

Through a letter received from a fellow minister I recently learned of his work among the 'Vietnamese boat-people'. There appears to have been a most remarkable response to the gospel among these immigrants and the letter I received mentioned eighty-five baptisms. Of particular interest for our study was the reference to Vietnamese family life. He writes, 'Many have spent hours reading their Bibles and the Lord has ministered directly to them through His Word. The New Testament pattern of families coming to the Lord together has been continuing, and increasingly baptisms have been of family groups ... The idea of the family is very important to the Vietnamese people and has been a recurring theme of our work with them. Our small family units are strange to these people who are used to large and close-knit family groups. It is not surprising that they have quickly grasped the idea of the church as a family and for many it has meant much to realize that they are now part of a new family.'

Dr E.A. Nida draws our attention to an example of solidarity in an overseas mission-field: 'When a man in West Africa told the missionary he would return the next week with his family, he did and brought forty-seven persons with him (five wives and forty-two children), all of whom insisted that they believed. In some of the mass movements in India entire villages have seemed to respond as a single person. We who lay so much stress upon individual action and decisions find it hard to conceive of people acting as a unit; yet in societies with a highly integrated social structure, people do act together in a remarkable manner. The missionary must not underestimate the importance of such socially conditioned decisions nor fail to appreciate the individual's part. There are both dangers and advantages to mass movements. However, they should not be judged in terms of our responses, but on the basis of the culture involved.'[15]

In our own situation the home group Bible study has proved to be particularly well-suited to evangelism within our working-class community. Recognition of the factor of solidarity appears to be a key feature in the development of the group's evangelistic potential. It is possible to identify a good number of reasons why the home group Bible study should prove a most suitable form of evangelism among the working classes.

1. The unbeliever is not required to face up to the matter of 'church' before he begins to understand the gospel.
2. Regular meetings with the group give him a sense of belonging and acceptance.
3. The form of the meeting allows and encourages a lot of participation. This, too, develops a sense of belonging. Questions put by the unbeliever or enquirer mean that the 'teacher' will be asked to deal with issues and problems which the working man *knows* he has, and not just those problems which *we think* he has — or ought to have!
4. By comments made and questions asked, valuable clues are given concerning the spiritual condition and outlook of the enquirer.
5. The home group provides a convenient situation in which the working man's distorted view of the Christian church can progressively be corrected.

6. When the enquirer has become part of the group, this activity then becomes a convenient stepping-stone on the way to attending gospel preaching in the church services.

7. Questions raised at a week-night group meeting can provide guidance for the kind of topics that need to be handled in the gospel preaching at church. There have been a number of times when discussion on an important and urgent matter has been left incomplete at the home group meeting. It has been a source of stimulus and encouragement to be able to say to the group, 'Make sure to be in church on Sunday evening when we will go into this subject more thoroughly.' It is encouraging to know on a Thursday evening that a number of folk have already 'booked their tickets' for the evening service! These are the times when both preacher and people look forward with increased expectancy to the 'appointed hour' on the Lord's day.

8. The pastor or elder who leads the group meeting is identified with the group as one who shares with them, rather than as the 'professional minister' who preaches to them on Sunday. The pastor or elder becomes a personal friend of the members of the group. Consequently, members of the group will the more readily share their thoughts, hopes and fears with him. In the course of time members of the group will discover for themselves what the minister of the gospel already knows about himself: he is every bit as human as they are! When members of the group confess their fears and failings, he will know what they are talking about. They share a common and frail humanity.

9. 'Faithful are the wounds of a friend.' The bonds of friendship which are developed within the weekly group meetings make it easier for the preacher on Sunday to speak more boldly and directly. A genuine friendship with another means that at times the truth must be spoken, even though it hurts. Where uncomfortable truths are suppressed in order to preserve the friendship, it is an indication that the relationship is only superficial and thus very fragile. If I truly love my neighbour, there must come a time when I say to his face that there is a heaven to be gained and a hell to be shunned. The willingness to 'risk the relationship' by directing attention to an uncomfortable issue is in itself a sign of the depth of the friendship. I believe that within our Thursday home group meeting I am, in part, earning my right to speak more bluntly on Sunday evening.

10. The home group is a convenient gathering into which enquirers can introduce their friends. It is not always the Christian who will be seeking new people to introduce to the group. An enquirer may discover real help from the group even before conversion takes place. Why should other friends of the enquirer not come as well and share in the blessing?

Sunday Schools

It may not appear immediately obvious why we are now to look at the matter of evangelizing children. As the study proceeds, it should become clear why this follows our consideration of the 'solidarity' factor and its bearing upon evangelism among working-class adults.

The Baptist church in which I am now pastor began as a Ragged School in 1859. In the final decade of the nineteenth century, following major expansion of the work, a new building was added to the first one built in 1875. For the special opening in 1896 a number of V.I.P.'s were present. One of the guests, Rev. A.W. Jephson, vicar, provided the assembled company with some 'Walworth statistics' for their interest and education. He said, 'On the 632 acres which composed the parish of Newington there were 120,000 persons packed away in 13,000 houses which meant that there were over 200 people to the acre. There were 23,000 children in the parish of whom not more than 14,000 attended Sunday School.'[16]

It would now be difficult to verify the accuracy of the figures quoted. We must hope that they are substantially correct because we need to make certain deductions from them. There are three matters of interest for our study.

In the first place, the figures indicate the population density at that time. In 1896 there were 200 people to the acre. Present regulations have lowered that figure considerably. 'In London 136 persons per acre is the rule for housing density on most large new estates, compared with 10 per acre in some privately-owned housing in the suburbs. In Singapore they are building for 1,800 persons per acre and in Hong Kong for 2,000.'[17]

Secondly, by dividing the population figure by the number of houses, we arrive at an average figure of over 9 persons per house. Stories of five in a bed and five under it are not so far-fetched after all!

Thirdly, it is the Sunday School attendance figure that is of most interest to us. If A.W. Jephson's figures are right, then in Walworth approximately two children out of three went to Sunday School. This we may find hard to believe, but it does fit other evidence we are able to put forward.

We have made mention of the work in Walworth which began as a Ragged School in 1859. At the very first meeting there were '*four* ragged urchins from the streets' who met, with their teacher, in the loft of a cow stable. By the year 1892 there were *over 1,000* children on the books of the 'Richmond Street, Walworth, Sunday and Ragged Schools' as it had then become. By no stretch of the imagination could over a thousand children get into our building at the same time. But we do know that after the opening of the new building in 1896 there were *nine* meetings every Sunday!

The figures quoted by the Rev. A.W. Jephson sound very encouraging when they are considered on their own. How we would rejoice if we had that kind of attendance today! But when we compare these figures with *adult* church attendance the figures then become disturbing. We must explain the method of our comparison. If the promise of early years is maintained we would have reason to expect that the attendance levels of children at Sunday School in one decade ought to be reflected later on in the adult church attendance in the next decade or two. It so happens that we do have the figures we need for the comparison. The Sunday School statistics are those quoted by A.W. Jephson in 1896. But we also have figures for adult church attendance in Walworth from the calculations of R. Mudie-Smith, with additional 'interpretation' by C.F.G. Masterman. According to these figures, adult church attendance in Walworth (in 1903) by the 'working-class people and the poor' of that area was about 2% of the local community. Masterman was well qualified to make his 'interpretation'. He was very familiar with the area and lived in Albany Road which forms the southern boundary of the Walworth area.

Even if we were to allow a margin of error, big or small, in the calculations of A.W. Jephson and C.F.G. Masterman, the disparity between Sunday School attendance in one decade and adult church attendance in the following decade is enormous.

For all the dedication of godly Sunday School teachers over many years, it appears that much of that effort was like pouring water into a badly holed bucket or, to be more biblical, like trying to catch fish with some badly torn gospel nets. Why was it that so many children who swam into the gospel nets in their earlier years had on the whole swum out again before adult years had been reached?

Are the statistics we have used and the conclusions we have drawn representative of Sunday Schools generally in working-class areas? The evidence we have strongly points to the view that this was the common experience of the churches. Historians and sociologists are in agreement on this matter. Hugh McLeod confirms our assessment. Writing of the late Victorian period, he says, 'In working-class districts Sunday School classes of varying degrees of roughness multiplied, and the main church services might be attended by more children than adults. The churches' functions were strictly delimited. Working-class Londoners regarded church as a necessary part of childhood; but as soon as a man or woman began to earn a living the compulsion was dropped and you only went to church because you had a reason for doing so.'[18]

Once again Richard Hoggart provides for us another valuable insight into working-class habits and values. In 1957 he wrote, 'Today, most working-class people go neither to church nor to chapel except on special family occasions once the parental order to attend Sunday School has been withdrawn. In some places one of the recognized signs of becoming adult, together with going into long trousers for the boys or permission to use make-up for the girls, is the freedom to leave Sunday School and read the *News of the World* at home like Dad. Few among the working classes seem to find their own way back to a church after adolescence. If old ties are cut, they are unlikely to be remade.'[19]

The reason why we have considered this topic immediately following the matter of 'salvation and solidarity' is because this cultural factor is a major influence in terminating Sunday School attendance for working-class teenagers. We must remember that although the working-class male did not 'get the vote' until he was 21 years of age, in practice he became a 'working *man*' at age 14! The 'long trousers', *News of the World* and 'no more Sunday School' were in effect the cultural symbols of his attainment of working-class adulthood. When the transition from adolescence to adulthood occurs, the impact and influence of class-awareness significantly increases. In those 'households' to which we referred in the book of Acts there was a 'solidarity in belief'; here we are encountering a 'solidarity in unbelief'.

Before we attempt to make any comments and positive proposals concerning the Sunday School situation we find today, it will be helpful if we sketch in some further historical detail, so that we can appreciate the changing role that Sunday School has had over the past two centuries.

Contrary to popular opinion, Robert Raikes was not the originator of Sunday Schools. There is evidence that they were in operation on the continent of Europe during the sixteenth century and John Knox was using them in Scotland at about the same time. However, to Raikes must go the credit for promoting the major advance of Sunday School work in England. L.E. Elliott-Binns corrects the false notion concerning the role of Raikes: 'In England, Robert Raikes of Gloucester is often regarded as the pioneer, but there were many before him and he himself was inspired by a Baptist, William King of Dursley. Raikes began by hiring four "decent women" to teach the children of the streets to read and to learn their catechism. The children were rewarded by buns and hot potatoes. This was in 1780. From that time Sunday Schools spread rapidly and have gone on spreading.'[20]

Sunday Schools were *not* established with the sole purpose of providing Bible instruction. There was no formal education for children in the time of Robert Raikes. The first aim of the Sunday Schools two hundred years ago was to provide children with some elementary education, in particular the ability to read and write. As the nineteenth century progressed and formal education of children became the increasing responsibility of the state, so the 'religious' aspect of Sunday School work became the dominant concern of the churches.

Although the development of the Ragged School movement did not occur until nearly a century after Raikes began his work, the pattern of development was similar. Initially, the social conditions of poor children were the concern of the pioneers of the Ragged Schools. 'Dr Barnardo estimated in 1876 that there were about 30,000 ... neglected children under the age of sixteen living on the streets of London.'[21] With the passing of the Education Act in 1870, the Ragged Schools Movement's work of providing elementary education ceased. Under its new name of The Shaftesbury Society it then turned its attention to other aspects of childcare.

How did the work of Sunday Schools generally fare throughout the nineteenth century? K.S. Inglis confirms that the 'drop-out' process that we saw in operation at the turn of the century was, in fact, occurring as a general characteristic of the whole nineteenth century. He says, 'In the case of the Sunday Schools, there is evidence that they were attended *mostly* by working-class children, that for most of the century more children attended them than attended day schools, and that they enrolled hundreds of thousands who belonged later in life to no church.'[22]

As we view the trend of Sunday School work from the beginning of the current century, we see earlier trends continued and the 'solidarity' factor robbing working-class Sunday Schools of most of their pupils just at the age when a credible profession of faith might be hoped and prayed for. Charles Booth observes that 'Elaborate doctrinal teaching may be inculcated in childhood, but its influence is not likely to last unless maintained by the atmosphere of the home or unless supported by social usage. It is to social usage that the upper classes trust, and it is in the union of home and church that we find the strength of the Nonconformists...Thus with regard to the working classes (and the poor) we seem to arrive at a deadlock. There is no hope of social usage, and to create religious homes a new generation of religious-minded parents must arise; while until we have the social usage or the religious homes all advance is stopped.'[23]

What Charles Booth is saying here is that there will be no widespread and lasting influence of the gospel among children until there is a God-sent revival of true religion among adults, particularly the parents of families. The history of urban Sunday Schools indicates that *normally*, where the character-forming influences of Christian example and Bible teaching are absent from the home in the earlier childhood years, the developing life is unable to withstand the social and secular pressures of adolescent and adult years. We know that Christian parents cannot automatically produce Christian children, but such is the strength of parental influence, for good or ill, active or passive, we dare not omit the supreme importance of the Christian home in all our thinking and planning on the best way to use our Sunday School opportunities.

What have we learnt about Sunday Schools which will help us in our future work? We shall tabulate some observations.

1. *The influence of Sunday Schools in the nineteenth century.* E.R. Wickham says that 'It is easy to decry the Sunday Schools, but it would be a grave misjudgement. As means of converting the masses to full Christian faith and practice, clearly, they were inadequate, but as the forerunners of schools for the masses, and as habitual places where the poor sent their children for such moral and religious instruction as many of them ever got, they constititute a major working-class institution in the nineteenth century.'[24]

K.S. Inglis makes a similar assessment. Like Wickham he is aware of the considerable influence of their work and yet at the same time of their considerable limitations. 'They were evangelical in origin and flourished best under evangelical auspices; and they may well have been the most important single means by which evangelical Christianity was brought to bear mildly on people who were otherwise out of reach of the churches.'[25]

2. *Workers.* Where did all the necessary Sunday School teachers come from to instruct the hundreds of children? Without having precise evidence to hand, it seems likely that there were several sources. Some workers were 'home-grown' and lived locally. That is, they were brought to salvation through the work in which they later assisted and taught. Others were equally 'home-grown' but, like so many, had moved out of the poorer slum areas to a more desirable residential location. Their debt of gratitude to the work that nurtured them in the gospel and their spiritual concern for the next generation of Sunday School children brought them to travel in to serve the Lord among working-class children. Relatively strong churches with a sizeable adult membership were also able to supply some workers for nearby 'Mission' causes.

3. *Decline.* Now we come to the hard facts. For the most part of the current century Sunday Schools have been in decline. In many cases the same trends would be apparent in the week-night recreational activities provided for the benefit of young

people in order to 'hold' them within the orbit of the church's influence and teaching. One obvious reason why these week-night activities have shown a parallel decline is that for a long time the right to attend on a week-night to enjoy the recreation has been coupled with an obligation to attend Sunday School. For many years this 'method of persuasion' succeeded in bringing children to hear weekly Bible teaching. This practice has now been modified or abandoned by many churches. A number now introduce a Bible-teaching element into the week-night activity in order to counter erratic attendance on Sundays.

4. *Crisis.* There are few urban churches which can still claim a thriving Sunday School and young people's work. To a greater or lesser degree among urban churches generally there is a crisis. The crucial question is 'If current trends of decline continue, for how much longer can the work survive?' The key factor in a church's ability to sustain a Sunday School and youth work is its ability to grow its own leaders for the next generation of the work. In earlier years, with larger numbers, although the majority of the children 'dropped out' from Sunday School in their teenage years, provided a few of them were brought to know the Lord, then there was good reason to be optimistic about the work continuing. Today's crisis question concerns future leadership. Are we growing new Christians and potential workers in sufficient numbers to be optimistic about the work continuing? Where decline continues, at a certain crucial stage, a point of policy will need to be considered. If a Sunday School has declined to a mere handful of children, does the 'grow-your-own-leaders' policy become no longer a viable option? Should some of the present Sunday School teachers switch their service to evangelism among adults, so that the church might look to that method as a more realistic approach to evangelism and as a better way of securing the future work of the Sunday School?

5. *Adults.* It is sometimes said that while a majority of church workers are engaged in bringing the gospel to children, there is always the hope that the parents might be reached with the gospel through the children. That sounds a hopeful policy and shows that a church is concerned about evangelizing adults as well as children. However, in view of what we have discovered so far about the nature of Sunday School work in urban areas, such a policy appears very unrealistic. Praise God for exceptions

and for those children who have been instrumental in introducing their parents to the gospel. But the weight of historical evidence is overwhelmingly against this kind of hope being realized in a working-class community. It has always been difficult to retain the children up to an age when a response to the gospel might be expected. But to reach the parents through the children cannot be regarded as a biblically demonstrable principle which works in common practice. Where God, in His grace, does work through the children I believe that it is an exceptional occurrence and not a biblical rule. If, however, we reverse the policy and speak of reaching the children through the parents, then that is a sound biblical principle and, therefore, one we should expect to work in practice. That order of gospel influence, from parent to child, should be normal and not exceptional.

6. *History.* The change of emphasis from evangelizing children to evangelizing adults may be viewed with a measure of apprehension. When we consider the spiritual gifts and Christian experience of all those who teach or assist in the Sunday School we may feel that only a minority of them would be prepared to engage in direct adult evangelism. Sunday School is probably where we still have our largest weekly number of hearers of the gospel; it is natural that this is where the majority of believers will exercise their Christian service. But a closer examination of the history of Sunday Schools should provoke us to reconsider our views.

The history of Sunday School work in this country goes back two hundred years. It was in 1780 that Robert Raikes began his work. This means that the Sunday School 'age' is virtually synchronous with the industrial period. During that period the role of the Sunday School has changed.

In the early days, the gospel priority for Christian witness was evangelizing adults. The church members were mobilized to carry the gospel to the people. The first concern of Sunday Schools at that time was educational and social. Evangelism was only a part of its wider work. This meant that the churches looked to converts gained in *adult evangelism* for the leadership and workers for the future. The Sunday School was *not* the chief evangelistic instrument through which new believers were recruited.

As the nineteenth century progressed, two very clear changes came about. First, the state became increasingly responsible for the educational and social needs of children. This left the churches free to concentrate far more on the gospel work among the children. Secondly, the Sunday School increasingly became the *chief agency* through which new believers were added to the churches. But that changed role in the Sunday School work did not come about as a policy decision. It happened as a consequence of the trend to 'introverted evangelism' which developed noticeably during the Victorian period. Throughout the nineteenth century, evangelism of adults by the *outreach* of lay members of the churches steadily diminished. In its place came an evangelism which looked '*inwards*' to believers' children, 'other' Sunday School children, friends, adherents and members of church organizations, to supply the church with its additions of new believers. This pattern of evangelism 'succeeded' in the days of large working-class Sunday Schools. Though most of the children had turned their backs on the church on approaching adulthood, a 'saved remnant' guaranteed a continuing work. We seem now to have come full circle. No longer does the level of conversions in our Sunday School work assure us of a future. Should we now return to the policy of our early industrial forefathers? In those days young men, in particular, viewed Sunday School teaching, not as a lifetime's service but a stage in their Christian development which led on to village preaching and aggressive evangelistic outreach among adults generally.

7. *Strategy.* What must we do now? The chief lesson of Sunday School and working-class history is abundantly clear. Apparent success in the Sunday School work of one decade is no guarantee of a thriving local church in the next. As a general rule, I believe that evangelism among adults ought to have the priority. But that is easier said than done! Those Christians who feel reasonably competent in Sunday School teaching may be hesitant and timid about 'launching out into the deep' to evangelize adults. We shall need a tougher breed of Christians, biblically equipped to face up to the challenge of witness and evangelizing away from the security and familiarity of the local church sanctuary.

I am sure that there is, and will continue to be, for most churches an opportunity to teach children 'the Holy Scriptures which are able to make them wise for salvation through faith in

Christ Jesus' (2 Tim. 3:15). In highlighting some of the difficulties we face I would not want to convey the impression that I have doubts on the value of presenting the gospel to children. While opportunities for this teaching may continue, it may well be that there should be a greater diversity in the *forms* such work should take. A uniformity of approach may suggest an inability, or an unawareness of the need, to tailor the form of the work to the particular characteristics of each local situation. For example, I am sure that the best time for some Sunday Schools is a week-night evening.

I realize that to promote or to provoke a full-scale investigation into the Bible-teaching and evangelistic work among children could well produce some headaches. Just what is the best strategy for bringing the gospel to local children? What is the most efficient deployment of Christian workers? Should there be any distinction in the way we cater for the needs of the children of believers and for those from non-Christian homes? We are not looking for techniques or formulae to produce a blueprint for a 'successful' Sunday School. The history of the work of urban churches among urban children is, strangely, both encouraging and disturbing. And it is positively unchristian to refuse to face facts (2 Peter 3:5,6). Better to have some minor headaches now, than to have some major heartaches later. Better to catch and keep fewer fish, than to enclose a much greater number who swim into our nets and out again. It is imperative that we find ways of mending the holes in the gospel nets we use for reaching children.

Reaching young people

My experience of working with young people does not qualify me to write with any real authority. I have had a limited involvement in a conventional work with a uniformed organization. I only write on this topic because to do otherwise would be to leave a gap in our thinking, and that in a field of gospel opportunity to which the churches look for the 'church of tomorrow'. In order to produce something constructive it may prove profitable for us to think through the following exercise. State the particular advantages of three different types of youth work by giving 'five points' in favour of each one. They are (a) a church-based uniformed organization; (b) a church-based youth club; (c) participation in a secular youth club.

Church-based uniformed organization — e.g. Boys' Brigade

1. *Object.* The object of the organization is clearly defined: 'The advancement of Christ's kingdom among boys, and the promotion of habits of obedience, reverence, discipline, self-control and all that tends towards a true Christian manliness.'
2. *Experience.* The Boys' Brigade celebrates its centenary in 1983. During the past ninety-eight years it has accumulated a wealth of experience of working for and with boys. An organization with that length of history has inevitably acquired established traditions and distinctive features. Leaders in this work need to have wisdom to know what proven practices should be continued and what traditions need to be changed so that Boys' Brigade is fully relevant for boys in today's world.
3. *Achievements.* The organization gives considerable attention to the development of various skills — e.g. physical training, first aid, communications, sport, music, camping and many more.
4. *Discipline.* Bishop Sheppard quotes the comment of a Boys' Brigade officer. He said, 'I couldn't cope with the problem of control of an open youth club. The discipline of the Boys' Brigade gives me just the leg up that I need. Then I can cope.' Sheppard adds, 'It was a humble and sensible remark.'
5. *Spiritual goals.* Attention to the spiritual objectives is built into the structure and regular programme of the Boys' Brigade. Attendance at weekly Bible class is still expected. The chaplain of the company is normally the minister of the church to which the company is linked. Some churches have a regular monthly parade service.

Church-based youth club

1. *Range of appeal.* Membership of a church-based youth club will almost certainly attract a wider range of young people. It is less selective than the uniformed organization. 'Churches often appeal only to a minority social grouping. A church which appeals to the young people who are better behaved, do well with books, like a highly organized programme, is almost certainly appealing to those who are going to move out of the (working class) area.'[26]

2. *Flexibility.* The week-to-week activities run by a Boys' Brigade Company are not optional. Membership of the Brigade involves wearing a uniform, parading for inspection, practising drill, working for badges in various skills, etc. Participation in these activities is required. They are a necessary part of Boys' Brigade life. By contrast, the open youth club offers a variety of facilities, but membership of the club does not involve compulsory participation. The greater flexibility in the youth club gives the leaders freedom to try to relate the club programme to the particular needs and interests of the current membership.

3. *Mixed club.* Uniformed organizations are usually for boys *or* girls, e.g. Boys' Brigade or Girls' Brigade. A single-sex youth work may be preferable if the main emphasis is on achievements, but where there is a desire on the part of the leaders to encourage normal and natural relationships between boys and girls in their adolescent years, then the youth club is better suited to do this.

4. *Relationships.* Where a uniformed organization has a full programme of activities it may mean that because of a strong emphasis on achievements, both by the company and the individual members, there may be little time left over to give proper attention to personal relationships, among the boys, with their leaders, and in life generally. What we are as people in relation to other people is more important than achievements. The person who is primarily interested in developing certain skills and earning awards may, at the same time, be immature in personal relationships.

5. *Keeping them longer.* A group of boys, who in their Junior School years find it exciting to march with other boys, all wearing the same uniform, are likely to find that at the onset of their teenage years the earlier enchantment with the uniform begins to wane. Nor will they respond so keenly to a regimented programme of activities as they did in their earlier years. Their growing group loyalties make them want to 'conform' in certain ways, while at the same time they want to reject the wearing of a uniform. For this and other reasons the average 'drop-out' age in the uniformed organization is likely to be lower than with the church-based youth club. Every additional year that the young people can be held within the church's influence is crucial in the attempt to secure a serious consideration of the Christian gospel before adulthood approaches.

Participation in a secular youth club

Although I do not know personally any Christian youth workers who have experience in this form of Christian service, in theory at least, it does offer some advantages over the other forms of Christian youth work.

1. *Location.* A youth club which meets in church halls, church rooms etc, will be aware that they meet on premises which are not for their exclusive use. Almost certainly the premises will be used for other church purposes at other times during the week. How a group of pensioners might use a church sitting-room might be very different from the way it would be used by a group of energetic and excitable teenagers. Inevitably a code of practice will need to be drawn up by the church authorities so that all users know what is permitted and what is not.

Where sponsorship and ultimate control are in the hands of the church, this may discourage some young people from attending because of the suspicion that sooner or later some form of pressure will be applied to encourage or persuade them to take an interest in the church and what it stands for. A youth club located in its own premises would avoid fears or suspicions about the church's involvement in the youth work. The secular youth club should appeal to the widest range of 'clubbable' young people.

2. *Facilities.* Where a secular youth club has its own purpose-built premises, it would be natural to assume that the building would be equipped for a greater range of activities than would the church-based club. A church club probably could offer table tennis, darts, snooker, billiards and a number of table games. A purpose-built club might also be able to offer basket-ball, badminton, gymnastics, swing-ball, weight-lifting and other sports and hobbies.

3. *Use of workers.* Christian workers who are prepared to go into the secular youth work are unlikely to be numerous. Those who do will have to be ready to meet the young people on their 'home ground' and without any form of church control. But these factors may well prove to be advantageous rather than disadvantageous. If Christians share in the work of a secular youth club they will be much more free from the ties of general administration, keeping an eye on the fabric, and maintaining

order in the club. If a youth worker is relieved from these responsibilities he will not be cast in a 'boss' role. His relationship with club members can be chiefly personal rather than organizational. The fact that the young person is in an environment where he feels at home and where the Christian is not seen as a representative of the church should make for an easier gaining of confidence, openness and deepening of the relationship.

4. *Costs.* The operation of a church-based youth club will inevitably involve the church in the normal items of expenditure for running a church activity — repairs, redecorations, heating, lighting, insurance, cleaning etc. While no church should want to involve itself in youth work 'on the cheap', a church with limited financial and personnel resources may regard involvement in the secular club as strategically and financially preferable, since the sponsoring body of the club would have to bear the financial responsibilities.

5. *Relationships.* As we have already mentioned, relationships are more important than achievements. Youth workers who are not actually 'running the club' should, in theory, have more time to give to the cultivation of relationships. They should be able more easily to identify with the club members and be accepted among them. Gospel opportunities are certain to be mainly in the informal witness occasions rather than in a religious 'slot' which might be allocated in an evening's programme. The Christian worker can over a period of time correct twisted ideas about the Christian church. He will also come to understand group loyalties and group pressures which will be felt most keenly when there is serious consideration of the claims of Christ. 'He who wins souls is wise,' says the writer in Proverbs 11:30. This spiritual wisdom will be particularly important for the Christian youth worker. He will want eventually to introduce young people to 'the church', but he must not do this too soon. An opportunity can be mismanaged. Some young people who show an interest in the gospel may need to be converted *before* they go to church, and not to go to church *in order to* hear the gospel and be converted. Where church-going is alien to the local culture, it makes good spiritual sense to introduce people to the gospel first: introduction to the church may have to wait. Only those who are 'born of the Spirit' can begin to understand what the church is all about.

In an earlier part of this chapter we considered how our work with the gospel should be affected by the cultural factor of solidarity and the influence of the group. From a wealth of experience in Canning Town in East London, Bishop Sheppard writes, 'The small group is often also the key to Christian youth work. A Church may decide to run its own youth organizations or open youth club, or it may choose to join in partnership with a secular youth club. Whichever is the case, young people of fifteen to twenty years of age need some sort of bridge where for them meeting, friendship and discovery can take place. It will need to be a mixed group. Often young people will prefer to sit on the floor of someone's home, listen to records and talk about life than go the best-equipped club which may be provided.

The open club has its point, but deep Christian discoveries are much more likely to be made in a small group which has something of a common life of its own. This can run parallel with a club or organization or within it, without taking members away from it.'[27]

Creation and the city

When the English poet William Blake (1757-1827) penned the words of his lyric 'Jerusalem', little did he realize that he was writing prophetically a national anthem for militant ecologists of the late twentieth century!

And did those feet in ancient time
Walk upon England's mountains green?
And was the holy Lamb of God
On England's pleasant pastures seen?

And did the countenance divine
Shine forth upon our clouded hills,
And was Jerusalem builded here
Among these dark satanic mills?[28]

Blake's ecology is better than his theology. At least, that is my impression! Evangelical Christians would certainly need to 'de-mythologize' his highly imaginative and mystical concepts to discover how near or far he was from orthodox belief. It will be safer for us to forget his theology and concentrate on his ecology.

In the words we have quoted from 'Jerusalem', Blake vividly portrays a clash of interests. Those who are concerned to preserve the beauties of 'England's green and pleasant land' are called to battle. The enemy is symbolized by 'these dark satanic mills' of the industrial barons and the system they represent. Blake saw the Industrial Revolution as 'an expression of mechanistic philosophy'. 'The "Satanic Mills" were not only or primarily those factories which in his day had scarcely begun to create their appalling and inhuman landscape, but the mechanistic philosophy of which these are an expression. He records the sufferings of the enslaved, the labourers in the brick-kilns and mills, of chimney-sweepers, prostitutes, soldiers. But man's enslavement, as Blake saw it, results precisely from those materialistic ideologies, both in England and France, of which Marxism is the ultimate triumph.'[29]

The conflict which William Blake, the poet, described in words was later portrayed on canvas by the artist L.S. Lowry (1887-1976). 'He was struck by the significance of the landscape of these manufacturing towns, the product of the Industrial Revolution and the first of their kind in the world. Here was a whole society of people surrounded by limited horizons — cobbled streets, red-brick houses, little shops, soot-covered churches, chimneys and factories — and driven by the acceptance of their particular destiny of work and play defined by the authority of the cotton mills whose steam-driven machinery set the pace of their lives.'[30]

It is probably true to say that whereas Blake was more concerned about the preservation of 'England's green and pleasant land', Lowry was obviously fascinated by 'these dark satanic mills'. He was gripped by the factories and fumes and the drab and dirty environment in which the multitudes of industrial workers had to spend their lives.

And so we come to the present day. How does modern twentieth-century urban man view the environment in which his life is placed? Changes have come since the days of Blake and Lowry. The smoke clouds have been reduced, if not eliminated altogether. Slums have been torn down and brighter and warmer homes have taken their place. But, for all that, is the city-dweller any more aware of God's creation, by which he is surrounded, than were his industrial forbears of earlier years?

Regrettably, the resident in the big city is still more aware of what man has manufactured than of what God has created. Urban dwellers on post-war high-rise estates are, so it seems, surrounded by monotonous mountains of greyness. From behind the blocks in which the people live, the sun peeps through from time to time as it plays its game of hide-and-seek from behind the columns of concrete. In the normal round of daily life the modern city-dweller is not in a position to 'consider the heavens', as the psalmist did. His environment hides them from view. Consequently, the reflections and conclusions which such an observation should provoke are lost to city-dwellers. From personal experience, I know that one of the pleasures I look forward to on our holiday journeys out of Inner London is the growing awareness of more and more sky. When the city is left behind I look forward to that exhilarating experience of 'considering the heavens' and delighting in their Maker.

How important is this topic we are now exploring? Is it just another aspect of the social deprivation which the city-dweller has to suffer, or is there more to it than that? On closer examination we find that this matter exposes a major factor of spiritual deprivation as well. The Scriptures teach that before a person becomes acquainted with the truth revealed in God's Word he has to rely on God's general revelation in creation for his inner awareness of the Maker to whom he is accountable. 'What may be known about God is plain to them, because God has made it plain to them. For since the creation of the world God's invisible qualities — his eternal power and divine nature — have been clearly seen, being understood from what has been made, so that men are without any excuse' (Rom. 1:19,20).

The impact of this general revelation is not automatic. It must be conditioned by the extent to which this revelation is normally visible to the human eye. 'The heavens declare the glory of God, the skies proclaim the work of his hands' (Ps. 19:1). But how can urban man appreciate this if he cannot see the 'whole canvas' on which God is displaying His glory? 'Day after day they pour forth speech; night after night they display knowledge ...Their voice goes out into all the earth ...' (Ps. 19:2-4). But how can the city-dweller hear God's 'sermon in the sky' when the city's dazzle and din blot out what God is trying to say? We should expect that man 'out of touch' with his Maker will behave differently from man 'in touch' with his Maker. The repercussions of this obscured revelation are greater than we realize. A modern city environment may largely blot out an awareness of God's creation, but what does that do to the people who live in it?

'The child of the concrete wilderness today grows up in surroundings almost entirely man-made. Outside the block where he lives, concrete stretches away as far as he can see. If small patches of grass have been sown, these are soon trampled into barren earth; the few trees planted are rapidly mutilated and torn down; there are no flowers. Even the air is so heavily polluted from local industries, petrol fumes, etc. as to remind one of man rather than of natural creation. The flat-dweller has no patch of ground 'belonging' to his home; and the child thus has no feelings of any bit of outdoors being particularly 'his', nowhere to be responsible for, to make decisions about, or to grow anything. And as it is against estate regulations to keep animals, most kids grow up without personal responsibility for any living creature.'[31]

Elizabeth Braund, to whom we made reference earlier in our study, has given much thought to this issue and its bearing on her work in Battersea, South West London. Speaking of young people in Battersea Miss Braund says, 'They are growing up with eyes that cannot see, and register anything beyond their own pitifully restricted vision of telly adverts, shops and estate life. Their own faculties are equally blunted. They cannot concentrate; their minds are tragically incurious; they have little control over themselves; ambitions, except in a strictly material sense, are nil, and ideals do not exist.'[32]

Miss Braund goes on to say, 'Nowhere in Scripture, before or after the Fall, is man exhorted to live in isolation from and ignorance of the rest of God's creation. Rather, we believe that a Scriptural doctrine of man lays down the principle that in order to be truly human and to develop a true humanity, conscious relationship with a responsibility for the rest of God's creation is a necessity; without it, human behaviour and development become sub-human.'[33]

The tragedy of urban man is that he is unaware of God *through* what God has created and this leads to a lack of reverence and respect for *what* God has created. In the beginning God placed man in an environment of 'living things' — trees, flowers and grass; insects, birds and animals. God made them. Therefore, man had to respect them. God entrusted their care to His highest creation — man. So man had to show responsibility for them. But the modern industrial city is a far cry from the Garden of Eden. Urban man is not surrounded by living things in the way that Adam was. Apart from the people in the city, it is a man-made environment of 'things' which are largely lifeless and inanimate. You cannot care for concrete and cars and colour television sets in the way that a farmer cares for his cattle! A child may care for a puppy — provide for its needs and protect it from danger. An animal's response of affection and trust makes a valuable contribution to the development of a child's capacity to care. But you cannot do the same with a motor-cycle! It requires no care and shows no response! Without this caring responsibility urban man becomes less than fully human. Francis Schaeffer says, 'The Christian is a man who has a reason for dealing with each created thing on a high level of respect.'[34] But the urban pagan has a tendency to do the opposite. Is the senseless vandalism by some people in cities not, in part, a protest by developing human beings against their environment for the way that environment is restricting and warping their progress towards mature adulthood?

In this context we might also ask what it is that impels industrialists to damage and disfigure some areas of natural beauty in 'England's green and pleasant land'? Such action would be defended in the name of material progress. Looked at in another way, it might be interpreted as legalized vandalism! A compulsive desire for more and more 'things' leads urban man to subordinate all other interests to his quest for material comfort. Where the economic arguments are all-powerful there will be scant respect for what God has created.

Schaeffer asks, 'Why does strip-mining turn the world into an absolute desert? Why is the "Black Country" in England's Midlands "black"? What has brought about this ugly destruction of the environment? There is only one reason: man's greed. If the strip-miners would take bulldozers and push back the topsoil, then rip out the coal, put back the soil and push back the topsoil, then ten years after the coal was removed there would be a green field, and in fifty years a forest. But, as it stands, for an added profit above what is reasonable in regard to nature, man turns these areas into deserts — and then pretty soon cries out that the topsoil is gone, that grass will not grow, and there is no way for hundreds of years to grow trees!'[35]

Providentially, the opinions of environmentalists and ecologists receive more attention than was formerly the case years ago. More thorough investigations are carried out, and public opinion is tested before the 'mechanical monsters' are let loose to perform their task of controlled destruction. We are learning from the mistakes of the past, but some of nature's industrial wounds will never heal.

When David the psalmist surveyed the heavens, under a night sky in Palestine, his soul was rapt in worship and wonder. 'O Lord, our Lord, how majestic is your name in all the earth! ...When I consider your heavens, the work of your fingers, the moon and stars which you have set in place, what is man that you are mindful of him, the son of man that you care for him?' (Ps. 8:1,3,4.)

Can we expect that sort of response from urban man in the industrial city today? The voice of God through ·His creation is muted amid the hustle and bustle of the modern metropolis. So what are we to do? A first step must be a readiness to think more deeply about the significance of the biblical doctrine of creation. Professor John Murray claims that, 'Without the concept of creation ...we cannot think even one right thought of God.'[36] We must talk about creation, think about creation and, as often as possible, take a good look at creation. A regular 'awayday' from the city should prove physically and spiritually refreshing. It would be a valuable scriptural exercise to discover in what ways the Bible writers use the teaching on creation to instruct and inspire God's people. For example, believers who feel cast down, neglected and powerless to defend their rights will find that Isaiah 40:21-31 offers a most wonderful tonic.

We must remember that it is creation itself, and not just the doctrine of creation, which makes its impact on the soul, disturbing the sinner and delighting the saint. That is why our study of 'creation and the city' has not been a diversion from the topic of evangelism. God's 'sermon in the sky' is meant to be seen rather than heard. But the man-made city obscures our view of God's handiwork. We shall need to guide people where to look.

The spacious firmament on high,
With all the blue ethereal sky,
And spangled heavens, a shining frame,
The great Original proclaim.

The unwearied sun, from day to day
Does his Creator's power display;
And publishes to every land
The work of an almighty hand.

Soon as the evening shades prevail,
The moon takes up the wondrous tale,
And nightly to the listening earth
Repeats the story of her birth;

While all the stars that round her burn,
And all the planets in their turn,
Confirm the tidings as they roll,
And spread the truth from pole to pole.

What though in solemn silence all
Move round this dark terrestrial ball?
What though no real voice nor sound
Amidst their radiant orbs be found;

In reason's ear they all rejoice,
And utter forth a glorious voice;
For ever singing, as they shine,
The hand that made us is divine. [37]

Joseph Addison, 1672-1719

Ten questions

We now conclude our discussion on evangelism. In order to help us apply the appropriate 'tests' to the gospel work in which we are engaged, a number of probing questions need to be asked. Our thinking now moves from theory to practice. We are to examine the particular gospel work in which we are currently active.

1. Are we placing the responsibility on the believers to evangelize or on the unbelievers to come and be evangelized?
2. Do our church members in their daily witness see themselves as the principal agents in evangelism, seven days a week and all hours of the day, or do they think that the chief responsibility lies with the preacher in his 'one-hour-a-week' gospel service and sermon?
3. Are *all* our church members capable of giving a 'reason for the hope' that is in them? Can they with simplicity and accuracy articulate their faith? If not, why not? Where does the fault lie? We have seen that John Bunyan, shortly before he became a Christian, was greatly impressed by 'three or four poor women sitting at a door in the sun ...talking about the things of God'. Are we to regard these women as peculiar and exceptional, in view of what the Scripture requires of us? How can we 'loose our stammering tongues to tell his love immense, unsearchable'?
4. Are our church membership and congregation socially representative of the community in which it is located? If not, why not?
5. How far has our gospel outreach become 'introverted' evangelism?
6. Are our methods of evangelism unfairly selective? Have we been guilty of a form of favouritism without realizing it? Apply this question to your own work among adults and also among young people.
7. In our evangelism generally do we make it our policy, as far as possible, to introduce people to the *gospel first* before we seek to introduce them to the church? Is it spiritually realistic to expect an unbeliever who is without spiritual life and understanding to share meaningfully in the worship aspects of an evangelistic service in order to hear the gospel?
8. If our church is located within a community which is partly or predominantly working class, do any aspects of our evangelism take into account the phenomenon of 'solidarity' which is an important feature of working-class culture?
9. Do the methods of evangelism we currently employ reflect an awareness of the need to have a careful balance between 'instruction' and 'persuasion'? Ideally, we need to explore or create opportunities for 'feed-back' following our preaching or witness. We need to be able to gauge whether or not we have carried our hearers with us in an understanding of the gospel

facts we have imparted. As we noted earlier, John Wesley warned against speaking in 'those kinds of technical terms that so frequently occur in Bodies of Divinity; those modes of speaking which men of reading are intimately acquainted with, but which to common people are an unknown tongue'. There is little point in adding further bricks of truth, until there is some evidence that the foundation of gospel thinking is beginning to be established.

10. The apostle Paul says, 'Be wise in the way you act towards outsiders; make the most of every opportunity' (Col. 4:5). Do we take those words seriously? Presumably he means that we should do all we can, all the time we can, for as many people as we can influence with the gospel of Jesus Christ. But time and energies are not unlimited. If we choose to become deeply committed to one form of evangelism, then this almost certainly means that we are not in a position to engage in some other forms of evangelism. We cannot do everything! But how do we go about choosing what to do and what not to do? Paul says, 'Make the most of every opportunity.' That means we shall need to make an assessment of the relative merits and potential of a number of opportunities that may be open to us. Paul told the Christians at Corinth, 'But I will stay on at Ephesus until Pentecost, because a *great door for effective work* has opened to me ...' (1 Cor. 16:9). Paul makes a very careful assessment of the opportunity he has and then, sensibly, arranges his timetable accordingly: 'I will stay on at Ephesus until Pentecost.' Do we in our local churches have any policy for regularly reviewing the opportunities that we have and those we ought to use? Are we able to make a calculated and spiritual assessment of the opportunities presented by a number of forms of evangelism?

In a lecture given to students at his pastors' college, C.H. Spurgeon said, 'Many a man, who is doing little, might, with the same exertion, do twice as much by wise arrangement and courageous enterprise. For instance, in our country towns, a sermon delivered on the village green would, in all probability, be worth twenty sermons preached in the chapel; and, in London, a sermon delivered to a crowd in a public hall or theatre may accomplish ten times as much good as if it had fallen on the accustomed ears of our regular auditors. We need, like the apostles, to launch out into the deep, or our nets will never enclose a great multitude of fishes.'[38]

In what ways should Christians evangelize a working-class community? The 'opportunities' should be tested by the criteria we have established in the ten questions we have just formulated. Here is a list for consideration: personal witness to neighbours; personal witness at work; evangelism through home groups; door-to-door visiting; open-air gospel preaching; gospel preaching in church services; Sunday School; church youth work; coffee-bar evangelism; witness in a local street market or shopping centre; distribution of a 'gospel paper'; contribution to a community paper; local radio; evangelistic films; gospel cassettes; careers in secular youth work; visiting homes for senior citizens; young mothers' group; men's group; women's meeting; contacts made through provision of social amenities — e.g children's pre-school playgroup; 'hospitality' evangelism.

To this list we might add those gospel opportunities which are created by what we might describe as 'sanctified imagination'. A couple of examples will explain the idea. A young mother chose to do her washing in the local laundrette because it was a useful meeting-point for developing links with local mothers. In her scale of values, deepening of relationships with neighbours was more important than the convenience of doing her washing at home, even though she possessed her own washing-machine. A senior missionary returned 'home' after serving the Lord for many years overseas. Rather than settle down to a quiet retirement in a village community, she chose to live in an urban community with a high proportion of immigrants. Her missionary experience had trained her mind to look for gospel opportunities. Shopping times provided natural and useful opportunities for developing contacts with people. In her scale of values effective evangelism was more important than efficient shopping. For her it was preferable to make her purchases from *two* shops even though she could have obtained all the items from *one*. Her approach to personal evangelism was determined by a matter of simple arithmetic. It is better to witness to two shopkeepers than to one! There is no intention to suggest that these opportunities represent a 'major discovery' in terms of evangelistic opportunity. What is important for us to copy and cultivate is the attitude of mind and heart that provoked these initiatives.

When a form of evangelism is assessed for its suitability in a local situation, it is important to consider more than the immediate opportunity of gospel witness that is afforded. A particular gospel opportunity may be explored with much trepidation and uncertainty and may even lack the wholehearted and enthusiastic prayer support of other Christians. Yet in the long term the harvest of souls reaped may be far in excess of what was first anticipated, whereas another form of evangelism may provide an immediate and very direct opportunity to present the gospel, but the fruit may be minimal. Sometimes believers are too easily discouraged by small numbers and, conversely, too easily encouraged by large numbers. We may misjudge a situation. There is a need for mature spiritual discernment here.

Jesus spoke about 'sowing' and 'reaping' (John 4:35-38). Paul talks in similar terms about 'planting' and 'watering' (1 Cor. 3:6-8). Normally, a harvest of souls will only be gathered when and where the earlier evangelistic spadework has previously been carried out. It is no doubt true that many people have been brought 'out of darkness into God's marvellous light' on their first hearing of the gospel. This would be particularly true during times of revival. But I would question whether it is the norm for pagans who have no knowledge of the gospel to come into a full experience of God's salvation on their first hearing of the good news. When Paul preached at Athens some of his hearers asked for a further opportunity of hearing the gospel explained. Some said, 'We want to hear you again on this subject' (Acts 17:32). Even the Roman governor Felix, who was already 'well acquainted with the Way' (Acts 24:22) sent for Paul and listened to him as he 'spoke about faith in Christ Jesus'. In my judgement the more useful evangelistic opportunities are those where there can be a continuing opportunity to declare and explain the gospel. This does not rule out the special occasion. Our biggest congregation is at our annual Carol Service. Our congregation more than doubles on that occasion. But that is only once a year.

Although the past two or three decades have witnessed the appearance of a variety of evangelistic innovations, a growing number of Christians continue to believe that preaching which is both expository and evangelistic is the ideal method of spreading the gospel. Where people can conveniently gather to hear the preaching, there the good news of Jesus Christ can be declared authoritatively and plainly. If that view is held as a basic conviction concerning biblical evangelism then the value of all other 'forms' and 'methods' is likely to be judged by that. The more nearly a form of evangelism approximates to the ideal, the more likely its potential will be explored with enthusiasm. The more distant it is from the ideal, the less likely it is that such an opportunity will win our approval and support. Between these two views there will be a range of opportunities which in turn will correspondingly either stir our zeal or dampen our enthusiasm.

It would not be at all surprising if we showed some caution and reluctance to investigate some of the evangelistic opportunities we have suggested. If that is the case, then the example of John Wesley may be an encouragement to help us overcome our natural reticence. To say that Wesley's thinking about evangelism underwent a radical transformation is certainly not an exaggeration. It is perhaps hard for us to imagine that this great evangelist who claimed, 'The world is my parish' found his thinking virtually 'chained to the pulpit' in his earlier gospel ministry. He says in his Journal, 'I could scarce reconcile myself at first to this strange way of preaching in the fields, of which he [George Whitefield] set me an example on Sunday; having been all my life (till very lately) as tenacious of every point relating to decency and order, that I should have thought the saving of souls almost a sin if it had not been done in a church.'[39]

After conquering his natural reluctance, Wesley said, 'I submitted to be more vile.' For the sake of lost souls, he was prepared to go into their situation and forego his natural preference for the decency and order to which he was accustomed. A 'sample' of those situations in which Wesley found opportunity to make known the gospel makes fascinating and challenging reading. He preached in a meat market, a corn market, a butter market, a shooting-range, a forge, a brickyard, a bowling-green, a malt-room, a room over a pigsty and a barn. He visited prisons, workhouses, hospitals and asylums. Much of his indoor preaching was done in private houses. Wesley's first open-air preaching in London was at Whitefield's sites at Moorfields, Blackheath and Kennington Common. Kennington Common was the place of execution most in use after Tyburn. It was not unusual to see men hanging there in chains. Wesley's last open-air sermon was delivered at the age of eighty-seven at Winchelsea. 'He covered nearly a quarter of a million miles in his lifetime, delivered forty thousand sermons and yet found time to write well over two hundred books.'[40]

6.
Lessons from Lystra

Who, where or what is Lystra? What is its connection with the subject of our study? This is where we must begin. The answers to our questions are found in the book of Acts 14:8-20. After healing a cripple, Paul and Barnabas were on the point of being venerated with divine honours. Paul dismissed this misplaced homage and used the incident as a base from which to proclaim the gospel. The visit to Lystra was cut short by the arrival of some Jewish 'bully boys' from Antioch and Iconium. They came to stir up opposition to Paul and his message. Paul was severely knocked about, dragged out of the city and left for dead. Providentially, he recovered. He paid a further brief visit to the folk at Lystra before setting off for Derbe. The church at Lystra was planted by Paul on his first missionary journey.

There are a number of features of the Lystran church and its city environment which have certain parallels with our urban situations today. A number of the principles we shall extract from the events at Lystra have a very clear application to our urban world. This is the purpose of our study.

1. *Location.* Lystra was founded as a Roman colony by Augustus, probably about 6 B.C. It was about 18 miles south-south-west from Iconium. It has been described as 'an obscure town on the high plains of Lycaonia (near modern Harun Sarai)'. Standing in a retired situation some miles away from the high road, it was not likely to participate strongly in the diffusion of Greek civilization. In the opinion of W.M. Ramsay

it is something of a surprise that Paul should have visited Lystra at all. He says, 'Considering the character of almost all other Pauline cities, the great places of the Eastern world, most of them centres of international intercourse and progress, one must wonder how Lystra came to be one of the list.'[1]

2. *Population.* The population of the colony consisted of the Latin-speaking colonists, a local aristocracy of soldiers; the native population, some of whom were doubtless educated in Greek and strong supporters of the Roman imperial policy; while the majority were evidently uneducated, not well acquainted with Greek, but more naturally expressing themselves in the Lycaonian tongue.

3. *Occupations.* The occupation of the majority of the population was in agriculture. As a farming community, their work demanded of them the development of manual rather than intellectual skills.

4. *Language.* 'The striking events which occurred at Lystra are associated mainly with the humbler class of the Lycaonian populace; and it is the only city of Asia Minor in which a native language is mentioned.'[2] Professor F.F. Bruce comments, 'The fact that the crowd cried out in Lycaonian is specially mentioned by Luke (who possibly got his information from Paul) for two probable reasons: in the first place, Paul and Barnabas recognized that this was a different language from the Phrygian which they had heard on the lips of the indigenous population of Pisidian Antioch and Iconium; in the second place, the crowd's use of Lycaonian explains why Paul and Barnabas did not grasp what was afoot until preparation to pay them divine honours was well advanced.'[3]

5. *Education.* 'Lystra is the only city in which Paul is brought into immediate contact with the uneducated Anatolian populace, wholly ignorant of Hellenic culture ...Everywhere else Paul's address was directed to the classes which had shared to some degree in Greek education and were familiar with the Greek tongue.'[4]

6. *Religion.* 'While the presence of Jewish residents in Lystra is clear (Acts 16:1), no synagogue is mentioned there; and the general tone of Acts 14:8-19 suggests surroundings more thoroughly pagan and less permeated by Jewish influence than in Iconium and Pisidian Antioch.'[5] The pagan majority of the community were 'much under the influence of the native

superstition'. Here alone the native Anatolian gods and the native religion are confronted with the new faith.

Although the first-century city of Lystra may seem poles apart from a twentieth-century industrial city such as Liverpool, what they share in common is probably greater than we would at first expect. The majority of the working people at Lystra were manual workers. To use the term 'working class' would be somewhat anachronistic, nevertheless, that would be a fair description. The pre-Industrial Revolution setting of Lystra does mean that the chief occupation involved the production of food. We have seen already that this was so in Britain prior to the eighteenth century. The advent of the industrial age brought with it a massive redistribution of the labour force. The proportion of the working population involved in food production diminished progressively throughout the eighteenth and nineteenth centuries. Whereas at the end of the seventeenth century only 20% of the working population were employed in non-agricultural occupations, by the year 1831 over 70% were employed in non-agricultural occupations. Today in this country the farming industry employs less than 3% of the total labour force.

The matters of 'language' and 'education' can be linked together. The majority of the Lystran population spoke the Lycaonian language: they were not familiar with Greek. Most commentators on life in Lystra also draw attention to the fact that this community was without the asset of education. When Paul spoke at Lystra he encountered for the first time a problem of communication, which was linked to the language and education of the people he was addressing. Where people are chiefly involved in manual occupations and do not require any particular educational standard or verbal skill for the kind of work they do, then those who need to communicate effectively with such 'working people' will need to develop a mental discipline in order to achieve this. The rules which apply here we have already discussed fully in chapter 3.

The religious condition of the general populace at Lystra has much in common with the bulk of the population of the inner urban area of a city like Liverpool. They are pagan Gentiles. We have already carefully distinguished between 'Jewish evangelism' as we see it in the New Testament, and particularly in the ministry of the apostle Paul. There are only two recorded sermons in the book of Acts which were preached to pagan Gentiles. They were the sermons preached by Paul at Lystra (Acts 14:8-20) and at Athens (Acts 17:16-34). It is in these two sermons in particular that we have detailed examples of the type of approach Paul used when he spoke to people who had no knowledge of Scripture. The sermon preached at Athens was preached to people who could be called 'middle-class intellectuals', whereas the sermon at Lystra was directed to ordinary 'working people'. In this sense Lystra is unique. It is the only example we have of detailed information concerning the social and spiritual condition of a New Testament working-class community and the structure and content of the evangelistic sermon which Paul addressed to them. The progressively more pagan our nation becomes, the more important Paul's experiences at Lystra become for our understanding of appropriate biblical evangelism.

Before we proceed to look further at Lystra, we need to say something about the size of cities mentioned in the New Testament. We shall be looking at the parallels between a first-century city and our urban situations today in order to obtain biblical guidance. The parallels are certainly there, but there is a major difference and contrast when it comes to the matter of size. 'Rome at the height of its power covered 6 square miles within the Aurelian walls in AD 274. Greater London now covers 677 square miles and New York 2,514 square miles.'[6] These statistics were calculated at least ten years ago. Any revision of them would only serve to highlight further the disparity of size between New Testament cities and those of the industrial age. In the United States the focus on the specialized needs of urban areas has spawned its own vocabulary. We are in the age of the supercity; megalopolis has arrived!

Our method of study will be to examine the content and structure of the message brought to the people of Lystra and how it related to their spiritual and social circumstances. In order to bring out in sharper relief the component parts of the sermon we shall set them out in tabular form alongside a similar analysis of the gospel message preached to the Jews and Gentile God-fearers in Pisidian Antioch and the gospel address preached to the middle-class pagans at Athens. The next step is for the reader to digest the information tabulated in Table 1. The left-hand column indicates the aspects of the analysis we are making.

Table I

Three evangelistic sermons preached by the apostle Paul to different audiences

Background:

	Pisidian Antioch	Lystra	Athens
1. Geographical location			
2. Bible portion	Acts 13:13-43	Acts 14:8-20	Acts 17:16-34
3. Religious status of the audience	Jews and God-fearing Gentiles	pagan Gentiles	pagan Gentiles
4. Social status of the audience	various?	working-class farming community	middle-class intellectuals

Sermons:

(a) Point of contact: gaining attention	synagogue worship and teaching (13:14-15)	idolatry and ignorance (14:13-15)	idolatry and ignorance (17:22-24, 29)
(b) Evidence of the nature of God	God's Word (13:15) and God's acts in choosing Israel as His people (13:15-20, etc.)	The 'living God' (cf. idols) created the world and every thing in it (14:15)	The 'living God' (cf. idols) created the world and every thing in it (17:24-25)
(c) Experience of the goodness of God (Rom. 2:4)	God's provision and protection for His people climaxed in the sending of the promised Saviour (13:17,32)	God has provided them with the necessary harvests, food and happiness (14:17)	All life is sustained by the providence of God. Nothing exists independently of God (17:25,28)
(d) Cultural identification	Paul is a Jew. He speaks of 'brothers' (13:15,26,38) and the God of 'our fathers' (13:17,32)	God's provision of rain, crops and food (14:17). A farming community would appreciate this.	World order and purpose considered. Quotation from one of their poets (17:21,26-28)
(e) God and history	The history of God's dealings with Israel (13:18-37)	In His grace and patience, God 'overlooked' their former ignorance (14:16)	In his grace and patience, God 'overlooked' their former ignorance (17:30)

(f) Spiritual obligation	God has kept His promises and sent them the Saviour they need (13:23,37-39)	God has blessed them with 'food ... and joy'. It is their duty to honour God 'as God' and give thanks to Him (Rom. 1:21)	As 'God's offspring' (17:29) they are completely dependent on him. They are to honour Him as God and give thanks to Him (Rom. 1:21)
(g) Evangelistic exhortation	They must 'believe' in the 'resurrected Jesus' through whom they receive forgiveness of sins and justification (13:38-41)	'We are bringing you good news, telling you to turn from these worthless things (other gods) to the living God' (14:15)	God demands immediate repentance from all people (17:30). God will one day judge the world through 'the resurrected Jesus' (17:18,31)

Three sermons from the book of Acts

The report which Luke gives of Paul's speech at Pisidian Antioch (Acts 13:13-47) affords us our only extended sample of Paul's missionary preaching to Jews and God-fearers. There are only three New Testament portions in which Paul's preaching and teaching deal exclusively with pagan Gentiles and their relationship to God. Besides the two sermons we have analysed, an early portion in the letter to the Romans (1:18-2:16) also covers the same topic. There is much common ground between the three portions: Acts 14:8-20; 17:16-34; Romans 1:18-2:16. These Scriptures are of particular importance for those Christians who are evangelizing in our almost wholly pagan environment today.

The two sermons for the Gentiles have a common starting-point: idolatry and ignorance. But the sermon for the Jews and God-fearers starts at an altogether different point from the other two. It refers back in history to that time when God, in His gracious electing love, chose Israel to be His own people. It is in the matter of the use of Scripture that the really major contrasts appear. The sermon preached in the synagogue followed the reading of Scripture. In fact, the major part of its content is really nothing less than a general summary of Israelite history from the people's initial deliverance from Egypt down to the coming of Jesus. The sermon is thus a broad outline of the contents of the entire Old Testament. To say that the sermon was thoroughly scriptural is certainly no understatement. When we come to look at the two sermons preached to the Gentiles, we find a very different approach. They do not begin with any particular Scripture. They make no quotation from Scripture. In fact, there is no indication in these two sermons that Paul informed his hearers that such a thing as 'the Scripture' existed!

Can we believe our eyes? When did you last hear a 'sound' evangelistic sermon preached for today's pagans in which there was no explicit reference to Scripture or quotation from Scripture? In defence of Paul's preaching we must say that the material for the two sermons for the Gentiles was entirely scriptural in that its content was fully in accord with the written Word of God.

Commenting on Paul's preaching at Athens (Acts 17) and Lystra (Acts 14), Michael Green says, 'To be sure he does not quote the Old Testament; that would have betrayed lack of sensitivity and would have been quite meaningless to them: insofar as he makes specific quotations they are from Greek poets — but, as at Lystra, his doctrine of God is entirely biblical, and so indeed is some of his language. This is true apologetic, and also true evangelism, where the content of the gospel is preserved whilst the mode of expression is tuned to the ears of the recipients.'[7]

How we know that God is there

The reason why the sermon to the Jews and God-fearers followed the reading of Scripture (from the Law and the Prophets) is because this was the recognized divine authority by means of which God ruled His people and ordered their lives. God had *acted* in choosing a people for Himself. He had *spoken* his directions and requirements to His servants. 'Men spoke from God as they were carried along by the Holy Spirit' (2 Peter

1:21). 'In the past God spoke to our forefathers through the prophets at many times and in various ways ...' (Heb. 1:1). When any query of faith or life occurred there could be only one way to settle the matter properly: what does the Scripture say?

This approach was all right for the Jews, but what about the pagan Gentiles? They do not know Scripture, but God has no less right to rule their lives than He had to rule the Jews. How is the divine authority to be brought to bear on their lives? Would it be advisable to give a simple and brief definition and summary of what the Bible is? Should we organize a crash course in Old Testament history? What does the Scripture say? How does the Scripture tell us to speak to people who have no idea of what Scripture is? The answer is that while *we* may have been privileged to understand what God is like through His special revelation in Scripture, the general revelation through God's work in creation is sufficient to convince *all* people of the existence and character of God. The Scripture says, 'What may be known about God is plain to them, because God has made it plain to them. For since the creation of the world God's invisible qualities — His eternal power and divine nature — have been clearly seen, being understood from what has been made, so that men are without any excuse' (Rom. 1:19,20).

Man's obligation to acknowledge and honour his Creator can adequately be demonstrated to the pagan without recourse to the Scripture. Man is already aware of this even before his attention is drawn to it. Made 'in the image of his Creator', man is so designed that creation around him and the voice of conscience within him combine to produce an ineradicable awareness of 'the God who is there'. Not only does man know of the existence of this God, he is also aware that this God demands moral action from him. Certain thoughts and actions are known by man to be right or wrong, good or bad. Whether he likes it or not, whether he denies it or not, conscience acts as an umpire in the soul. With irritating persistence this umpire continues to register approval or disapproval where moral decision is required. The voices of creation and conscience cannot be silenced. But by the conspiracy of sin their message is muted. What they now convey is less than compelling and less than infallible.

It is most important that we allow God's special revelation in Scripture to determine our understanding of the weight of conviction that can be conveyed through God's general revelation in creation. It would be far from the truth to imagine that an occasional glance at a clear night sky or a wondering gaze at a majestic sunset merely provide faint hints and scattered clues to the existence of a great 'Someone' who is behind it all. The force and clarity of God's 'handwriting in the heavens' is spelt out plainly in the first part of the letter to the Romans. Sin provokes the unbeliever to *suppress* the truth (Romans 1:18) that is conveyed to him through 'general revelation', precisely because it disturbs his conscience. Before the Gentiles heard the Holy Scriptures, 'although they knew God, they neither glorified him as God nor gave thanks to him' (Rom. 1:21). 'They exchanged the truth of God for a lie' (Rom.1:25). 'They did not think it worthwhile to retain the knowledge of God' (Rom. 1:28). 'They know God's righteous decree' (Rom. 1:32). The inner voice will not stay silent. They are without excuse. The truth stings. So the wasp in the conscience must be crushed. Professor John Murray says, 'We must not tone down the teaching of the apostle in this passage. It is a clear declaration to the effect that the visible creation as God's handiwork makes manifest the invisible perfections of God as its Creator, that from the things which are perceptible to the senses cognition of these invisible perfections is derived, and thus a clear apprehension of God's perfection may be gained from his observable handiwork.'[8]

As the writer, Thomas Watson (1620-1686) put it, 'The world could not make itself. Who could hang the earth on nothing but the great God? Who could provide such rich furniture for the heavens, the glorious constellations, the firmament bespangled with such glittering lights? We see God's glory blazing in the sun, twinkling in the stars. Who could give the earth its clothing, cover it with grass and corn, adorn it with flowers, enrich it with gold? God only. (Job 38:4.) Who but God could make the sweet music in the heavens, cause the angels to join in concert, and sound forth the praises of their Maker? (Job 38:7.) "The morning stars sang together, and all the sons of God shouted for joy." If a man should go into a far country, and see stately edifices there, he would never imagine that these built themselves, but that some greater power had built them. To imagine that the work of the creation was not framed by God, is as if we should conceive a curious landscape to be drawn by a pencil without the hand of an artist.'[9]

'The notion of a Deity is engraven on man's heart; it is demonstrable by the light of nature. I think it hard for a man to be a natural atheist; he may wish there were no God, he may dispute against a Deity, but he cannot in his judgement believe there is no God, unless by accumulated sin his conscience be seared, and he has such a lethargy upon him, that he has sinned away his very sense and reason.'[10]

Good news for the workers

The circumstances in which the apostle Paul preached his gospel address at Lystra have some remarkable similarities with those in which the apostle Peter preached an evangelistic address in Jerusalem soon after the Day of Pentecost. The occasion of both addresses arose from the healing of two crippled men who had endured that condition from birth (Acts 3:2; 14:8). When God's servants pronounced healing for these men both of them 'jumped' and 'walked' (Acts 3:8;14:10). Not surprisingly these miracles produced astonishment in all who had observed what had happened (Acts 3:10;14:11). Both apostles needed to explain that it was not their own power which had brought about the healings (Acts 3:12;14:14,15). The explanation of these healings provided a convenient introduction for both evangelistic addresses.

It is at this point that the similarities between the two events cease. The sermon which Peter preached was from first till last full of Jesus Christ. The sermon was addressed to Jews. It explained why and how salvation from sin had been accomplished through Jesus Christ. The fulfilment of Old Testament prophecy was explained. The personal involvement of the hearers in the events of the death and resurrection of Jesus Christ was plainly demonstrated. The need for repentance was clearly expounded. By any standard this was a first-class gospel sermon which exalted Christ and abased the sinner.

When we turn to the sermon which Paul preached at Lystra, we find that it could hardly have been more different from Peter's sermon in Jerusalem. The sermon began with the assertion that there is but one Creator God — the living God who has made heaven and earth and sea and everything in them. Following this, Paul then moved to explain God's dealings in providence with the people of Lystra. Then the address finished. Presumably Paul would have gone on to speak about Jesus Christ and the way of salvation, but we are obviously in an area of speculation if we attempt to say what he should have added in order to present a balanced and biblical gospel address. What we can say is this: whatever was spoken but has not been recorded was not necessary for us to know. But what the Holy Spirit has caused to be recorded is necessary for us to know. It has been written for our edification.

Since the content of Paul's sermon was so very different from that which Peter preached in Jerusalem, we need to ask a particular question: 'Is the address at Lystra an example of something we should copy or is it a warning of something we should avoid?' We must remember that the Scriptures are infallible, but men of God are not! They can make mistakes. However, since there is no suggestion within Scripture to indicate that Paul was wrong in his approach to the Lystrans, then we must conclude that what has been written is for our instruction. We shall now examine in more detail this Lystran address and attempt to elucidate the biblical principles it exhibits.

1. *Scriptural content.* The address was entirely scriptural in that its content was in full accord with the written Word of God, even though no explicit reference to Scripture is contained within the sermon.

2. *Pagan audience.* The spiritual condition of the people at Lystra was so vastly different from those who listened to Peter in Jerusalem that an altogether different approach was necessary.

'If it be asked whether Paul would have expressed himself in this way, even to a pagan audience, it may be pointed out that his description of the Thessalonians' conversion from paganism in 1 Thessalonians 1:9f presupposes preaching very similar to that given here at Lystra. To Jews, who already know that God is one, and that He is the living and true God, the gospel proclaims that Jesus is the Christ, but pagans must first be taught what Jews already confess regarding the unity and character of God. "God is one", they are told, "and has not left Himself without witness; His works of creation and providence show Him to be the living God who supplies the needs of men;

therefore abandon those gods which are no gods but utter vanities, and turn to the true God".'[11]

3. *Explaining Christ.* Even if Paul had intended to speak about Jesus Christ, why was reference to the Saviour not made much earlier in the address? When the crowd jumped to the wrong conclusion that the gods had come down in human form, was this not a golden opportunity for Paul to speak of the incarnate Son of God who had come down to accomplish the work of salvation? Why did Paul turn aside from what appeared to be such a useful situation to introduce Jesus Christ? Just how easy is it to explain and teach about Jesus Christ to people who have no knowledge of Scripture at all, and whose lives are steeped in a background of ignorance and idolatrous paganism? Even those who closely followed Jesus while He was here on earth found themselves baffled by the events of the first Easter. When Jesus walked with two disconsolate disciples on the Emmaus Road, He said, 'How foolish you are and how slow of heart to believe all that the prophets have spoken! Did not the Christ have to suffer these things and then enter his glory? And beginning with Moses and all the Prophets, he explained to them what was said in all the Scriptures concerning himself' (Luke 24:25-27). It took a major Bible study from the Saviour Himself to clear their confusion and set their hearts at rest. It is interesting to note that in his initial evangelism at Athens Paul's earliest references to Jesus were misunderstood. 'Some of them asked, "What is this babbler trying to say?" Others remarked, "He seems to be advocating foreign gods." They said this because Paul was preaching the good news about Jesus and the resurrection' (Acts 17:18).

4. *Point of contact.* He started his address at the point his hearers had reached in their understanding — or misunderstanding! Paul turned their attention from the many gods to the one living God. In his thinking with them he moved from the known to the unknown. This is a sound educational principle.

5. *Personal experience.* He focused their attention on their personal experience of God's dealings in their lives: 'He has shown kindness by giving *you* rain from heaven and crops in their seasons; he provides *you* with plenty of food and fills *your* hearts with joy.'

6. *Practical relevance.* Paul spoke in a way which demonstrated the practical relevance of his subject to their lives. The point

which Paul made about their personal experience of God's provision of food could apply to any group of people whatever their occupations — carpenters, tent-makers, tax-collectors, and so on. But the provision of rain and crops and harvests were of particular interest to the Lystrans because farming provided their livelihood. Without adequate rain their crops were jeopardized because they were virtually without alternative sources for the watering of their crops. The area of Lystra was in a 'bare and dreary region, unwatered by streams, though in parts liable to occasional inundations. Strabo mentions one place where water was even sold for money.'[12] Paul's words had direct relevance for everyday living in that farming community.

7. *Style of preaching.* The style of Paul's sermon was well suited to the capacity of his hearers. His address was simple and uncomplicated. There was no abstract reasoning with concepts. The content of the sermon was accompanied by permanent visual aids!

8. *Urging repentance.* The motivation for repentance was presented in a way that showed great spiritual wisdom. The Scriptures show that it is possible to argue the need for repentance and turning to God from two different points of view. It can be argued from (i) *future events* — what God will do to us in a coming day; or (ii) *past experience* — what God has already done for us in the past. These two approaches complement each other, but there are times when it is preferable to reason from one point of view rather than the other.

When Paul preached to the Athenians, he chose to argue from 'future events': 'In the past God overlooked such ignorance, but now he commands all people everywhere to repent. For he has set a day when he will judge the world with justice by the man he has appointed. He has given proof of this to all men by raising him from the dead' (Acts 17:30,31). By contrast, his approach to the pagan Gentiles at Lystra was from the aspect of past experience. Paul called them to turn to God because they are utterly dependent on Him and deeply indebted to Him. 'He has shown kindness by giving you rain from heaven and crops in their seasons; he provides you with plenty of food and fills your hearts with joy' (Acts 14:17). These good gifts do not come from Zeus or Hermes. They come from the living God. How should pagan man react to this awareness of God's unfailing goodness to him? 'Do you show contempt for the riches of his kindness, tolerance and patience, not realizing that God's kindness leads you towards repentance?' (Rom. 2:4.) Arguing for repentance on the basis of future events is a more detailed mental exercise. It requires the imparting of new facts; it does involve a process of reasoning, and necessarily it is beyond present experience. Paul's approach at Lystra was direct, simple, persuasive and rooted in personal experience.

The example of Paul's address at Lystra does have much to help us in our work of spreading the gospel among the working classes. In particular, the emphasis on personal experience of God's providential dealings can exert a strong moral pressure on the conscience. It has been my advice to Christians who are keen to witness for the Lord that where the conversation seems to be running into an intellectual cul-de-sac it may prove helpful to shift the emphasis to personal experience. The change of tactics may break the deadlock. For a Christian to testify to what God has done in his life demands no great reservoir of doctrinal knowledge nor any great ability to out-reason the sceptic or cynic. When a Christian simply and sincerely relates how life was before God graciously intervened and what life is like now, this can open minds and hearts where the doctrinal dialogue may seem to fail. This move can cool aggressive debate. The believer's experience cannot be taken away from him. It might be challenged, but it cannot be refuted. The unbeliever can be disarmed. When his intellectual defences are no longer under siege, he may relax and be more open to the gospel. This is an emphasis on the personal experience of the *believer*.

What Paul did at Lystra was to emphasize the experience of the *unbeliever*, and remind him of God's providential goodness to him. In our evangelism among the working classes, should we not remind our neighbours of the goodness of God in their lives? It is a simple and direct approach. It steers clear of a 'word battle' and the struggle to grasp difficult concepts. Who can number all God's mercies? The blessings of the daily provision of food, clothing and shelter; the blessings of health, sleep and work; God's protection in dangers seen and unseen; the amazing patience of God who extends His mercies and withholds His wrath in spite of many provocations — all these and more should lead twentieth-century pagans, like those of the first century, towards repentance and a new relationship with the living God.

Ritual or repentance?

The opening words of the apostle Paul's address to the people of Lystra established the fact that the living God is primarily concerned with 'repentance' and not 'ritual'. Zeus, Hermes, the bulls, wreaths, garlands, sacrifices and the rest of the pagan paraphernalia had to be abandoned. In sum they were nothing but 'worthless things'. The living God, Creator of all things requires His creatures to turn from the error of their ways and demands that they set their lives to serve and honour Him.

All religions have some place for rites which are to be performed by the adherents. This is true of biblical religion as well as all false faiths. Under the old covenant the Jewish nation was required to perform certain sacrificial offerings as instructed by the law of God. God's people of the new covenant are required to observe the ordinances or rites of believers' baptism and the Lord's Supper. Adherents of false faiths tend to view the performance of certain rituals as the centre and essence of their religion. Neglect of these duties may incur the disfavour of an offended deity, whereas in the Christian religion ritual is never of the essence of the faith. Where it is required, Christian ritual must be strictly controlled and carefully explained. Note the solemn warnings linked with scriptural teaching on the Lord's Supper (1 Cor. 11:23-32). At most, rites may be regarded as symbolic and secondary in the Christian faith.

A general survey of the history of the Christian church would reveal just how much in thought and practice 'ritual' and 'repentance' have become polarized. In practice, ritual and repentance do not go happily together. Either one or the other will tend to dominate, to the virtual exclusion of the other. The reasons for this are not hard to find. Ritual and repentance are fundamentally different. A summary of contrasts will make this clear.

1. Ritual in itself is no more than an external action. Repentance is essentially an inward disposition of the human soul.
2. Ritual may say nothing to the mind. Where it is unexplained, it may be shrouded in religious mystery. For the performance of the ritual there are times when the mind could, without disadvantage, be switched off. Repentance is, by definition, a change of mind leading to a new outlook on life.
3. Ritual may provoke certain favourable feelings, which tend to

operate in the sphere of the aesthetic. Repentance should provoke certain feelings which operate in the realm of the conscience and moral behaviour.
4. Religious ritual may have no connection whatever with daily living. Genuine repentance must affect the moral quality of daily living. If it fails to do so, its genuineness must be challenged.
5. Ritual may ease and yet deceive the conscience. Repentance should disturb and then heal the conscience.
6. Ritual is seldom costly. It may be easily done and quickly forgotten. Repentance can be very costly. Obedience to God may lead to conflict with family, friends and colleagues: sometimes even with the civil authorities.
7. Religious ritual may serve to provide an escape from the harsh realities of a sinful world. Repentance exposes to us the harsh realities of a sinful world, casts us upon the mercy of God, and equips us to go to our fellow men with a message of hope.

These contrasts between ritual and repentance explain why they tend to polarize. Genuine Christian conversion demands both faith and repentance. When Paul spoke to the Ephesian elders he described the precise response that God requires to the gospel of His grace. He says, 'I have declared to both Jews and Greeks that they must turn to God in repentance and have faith in our Lord Jesus' (Acts 20:21). Ideally, repentance and faith should be present together like the two sides of one coin. But this is not always the case, and faith may be present even where repentance is still absent. Simon, the sorcerer from Samaria, is a case in point. When he heard the preaching of Philip, 'Simon himself believed and was baptised' but subsequently his desire to purchase the gift of the Holy Spirit exposed an unrenewed heart. The apostle Peter urged Simon to 'repent of this wickedness and pray to the Lord. Perhaps he will forgive you for having such a thought in your heart. For I see that you are full of bitterness and captive to sin' (Acts 8:22, 23).

How do the matters of ritual and repentance bear on our concern to evangelize the working classes? We are all too aware that the average working man has next to no contact with the Christian church. But what contact he does have tends to present the Christian faith as primarily a matter of religious ritual. Only rarely will he get the impression that it is repentance which is fundamental. There are predictable, if rather infrequent, occasions when the working man and his family actively seek contact with the Christian church. For the events of birth, marriage and death the local vicar is usually the one to be contacted and the appropriate services arranged. Since these occasions when the working man comes to church are for something special, there tends to be an even greater prominence of ritual than would be the case for normal Sunday worship.

Added to this 'special occasion' emphasis, there is also a historical factor. During the nineteenth century, High Churchmen in the Anglican communion appear to have had more success in urban parishes where other shades of churchmanship have fared less well. A.D. Gilbert speaks of a particular strand of 'the reform movement' which 'began with Tractarianism and can be traced more or less directly to the Ritualist clergy of the later Victorian era whose efforts contributed most to the modest achievements of the Church in urban working-class parishes'.[13]

In 1904, C.F.G. Masterman observed that 'The High Church clergymen have no monopoly of devoted work, nor do they give in charity more than the missions which endeavour to stem their influence. The working man has no affection for elaborate ritual; he accepts with resignation, as part of an inexplicable activity, the ornaments, the processions, and the ceremony. If they processioned round their churches standing on their heads, he would accept it with the same acquiescence. But they have gone down and lived amongst the people; they have proclaimed an intelligible gospel of Christian Socialism; they have demanded not charity, but justice.'[14]

The special family occasions which bring the working man to church and the historic emphasis on ritual all serve to produce in the working man's mind an image of Christianity which is very much taken up with certain religious actions and gestures in a special building where those things have to be done.

Christenings, weddings and funerals all have to be 'done' in church otherwise they just would not be done 'properly'. These occasional visits to church for the appropriate rites to be performed confirm to the working man that what goes on inside a church building has next to nothing to do with ordinary everyday life. It is a world apart from work in the factory or life in the family. Ritual is far removed from Monday morning. And so, for that matter, is repentance. Anyone who really took seriously all that the Bible says must be an 'odd bod' or a crank. It is just attempting the impossible!

'Working-class people, when they insist on a church wedding or funeral, are drawing upon beliefs which, though rarely considered, are still in most cases firmly there. These beliefs, some of the basic Christian doctrines, they hold but do not examine. Nor do they often think that they have much relevance to the day-to-day business of living. That is thought of as an altogether different matter, a hard and unidealistic matter; if you tried to "live according to religion", well, you would soon find it was "a mug's game", would soon be "done for". They know that they and other people often do wrong, but by that they usually mean doing wrong towards other people; the sense of sin, of original sin, is on the whole alien to them. If one of their number is strikingly affected by the dogmas of religion, they are quick to say, "Oh 'e's got religious mania," and to regard him as a harmless crank or near lunatic. Sometimes he is, but not always, and they draw few distinctions here.'[15]

The Christian person who knows that he has been brought into an experience of regeneration and repentance by the work of the Holy Spirit must not allow himself to drift into a relaxed and casual approach to the Christian life once the milestone of conversion has been passed. There can be a tendency for the believer to move away from the position of repentance towards one in which ritual gains the ascendancy. Heart religion becomes a mere husk of its former self, even though the routine of ritual is perpetuated. The prophets of the Old Testament repeatedly sounded warnings against this. David, the 'man after God's own heart', bares his soul in his great psalm of confession and repentance:

> 'You do not delight in sacrifice,
>   or I would bring it;
> you do not take pleasure in burnt offerings.
> The sacrifices of God are a
>   broken spirit;
> a broken and contrite heart,
>   O God, you will not despise'
>   (Psalm 51:16,17).

There may be those who view a continuing emphasis on repentance as undesirable. They may see it as something which is too introspective, too sombre and likely to produce an unhealthy guilt complex. It may then be argued that a measure of ritual may add lightness and colour to worship, helpfully counterbalancing any trend to spiritual morbidity associated with a call to repentance. There is an element of truth in what is being argued, but any trend to increase ritual must be guarded with spiritual vigilance. It may be claimed that ritual is morally neutral, but that cannot be proved. From Bible history we learn that increasing ritual tends to be associated with idolatry. Idolatry is often the forerunner of immorality. Ritual does not check sin: therefore it tolerates sin and thereby forfeits its claim to moral neutrality. The Greek god Hermes, whom the people of Lystra identified with Paul, had a moral pedigree a million miles apart from the apostle: 'Hermes was the messenger of the gods and of Jupiter in particular; he was the patron of travellers and shepherds; he conducted the souls of the dead into the infernal regions; he presided over orators, and declaimers and merchants; and he was also the *god of thieves, pickpockets, and all dishonest persons*'![16]

Spotlight on superstition

When Paul evangelized the Jews he had a standard procedure in the synagogues. He 'reasoned with them from the Scriptures, explaining and proving that the Christ had to suffer and rise from the dead'. The word translated 'reasoned' also appears in Acts 19:9 where it is translated 'had discussions'. People who were used to hearing the Scriptures expounded had their powers of reason exercised and developed by listening to the preaching. This also tells us that the Christian gospel has a very solid rational content. In the glory of its full dimensions the Christian gospel transcends reason; nevertheless, God does invite man to come and reason with his Maker about the matter of sin and how it is to be dealt with (Isa. 1:18). This in turn explains why the Scripture requires Christians to be ready to give a 'reason' (logical defence — Amplified Bible) for the hope that is within them (1 Peter 3:15).

If that is what we can expect from Jews and Gentiles who have become Christians what can we expect fron Gentile pagans? A

Lessons from Lystra

reasoned appeal may elicit a very different response where the hearers are largely uneducated, and their thought and life are generally described as primitive. When Paul healed the cripple at Lystra the reaction of the inhabitants was astonishing, to say the least. They said, 'The gods have come down to us in human form.' Convinced of the reality of this totally unexpected visitation, the people prepared to offer sacrifices to these deities who had 'dropped in'. In spite of all the protestations, in word and action, on the part of Paul and Barnabas, 'they had difficulty keeping the crowd from sacrificing to them'. 'The use of the Lycaonian language shows that the worshippers were not the Roman *coloni*, the aristocracy of the colony, but the natives, the less educated and more superstitious part of the population.'[17]

Reason is a God-given faculty which is not to be ignored or neglected or abused. But it is clear that where people still live in pagan darkness then all sorts of religious superstitions exist and they are not easily shifted by the use of reason. Educated pagans may more easily be persuaded by reason, but this is not to say that they are largely unaffected by irrational superstitions. These may still exercise a very powerful hold over unbelievers, regardless of their educational attainments.

What is superstition? How broad or narrow is the definition? The *Oxford Dictionary* defines 'superstition' as 'credulity regarding the supernatural, irrational fear of the unknown or mysterious, misdirected reverence, a religion or practice or a particular opinion based on such tendencies'. In view of the fairly comprehensive description of this phenomenon, what we shall be examining now falls well within the definition given. In relation to the matter of religious superstitions, what was true of the local people of Lystra is generally true of working-class people today. In their religious views they hold ideas and attitudes which may be totally illogical and yet irritatingly immovable. In his study of working-class life in the North of England earlier this century, Professor Richard Hoggart observed the minimal amount of rational content in the religious views held by working-class people: 'In general most working-class people are non-political and non-metaphysical in their outlook. The important things in life, so far as they can see, are other things. They may appear to have views on general matters — on religion, on politics, and so on — but these views usually prove to be a bundle of largely unexamined and orally-transmitted tags, enshrining generalizations, prejudices, and half-truths, and elevated by epigrammatic phrasing into the status of maxims ...These are often contradictory of each other; but they are not thought about, not intellectually considered.'[18]

The superstitions shown by the people of Lystra in their actions towards Paul and Barnabas were of a much more serious nature than those which we may discover in working-class thought and life today. The consternation of Paul and Barnabas at the intended sacrifice and worship was quite understandable. The people of Lystra believed in many gods. Their polytheism was intolerable. Although they did not realize it, their action was an open defiance of God's first commandment. The people of Lystra did not yet realize the gravity of their sin. But to make matters worse, the two servants of the living God were now being regarded as gods themselves. The thought that they should be the objects of worship and reverence horrified Paul and Barnabas. The apostles vigorously protested their humanity and urged the people to 'turn from these worthless things to the living God' (Acts 14:15).

The superstition we may encounter among working-class people today is very different from that which we have observed at Lystra. It is not polytheistic but rather it views monotheism as a sane and sensible approach to life: 'There *must* be *Someone* up there.' The inevitability of the existence of God is their very limited but reasonable defence of their monotheistic outlook. What this God is like, what He expects of us, and what He can do for us, are other things altogether. How do working-class superstitions show themselves? There are a variety of ways and we can only mention a few examples. A frequent visitor to our church is a lay preacher from a suburban church who spent his boyhood in this part of south-east London. He was not brought up in a Christian home, nevertheless, Sunday was observed as a different day from the other six. One Sunday, father caught his son John cleaning his shoes in the kitchen, whereupon father 'blew up' and knocked his boy 'from one end of the kitchen to the other'. There were things you just did not do on Sundays. But the father made no claim to be a Christian. A year or two ago a young husband with a history of depressive illness took his own life. The widow decided that it had to be a no-expense-spared funeral even though, at the time, she did not have the funds to pay for it. She requested that the coffin should be brought to her flat a few days in advance of the funeral. Before the lid was sealed, she placed inside the coffin a betting slip and a pound note. Why did she do it? 'He always liked to have a bet.'

Superstition is most manifest in people's very unreasoned approach to the doctrine of providence. Of course, that is not how they see it. There are certain things that happen to them which are indicators of impending 'good luck' or 'bad luck'. If a person walks under a ladder, or spills salt, or breaks a mirror, then any of these portends something unwelcome. But if a black cat walks across the path, or if a person tempts misfortune by saying, 'Touch wood', then these signal a lucky outcome. How firmly are these beliefs held?

The views we have just mentioned are often dismissed by working-class people as 'all superstition'. Yet at the same time they do not discard these fables. Horoscopes are still popular. Inconsistencies of belief seem not to matter. Oral tradition is strong and guarantees that the 'old tags' are repeated and handed on from generation to generation.

David Martin claims that 'Faith in the power of luck and in the usefulness of the devices for controlling it in one's favour is very widespread. One in three of those in the wartime services carried some form of tangible protective magic on their persons. Nearly half the population has consulted a fortune-teller, and four out of five read weekly horoscopes, though half of these describe it as "a diversion". Yet nearly two men and over three women out of ten sometimes follow astrological advice.'[19]

In so far as they feel they can have some influence on these 'bad luck' or 'good luck' occurrences, so working-class folk practise their 'beliefs'. What it really amounts to is a hope that they can 'tip the scales of providence' in their favour. Because they do not have a personal relationship with the 'Someone' up there, their actions are just a little reminder or persuader to the Almighty about what they would like to see happen. This kind of thinking (or lack of it) we may view with a condescending smile. It all seems so trivial. But I have discovered that not all Christians have shed this 'give-God-a-hand' view of divine providence.

In a home Bible study group which I was leading, an adult Christian said in the course of conversation: 'Please God' and 'Touch wood'. Normally a placid man, I erupted with astonishment. My somewhat uncharacteristic reaction was deliberate. People are not easily reasoned out of unreasonable superstitions. If I could not disturb these views by sober reason, then I judged it best to crack the obstinate nut of superstition with a fourteen-pound sledge-hammer of horrified amazement! This is not to suggest that the almost innocuous 'Touch wood' or 'fingers crossed' are the seeds or signs of blatant heresy. But they are part of the sentimental rubbish of an unregenerate way of thinking. The Christian mind needs a good spring-clean from time to time. Unless these unbiblical views and ideas are swept out of our minds, we may find that at some later date they act as a clog on clear thinking about the doctrine of providence.

These particular superstitions of the working class need to be set against a background of mushrooming superstition in society generally. The decline in the presence and power of true religion has left a spiritual vacuum which the devil is only too ready to fill with confused thoughts and feelings. The unbeliever senses an appetite for something he cannot define. In his confused ignorance he can so easily be lured to scavenge around the devil's dustbins for crumbs of comfort to ease the spiritual hunger of his sin-sick soul. We must be ruthless in our exposure and condemnation of anything that either clearly or remotely suggests a dabbling in the veiled areas of the devil's darkness. Manifestations of occult powers in such things as spiritism, divination, astrology, witchcraft, mysticism, magic and even Satanism are all part of the sticky web into which the unsuspecting unbeliever can be drawn. When set alongside the 'powers' we have just mentioned, the working-class 'Touch wood', crossed fingers, walking under a ladder, breaking a mirror and all the rest seem trivial, and perhaps they are in terms of the degree of spiritual hazard they represent. The idiosyncracies of working-class superstition are fascinating but not threatening. More often than not, the particular superstition has no objective reality to which the mental image relates. Such superstitions are, therefore, 'all in the mind'. But that is not so with superstitions related to occult practices. Here we encounter exceedingly dangerous devices of the devil. No longer are we up against figments of the imagination; this time it is for real. 'For our struggle is not against flesh and blood, but against the rulers, against the authorities, against the powers of this dark world and against the spiritual forces of evil in the heavenly realms' (Eph. 6:12).

'Human like you'

'We too are only men, human like you,' protested Barnabas and Paul to the people of Lystra (Acts 14:15). But their hearers were not easily persuaded. In spite of the simple gospel address given by Paul, the 'primitive' farming folk of Lystra were determined to hold on to their own views about the true identity of Barnabas and Paul. They were convinced that their visitors were none less than 'the gods come down in human form' (Acts 14:11). Paul's powers of persuasion were fully stretched. 'Even with these words, they had difficulty keeping the crowds from sacrificing to them' (Acts 14:18). But there was a particular reason for the people's extreme reluctance to accept what Paul said about God's servants.

A local Lycaonian legend sheds light on their behaviour. The story goes that once Zeus and Hermes had come to this earth in disguise. But nobody would offer them hospitality. At long last two old peasants, Philemon and his wife Baucis, took them in and cared for their needs. These gods did not forget the reception they had received. Consequently, the whole population was destroyed by the gods, except Philemon and Baucis, who were made the guardians of a splendid temple and were turned into two great trees when they died. When Paul healed the lame man, the people of Lystra immediately guessed who their two visitors were. This time they were not going to make the same mistake as before. Behind their eagerness to sacrifice to Paul and Barnabas was their understandable concern to avoid a second experience of the wrath of the gods. The legend certainly adds to our understanding of events at Lystra. But there is no indication that either Paul or Barnabas were aware of this legend before they arrived at Lystra.

'We too are only men, human like you,' said Paul. But his hearers did not want to believe what they heard. Ultimately, we cannot force people to believe what we tell them, regardless of the depth of conviction and persuasion with which we may speak. But should we be concerned about this? Does not our Lord warn us that we are likely to be misunderstood and misrepresented both unintentionally and intentionally? It is all part of the cost of Christian discipleship. Jesus said, 'Blessed are you when people insult you, persecute you and falsely say all kinds of evil against you because of me. Rejoice and be glad, because great is your reward in heaven, for in the same way they persecuted the prophets who were before you' (Matt. 5:11,12). We may consider it unwise to enter a contest solely to defend and preserve our personal reputation (1 Peter 2:23). But where slander or prejudice, lies or gossip may seriously hinder the advance of the gospel, we cannot remain indifferent and stay silent. When Festus, procurator of Judea, claimed that Paul's great learning was driving him insane, the apostle was swift to counter this charge with a courteous, powerful and reasoned answer, which exposed the nonsense of Festus' accusation (Acts 26:24-27). Where the 'popular image' of the ambassadors of the gospel proves to be a threat to the credibility of the gospel and a hindrance to its progress, it is only sensible that thought be given to ways of remedying the situation.

'We too are only men, human like you.' So say the ministers of the gospel today. But does the working man take that claim seriously? 'We face the same temptations, we experience the same trials, we have the same weaknesses, as other people. We are neither more than, nor less than, human like our neighbours.' But do they really believe what we say? I made mention in an earlier chapter of a conversation I had with a cable-layer several years ago. 'It's all right for you,' he said, 'you are a professional Christian!' It is not at all easy to find a simple yet convincing answer to that comment. How do working-class people generally view a minister of the gospel, whether he be the local Anglican vicar or the Free Church pastor? Obviously, there is no 'standard' image of a minister of the gospel, although the vicar in the television programme *Dad's Army* seems to be a fairly popular caricature. It is interesting to note that the way people viewed the apostles spanned a range of opinion from the *superhuman* (Acts 14:11; 28:6) to the *subhuman* (1 Cor. 4:13). In the interests of removing or minimizing barriers to an acceptance of the Christian gospel it will be helpful for us to make a brief historical survey of working-class views of ministers of the gospel.

Writing of the years 1800-1850, and the evidence of unfavourable attitudes towards the clergy, R.F. Wearmouth, the Methodist historian says, 'Another factor that must not be ignored was the disfavour in which the Established Church seemed to be held by a large section of the working-class community. In all the Radical movements of the first half of the nineteenth century, the Church was held up to ridicule. The high stipends obtained by the bishops and the anti-democratic attitude of most of the clerical magistrates were causes of constant complaint.'[20]

During the latter half of the same century it was still apparent that the Anglican clergyman was expected to be a 'gentleman'. Even recruits drawn from a lower social rank still found a wide gulf in status between themselves and ordinary people of a working-class parish. Writing of these 'recruits' K.S. Inglis says, 'Few among the remainder were of birth humble enough to approach the artisan or docker or miner without crossing a wide social gap. Although the theological colleges took men from lowlier homes than supplied the universities, they were still thoroughly middle-class institutions. They reduced the difference in rank between the clergyman and the Nonconformist pastor; but no serious effort was made in the Church of England, or in the larger Nonconformist bodies to reduce the difference in rank between ministers of religion and the working classes. "The Reformation", wrote a French observer in England in 1867, "desired to bring the priest nearer to the people, in order to bring men nearer to God, but birth, education and fortune, still create a gulf between the Protestant minister and the most humble of his congregation." '[21]

Estimates of working-class views of ministers of religion at the dawn of the current century were not uniform. Charles Booth claimed that 'The average working man ... despised the professionalism of the clergy.' Added to this there was a sense of grievance against ministers of religion in general for their failure to take positive and persevering steps towards securing social justice for the deprived masses. Men who dared to campaign actively for the rights in question often found 'open opposition from larger religious organizations'. In spite of these views, C.F. Masterman felt able to claim that 'the clergy are frequent and often welcome visitors' to the homes of working people.

There is one more factor which has a major bearing on our enquiry. It concerns the matter of indigenous leadership in local churches. Almost without exception, the ministers of religion, the leaders of the churches, were not native to the areas in which they served. The churches did not have an indigenous leadership, whereas the local churches of the New Testament period had wholly indigenous leadership. This is a subject we shall look at in more detail in the next two chapters.

K.S. Inglis has drawn our attention to the wide social gap which existed between the ministers of religion and their urban congregations. This social gap understandably produced a credibility gap. Ministers of religion were inevitably 'outsiders' who came into a different kind of community from that to which they were accustomed. They thought differently, spoke differently, dressed differently and lived differently from their urban neighbours. It is difficult for us to appreciate the kind of enigma the Christian minister presented to the working man.

Masterman, writing in 1904, comments, 'Our movements and inexplicable energies are received with a mixture of toleration and perplexity. We are recognized as meaning well, but our aims and ideals never become clearly intelligible. "What is he after?" "What does he get?" "What is behind it all?" — are questions I have heard frequently asked as some church has burgeoned out into fresh and ingenious enterprise ... Funds from outside raise churches and chapels; funds from outside provide clubs and material relief. We appear and we vanish. After a few months of this perplexing enthusiasm the curate or minister is called to another sphere of work, and disappears from the universe of those who had just, perhaps, commenced to realize that he possesses *some traits of ordinary humanity*!'[22]

As the twentieth century progressed, any hostility to the clergy faded and disappeared, even though the 'enigma' remains. Richard Hoggart claims that working-class people are 'not consciously anti-clerical'. David Martin amplifies Hoggart's mid-century assessment: 'The cleric is at the same time an object of respect and suspicion, as well as being a figure of derisive affection in the world of the comic cartoon. He presides at the rights of passage, like the churching of women, which are often of very great importance in working-class life, especially those which provide the major gatherings (or even bickerings) of the wider kin. But since this is the only "visible" portion of his work he is regarded otherwise as a man whose rather easy task is that of entertaining the womenfolk. Add to this the fact that he not only has a white collar but one which is turned round the wrong way, and he becomes defined as a man with a "cushy number". Even the industrial chaplain intruding delicately into the factory structure will be asked how he would like to work for a living.'[23]

'We too are only men, human like you,' say God's ministers in the nineteen-eighties. Do working people believe that is true? While they may be willing to concede that ministers of the gospel are no more nor less than fully human, like themselves, the charge of being 'professional Christians' is difficult to refute convincingly. This particular problem brings us back to the topic of communication and the matters of 'reason' and 'impression' which we examined in the context of the 'battle for the mind' (see Chapter 3). There we discovered that the working man's opinions are largely determined by the sense impressions he receives from the world about him. It is very difficult, by reason alone, to persuade the average working man to abandon opinions which are not true to fact. If we would change the mind we must correct the impression.

Paul and Barnabas faced the same problem at Lystra. When Paul healed the cripple, the crowd immediately were under the *impression* that the gods had come down to them in human form. We can appreciate how these primitive farming folk gained that impression. In order to correct the misunderstanding, Paul presented an elementary summary of the Christian gospel. But his address, so simple in its structure and so uncomplicated in its *reason*, almost failed to convince his hearers (Acts 14:18). It is worth noting that Paul, in his effort to communicate effectively, did not rely on reason alone. He was also mindful of impression. When the apostles first realized the ritual intentions of the people of Lystra, they 'tore their clothes and rushed into the crowd shouting' (Acts 14:14). The tearing of clothes among the Jews was a gesture of horror at blasphemy (cf. Mark 14:63). What impression this produced in the minds of the people we cannot accurately measure. A particularly Jewish gesture necessarily had a limited impact on people who were largely pagan Gentiles.

A minister of the gospel is all too human when trials and temptations expose his fallen nature and his frail humanity. He knows it, but whether the people in his urban community recognize it is another matter. It must be admitted that it is not difficult to see how people get the *impression* that he is a 'professional Christian'. Is there any sure way of correcting these false notions? A further 'lesson from Lystra' is that we need to be aware of the way our neighbours' thinking is influenced by 'reason' and by 'impression'. Whether there will be any positive and immediate steps that can be taken to correct an erroneous impression will vary from time to time and place to place according to the topic being considered. To rely on reason alone is almost certainly to prolong indefinitely our attempts to communicate effectively, and particularly where a strong and enduring impression appears to be an open contradiction of what is being said by reason.

Consider what impression would be gained from David Martin's description of a minister of the gospel, which we have just quoted. At Lystra the apostles 'tore their clothes' to convey a truth and to create an impression. By what we wear people often know what job we do and the kind of people we are. Did New Testament pastors or elders wear any particular clothes for their participation in the services of worship? Did they wear any distinctive clothing when pursuing their everyday duties? For whatever good reasons ministers of religion may choose to wear various pieces of clerical attire, as far as the working man is concerned they only serve to shield and distort his humanity. Were New Testament church leaders recognized more by the quality of their character than by the distinctiveness of their dress?

The Most High God

After the apostle Paul's visits to Lystra (Acts 14) and to Athens (Acts 17) how did he view, in retrospect, the progress of the gospel among the pagan Gentiles? In the new situations he faced, speaking to people with no knowledge of the Scriptures, was he convinced that his policy had been the right one? Opinion is divided here. The subsequent events are interpreted in different ways.

There are those who believe that Paul made an error of judgement in speaking to pagans from God's general revelation in creation. This was a considerable departure from his approach in the synagogues. It is contended that his subsequent and firmly declared preaching policy, which appears in his first letter to the believers at Corinth, signals a change of mind and a return to the heart of the biblical gospel. We are no doubt familiar with Paul's strong defence of the message of 'Christ crucified': 'When I came to you, brothers, I did not come with eloquence or superior wisdom as I proclaimed to you the testimony about God. For I resolved to know nothing while I was with you except Jesus Christ and him crucified. I came to you in weakness and fear, and with much trembling. My message and my preaching were not with wise and persuasive words, but with a demonstration of the Spirit's power, so that your faith might not rest on men's wisdom, but on God's power' (1 Cor. 2:1-5).

Some people argue that these words to the Corinthians concerning the gospel message reflect a revision of his preaching policy following his visit to Athens. It is said that the reason why the Lystra and Athens sermons are markedly different from his typical preaching is that 'they are speeches made under exceptional circumstances at dramatic moments in St Paul's career'.

I believe those who claim that Paul made mistakes at Lystra and Athens are wrong. It would appear that those who challenge Paul's method of approach to the Gentile pagans are forming a conclusion first and then arranging the evidence to support the view they have taken. Arguments which question and reject Paul's manner of approach to the pagans do not have a foundation which takes account of *all* Scripture that has bearing upon this issue. Surely the Holy Spirit did not lead Paul to contradict himself in the first letter to the Corinthians! 1 Corinthians 2:1-5 must be consistent with 1 Corinthians 9:19-23. Would the Holy Spirit cause so much detail of the sermons at Lystra and Athens to be recorded for us without any word of warning if, as some claim, Paul made an error of judgement here? Are we really meant to believe that the Lord blessed the gospel preaching in Lystra with conversions in spite of the way Paul preached and not because of the way Paul preached? The Scripture does not say so, and neither is it implied.

Far from leaving us with a questionable model for evangelistic preaching to pagan Gentiles, the sermons at Lystra and Athens present an emphasis from which we should learn. It has something special to say to us. I would want to describe the sermons at Lystra and Athens as being deliberately 'God-centred'. The major part of the content of these addresses is taken up with a description of the character of God. If the scriptural summaries of these sermons accurately reflect all that was said by Paul in these situations, then we may say that in both cases the prime object was to present clear teaching on the nature of God before there was an attempt to explain the person and work of Christ. I believe there is a very sound theological reason why these two sermons preached to pagan Gentiles are so 'God-centred'.

The fool says in his heart, 'There is no God.' The people at Lystra and Athens were not fools, but they were deceived into believing in many gods rather than one. Paul's first task was to call the people to put away their superstitions and erroneous beliefs in a pantheon of deities. He called them to turn to the 'living God', beside whom there is no other. Man is aware of God, dependent upon God, accountable to God, alienated from God, and inexcusable before God. How can he find a way back to God? By the preaching of the gospel — the good news of Jesus Christ. So initially, it is the *work* of God in creation that tells him of his accountability to God. But it is the *Word* of God in Holy Scripture which tells him about Jesus Christ and the way back to God. Creation alone, which tells us much about God, tells us nothing about Jesus Christ. Perhaps it is a distinction which we often overlook because it may seem to have little significance. But I believe it is vitally important.

Why do people need Jesus Christ today? There are several ways of answering that question. My first answer, without hesitation, would be 'Because of what God is like.' The more I know about God, His greatness and His glory, and my utter dependence upon and accountability to Him, then the more I understand the Saviour whom God has provided to bring me back into a right relationship with Him. A sermon that is full of God is bound to be the best preparation for understanding the kind of Saviour I need. Only that type of emphasis is likely to lead to a contrite response from a sinner's heart. Tell me as much as you can about what God is like, then I shall truly appreciate the kind of Saviour I need. Then I shall adore and obey this gracious God for providing just such a Saviour.

The privilege we have of knowing God's self-disclosure through Scripture may cause us to overlook the importance of

Lessons from Lystra

God's revelation through creation. Since we have received God's supreme revelation and redemption through His Son Jesus Christ, we may be inclined to allow creation's earlier glory to be pushed into the shadows and ignored altogether by the coming of the 'Sun of Righteousness'. We must be careful in our thinking at this point. What God has revealed to mankind through His work of creation does not become irrelevant and superseded by the new and complete revelation through Jesus Christ. It is of great importance that a Christian should think correctly about his sovereign Maker.

Professor John Murray claims that 'The thought of creation, the thought of our dependence upon God, is implicated in any true thought we entertain with respect to God. *Without the concept of creation, (then) we cannot think even one right thought of God.* Hence, the significance of creation for our conception of God and therefore for the Christian position.'[24]

Added to this, we must say that much contemporary theology is too weighted on the side of God's immanence and this has unfortunate consequences. We need to recover a more transcendent view of God — the Creator God whose name alone is majestic in all the earth. The late Dr A.W. Tozer, a twentieth-century preacher whose ministry has been a blessing to many, was very troubled about the inadequate views of God held by many Christians today. In his book, *The Knowledge of the Holy*, Tozer expressed his deep concern in the following words: 'A right conception of God is basic not only to systematic theology but to practical Christian living as well. It is to worship what the foundation is to the temple; where it is inadequate or out of plumb the whole structure must sooner or later collapse. I believe there is scarcely an error in doctrine or a failure in applying Christian ethics that cannot be traced finally to imperfect and ignoble thoughts about God.

'It is my opinion that the Christian conception of God current in these middle years of the twentieth century is so decadent as to be utterly beneath the dignity of the Most High God and actually to constitute for professed believers something amounting to a moral calamity.'[25]

In a day of growing spiritual darkness, evangelistic sermons which say a lot about Jesus Christ and not enough about God may lead to the kind of response about which we warned in the previous chapter on the matter of 'instruction and persuasion'.

If a sinner responds to the gospel and believes in Jesus Christ because the Saviour does seem to have the answer to his problems as he, the sinner, sees them, then his response may be suspect. When a sinner believes in Jesus Christ then he needs to do it for the right reasons. It is all too possible for people to follow Jesus Christ for entirely selfish reasons. We should remember what happened after Jesus had performed the miracle of feeding over five thousand people. Later He had to say to them, 'I tell you the truth, you are looking for me, not because you saw the miraculous signs but because you ate the loaves and had your fill' (John 6:26). It is not surprising that within a short time most of the crowd had deserted Him. He had exposed the selfishness of their motives.

When a sinner turns to Jesus Christ because God is the kind of God that He is, then that sinner will not fall away. Because our nation does have a Christian heritage we tend to assume far too much. Sermons with inadequate content concerning the being of God are more likely to lead to a suspect response to the person of Christ. Paul's 'God-centred' sermons at Lystra and Athens are a healthy corrective to lopsided preaching in a pagan society.

Signs of the times

In his missionary travels Paul's alertness in detecting just how widely situations differed from one another, and his ability to suit his message accordingly reveal a depth of spiritual insight and a display of spiritual skill which are all too rare today. So often churches appear very stereotyped and mechanical in their approach to spreading the gospel. Changes are taking place in our society more rapidly than we realize. More often than not the churches are slow to discern this and even more lethargic to produce an appropriate response. Our Lord's rebuke to the religious leaders of His day is warranted equally by many Christian leaders today. Jesus said, 'When evening comes, you say, "It will be fair weather, for the sky is red," and in the morning, "Today it will be stormy, for the sky is red and overcast." You know how to interpret the appearance of the sky, but you cannot interpret the signs of the times' (Matt. 16:2,3).

'Lessons from Lystra' is the title of the chapter we are now concluding. But how like or unlike Lystra are our British urban and pagan communities today?

The primitive and poorly educated farming community of a relatively unimportant New Testament city is a far cry from our modern highly complex urban communities of an advanced industrial society. Can there be a meaningful comparison? The difference between first-century communities and twentieth-century society, in terms of knowledge and material comfort, presents a gulf that is ever widening. But when we make the comparison in spiritual terms the gap is closing, and the rate at which this change is occurring is much faster than most people would imagine.

Dr Francis Schaeffer, in his book *Death in the City*, alerts our attention to the rapidity of our drift in Western civilization towards pagan darkness. He says, 'Having turned away from the knowledge given by God, man has now lost the whole Christian culture. In Europe, including Britain, it took many years; in the United States only a few decades. In the United States in the short span from the twenties to the sixties we have seen a complete shift. Of course not everyone in the United States in the twenties was a Christian, but in general there was a Christian consensus. Now that consensus is completely gone. Ours is a post-Christian world in which Christianity, not only in the number of Christians but in cultural emphasis and cultural result, is now in the absolute minority. To ask young people to maintain the *status quo* is folly. The *status quo* is no longer ours. In the last four decades the change has come in *every portion* and in *every part* of life. If in the twenties you had distributed a questionnaire in a place like Columbus Circle in New York, you would have found that most of the people may not personally have been Christians, but they at least would have an idea of what Christianity was. Trafalgar Square about 1890 would have been the same. But if today you distributed a questionnaire in these places, you would find that almost every man you asked would have little or no concept of true Christianity.'[26]

If Francis Schaeffer is correct in his assessment then we have some hard thinking to do. If I am asked the question: 'How would Whitefield and Wesley preach if they came back today?' I am forced to conclude that their messages would be much closer to Paul's sermons at Lystra and Athens than to his Pisidian

Antioch sermon. Part of me wants to think that provided the Holy Spirit anointed their ministry all they would need to do would be to 'preach Christ', just as they did two hundred years ago, and the rest would follow. But another part of me leads me to believe that Whitefield and Wesley, being the spiritual giants that they were, would understand the situation and, like Paul, would adapt the approach of their preaching accordingly. In the book by Francis Schaeffer to which we have just referred there is a chapter with the title, 'The Man without the Bible'. Some of the issues we have just been exploring are discussed in that chapter. In particular, Schaeffer refers to Paul's sermons at Lystra and Athens, and says, *'Here, I believe, is where God gives us the method of preaching to our generation, for our generation is largely made up of men without the Bible.'*[27]

7.
Growing together

What is the Christian church for? Why does it exist? One of the classic answers to these questions says that the church exists for 'the gathering and perfecting of the saints'. In the last three chapters we have been considering the 'gathering' of the saints through the work of evangelism. In the next three chapters we are to consider the 'perfecting' of the saints — how Christians grow up to spiritual maturity as individual believers and how their perfecting is advanced through their active participation in the life and witness of a local church. Our first concern will be to understand why a local assembly of believers ought to be an indigenous church.

What is an indigenous church?

The missionary principle of the indigenous church traces its origin back to the New Testament, and its definition and development back to a Dr John L. Nevius (1829-1893), an American Presbyterian missionary who worked in China in the latter part of the nineteenth century.[1] An elder statesman in missionary work, Dr Nevius received an invitation to instruct some new missionaries who were about to begin their service in Korea.

The 'Nevius' or 'indigenous' principle was developed along

four particular aspects of church life. The word 'indigenous' means 'native to', or 'belonging naturally'. Dr Nevius contended that when a church has been planted and established according to the New Testament pattern, then it will, in God's time, face up to the full responsibilities of a mature church and aim to become self-supporting, self-governing, self-educating and self-propagating. As these spiritual goals are pursued the church will become progressively less dependent on outside church bodies. The aim is not so much to bring the church to 'legal' independence, but rather to a position of voluntary interdependence with other groups of believers. The Korea Mission, to whose missionaries Dr Nevius expounded these teachings, considered them so important that they adopted them as mission policy, and in the early days gave all new missionaries a copy of his booklet and required them to pass an examination on it.

Does the indigenous principle apply to the work of churches in the urban working-class areas of our country today? It is not difficult to demonstrate that these areas are just as much pagan mission-fields as those places overseas where we have been sending missionaries for nearly two hundred years. It is also possible to show that the application of this principle overseas has been hindered, or even avoided, for the same reasons which we shall discover here in the 'home mission-field'. We must now develop this further. From missionary experience it is known that biblical principles can become overlaid with cultural accretions.

'The history of missions shows a great diversity in motivation. Some missionaries were motivated by an ascetic view of life, and chose missions as a form of self-denial; others were stimulated by a desire to hasten the return of Christ; and frequently missionary work has been connected with a tendency to spread Western culture, regarded as far superior to all other forms of life. At times missionary activity became a part of colonialism, a task of the government more than of the church.'[2]

In order to see what the application of the indigenous principle really involves in a working-class church and community, we need to distinguish carefully between biblical requirement and cultural accretion.

Self-support

By this we mean that the local church must eventually reach a stage in its development when it is able to assume full responsibility for all its financial commitments. This is New Testament practice. It is true that Paul often chose to work at his tentmaking rather than place any undue financial burden on the people among whom he was working, and also to avoid having his motives impugned. But it is the same apostle who defended very clearly the responsibility of a local church to meet its own financial obligations (1 Cor. 9:7-14; Gal. 6:6; 1 Tim. 5:17,18). Obviously, the stage at which groups of believers will become self-supporting will vary from church to church. But the ideal of self-support must be a definite goal towards which the growing church moves with determination. Where this responsibility is not faced with realism, there can be at least two detrimental effects upon the groups of Christians concerned.

Firstly, if the local Christians find it convenient to have their work subsidized indefinitely, this will retard their spiritual growth. If the obligation to face up to the realities of church life is postponed and the demands of responsibility are gently cushioned, this will produce nothing but a flabby faith. It must be avoided.

Secondly, the 'parent church' or denominational body will continue to retain a measure of control over that group of believers for an indefinite period. This is not good. A parent church may be well equipped to provide money for a developing cause and at the same time it may be ill equipped to influence or advise on certain aspects of church policy in a community which, socially, may be in marked contrast to the area in which it is located. A strong parent church which draws its main support from an 'owner-occupied' housing professional community may have its 'mission' in a local council estate or on a modern 'high-rise' estate. The readiness to encourage and allow that 'mission' to become self-supporting will reflect on the spiritual wisdom and mature faith of the senior church.

Self-government

One verse in the book of Acts gives us a definite statement about the nature of the government among the churches in the apostolic age. Paul and Barnabas, on their return to Antioch from their first missionary journey, visited the places where the seed sown by them had borne fruit. On these visits they made provision *from within* these local fellowships for their future leadership. 'Paul and Barnabas appointed elders for them in each church' (Acts 14:23). Paul's letters to Timothy and Titus deal with the appointment of elders and indicate that such men are to come from within the local churches they serve. Only within the life of a local church can the prospective elders reveal their character and develop their spiritual gifts in such a way that the church members will be able to observe and assess their ministry and, in due time, ratify their appointment to the eldership.

Here again we can suggest reasons why a local company of believers may choose to avoid full responsibility in this respect. The members of the 'infant' church may find it more to their liking if difficult issues, controversial matters and hard decisions are the ultimate responsibility of the parent church. Added to this, we may find that the parent church is not anxious to offer autonomy to its growing infant. A parent church in a middle-class area will probably have a pastor and a number of church officers who are professionally qualified. From their experience as church leaders they may find it difficult to see a number of men in the growing working-class church who show sufficient spiritual maturity and a degree of practical competence to warrant the offer of autonomy. Unfortunately, their assessment of a potential eldership for the young church, though governed by the highest motives, may, in fact, have more to do with the traditionally accepted standards of the 'professional' ministry than it has to do with biblical standards of eldership within a local church.

How young 'in years' and 'in the faith' were some of the first elders in the New Testament churches? This would be an interesting investigation to pursue. The time which elapsed between the gathering of the first converts and the appointment of the first elders, under the direction of the apostles, seems to have been comparatively brief. The paradox of 'young elders' may have been more common than we would expect. 'Recent converts' were not eligible for appointment to the eldership. Timothy, though not a local church elder, was called to an important teaching and pastoral ministry while still a young man. Paul urged the somewhat timid Timothy not to lack confidence in the tasks to which he was called: 'Don't let anyone look down on you because you are young, but set an example for the believers in speech, in life, in love, in faith and in purity' (1 Tim. 4:12). Obviously, the first elders in a new church were at some disadvantage. They had no previous example to follow: there were no precedents by which they could be guided. Some of the New Testament letters and subsequent apostolic visits to the churches already established helped to compensate for any comparative inexperience among any 'younger' elders who may have been among the first leaders of the new churches. It ought also to be said that new churches without leadership precedents are not always at a disadvantage. They can be gloriously free from the tyranny of traditions which have no biblical base. At times, the religious customs of our forefathers in the faith restrict and retard. Ideally, the past should galvanize the present; sometimes it paralyses it!

Self-education

The New Testament provision for the instruction of believers in 'the whole counsel of God' is quite plain. Timothy is directed by Paul to ensure that he trains other men who can continue this teaching ministry. He says, 'The things you have heard me say in the presence of many witnesses entrust to reliable men who will also be qualified to teach others' (2 Tim. 2:2). In the first letter to Timothy and in the letter to Titus the character and abilities of elders are defined. Apart from a godly life, such men must also have an aptitude to teach. 'He must hold firmly to the trustworthy message as it has been taught, so that he can encourage others by sound doctrine and refute those who oppose it' (Titus 1:9).

The provision for the instruction of believers in the local churches today is very different from that which we find in the New Testament. As soon as New Testament churches became established, their continuing instruction in the faith came from a wholly indigenous ministry — a local eldership. By contrast, it is still the practice for many evangelical churches today to have one man almost exclusively responsible for the instruction of a local company of believers. Usually this one man, a full-time pastor, does not come from within the church and community in which he now serves. There is, however, a growing realization that the 'one-man ministry' cannot be defended from Scripture.

The practice of appointing elders within local churches is increasing. Good as this is, it is most important that today's elders should not be that in name only. They must fulfil New Testament qualifications; they must perform New Testament functions. A vital supplementary teaching role, rather than a subordinate teaching role, is the ideal in eldership towards which churches should be working.

It would be foolish to deny that some major problems have to be faced realistically if we are to move towards the biblical ideal. The principal role of those who tend God's flock is the teaching of the believers. To do this effectively would seem to require some measure of academic competence. But churches situated in wholly working-class communities tend to produce men whose gifts are other than academic. Can we expect God to raise up working-class men who will be adequately competent to instruct their fellow believers in the whole counsel of God? I believe God can and will do that in those churches which see such a policy for the teaching ministry as a biblical necessity, and not just desirable but optional. This claim leaves a number of questions unanswered. We shall look further into this in our consideration of 'home-grown leaders'.

Self-propagation

Need more be said on this? A recurring note throughout our study so far has been the contention that the 'ordinary church members' are to be the principal ambassadors of the gospel, and not the pastor-preacher. His task is to preach the gospel and to equip the church members to witness and to be able to give a reason for the hope that is within them. The best people to reach working-class folk with the gospel are working-class folk. They have proved that it is possible to lead a normal and consistent Christian life in a working-class community. It really works! A pastor who has come into this situation 'from outside' will, at first, be at some disadvantage here. The church and community he serves may treat him with a measure of reserve until his 'outsideness' has worn off and he is really accepted as 'one of us'.

The indigenous church principle is particularly important in working-class communities. Parent churches or denominational bodies who neglect or choose to ignore this principle are likely to produce immature and over-dependent companies of working-class believers. They also perpetuate the long-held grievance that churches usually fail to give working men positions of status and responsibility. 'Church', like so many other things in working-class life, is run by 'them' for 'us'. The over-protection of the young church may stem from the best of motives, but it may prove to be a recipe for weakness rather than strength. It is no use a mother bird (or church) saying to its offspring, 'You are not leaving this nest until you have proved to me that you can fly.' God does not make parachutes for birds or churches! As soon as it is right, the mother should gently but firmly ease the young life out of the security of the nest. The wings of faith will do the rest!

A lesson from John Wesley: the importance of the 'group'

How can working-class converts be nurtured in the Christian faith? What forms or methods are best suited to produce a growing spiritual maturity for those who are as yet 'babes in Christ'?

A man of God well qualified to answer these questions was John Wesley. While his phenomenal endeavours in the field of gospel preaching are perhaps his best-remembered contributions to the cause of Christ, surely his most distinctive contribution was his genius for organization in the way he promoted the spiritual growth of the Christian believers who became known as 'Methodists'. I am sure that we can gain much help from an understanding of the pattern and purpose of the Wesleyan 'class meetings' for our pastoral responsibilities among working-class converts today. If we think that a 'class meeting' was nothing more than an informal discussion group where everyone could have his say and the spiritual nourishment was minimal, then we are far from the truth. We need to do our homework. Nothing Wesley did was casual or haphazard. He was at his methodical best in directing and supervising the spiritual objectives of the class meetings.

'Wesley had manifestly inherited many of the qualities of his parents — his mother's vigour of mind and talent for discipline, and his father's aptitude for learning and intensity of purpose —

and these faculties, granted him in birth, had been brought to a state of fine concentration during his years at Oxford and in the strict regimen to which he had long accustomed himself. He was a man of wide reading, native poetic abilities, rare force of intellect, unusual powers as a preacher and a rich emotional nature. But superior, perhaps, to all these was a further faculty: a natural talent for administration and government. He seemed born to take the oversight of his fellow men, to bend them to his will and to lead them with a benign but also an inflexible authority.'[3]

In a letter to the vicar of Shoreham in Kent in 1748, John Wesley explained in great detail the origin and development of the class meeting, as well as other aspects of Methodist life and witness. In his letter he also answered a number of objections levelled against the pattern of pastoral care he employed. The contents of this letter have now been reproduced in booklet form with the title *A Plain account of the people called Methodists*.[4] It is a small document with a value far beyond its size: it contains much pastoral and practical wisdom.

It appears that the seed thoughts for the class meeting were sown in Wesley's mind when he was approached by those who were newly born again, and were being harassed and hindered by their worldly friends and colleagues. 'One, and another, and another came to us, asking what they should do, being distressed on every side; as every one strove to weaken, and none to strengthen, their hands in God. We advised them, "Strengthen you one another. Talk together as often as you can. And pray earnestly with and for one another, that you may 'endure to the end, and be saved'." '[5]

At first Wesley began to meet with a group on Thursday evenings in order to guide the spiritual exercises he had encouraged. As numbers grew, so did the number of class meetings. Wesley appointed men to lead these groups and they were accountable to him.

What was the aim of a class meeting? 'They united themselves in order to pray together, to receive the word of exhortation, and to watch over one another in love, that they might help each other to work out their salvation'.[6] Who could attend and belong to a class meeting? There was only one condition for membership: 'a desire to flee from the wrath to come, to be saved from their sins'.

What was the role of the leader? Here, as usual, Wesley is most definite in his instructions. The 'job-description' for the class leader could hardly be more explicit: 'It is the business of a Leader, (1) To see each person in his class, once a week at least, in order to enquire how their souls prosper; to advise, reprove, comfort, or exhort, as occasion may require; (2) To meet the Minister and the Stewards of the society, in order to inform the Minister of any that are sick, or of any that are disorderly and will not be reproved; to pay to the Stewards what they have received of their several classes in the week preceding.'[7]

Did the class meeting achieve the ends for which it was designed? No system in itself, however biblically accurate in its design, can guarantee spiritual results automatically. All systems are fallible and no less are the men who design and use them. Yet, within a comparatively short while after the inauguration of the class meetings Wesley could say, 'It quickly appeared that their thus uniting together answered the end proposed therein. In a few months, the far greater part of those who had begun to "fear God, and work righteousness", but were not united together, grew faint in their minds, and fell back into what they were before. Meanwhile the far greater part of those who were thus united together continued "striving to enter in at the strait gate", and "to lay hold on eternal life".'[8]

One writer who has made a special study of the class meeting describes a typical spiritual benefit these meetings were intended to secure: 'Many a raw, uncultivated lad has been led into the class meeting under strong religious feeling. There, at first, he would scarcely have sufficient command of his native tongue intelligibly to express the feelings of his soul, and perhaps under ordinary circumstances, would never issue a pure or correct sentence; but, unaccountably to all but those who acknowledge the work of a Divine Teacher, that same lad in his weekly intercourse with his Leader and Classmates begins to talk with propriety about spiritual things, and at length by dint of exercise in sincere prayer, he learns to "pray with the Spirit and with understanding" and might gracefully and with holy effect lead the devotions of an intelligent and even educated congregation. The praying ranks of Methodism derive their most useful power from such trained recruits, and must always depend upon such strength for the fulfilment of the work which is dearest to its heart, and most necessary to the completion of its first and only purpose. When its class meetings are dissolved its real praying power will be lost.'[9]

What of the doubts and objections concerning the class meeting? Some objected that this form of meeting was not commanded or sanctioned within Scripture. But it is more than probable that the class meeting as a form of Christian gathering was much nearer to a New Testament pattern than the critics realized. The earliest Gentile Christians had to meet together in the homes of the Christians. There were no church buildings. Very few Christians actually possessed copies of the Scriptures, and for those who did few would have possessed copies of the entire Old Testament. If we think of the 'average' New Testament believer reading the Scriptures and praying in the quiet of his own bedroom, then we are mistaken. Reference to the *written* Word of Scripture could only take place when Christians met together in groups in their homes and had access to the written Scriptures owned by a senior or rich Christian. This would have been the norm as a pattern of gathering for regular instruction from the Scriptures.

Some critics pointed to Wesley's authoritarian supervision of the network of class meetings. They charged John Wesley with 'papal' tendencies. Other critics showed a rather condescending attitude towards those of the labouring class who shared in these meetings. During our Lord's ministry there were those opponents who were envious and irritated by the content and impact of His teaching. There is good evidence to show that Wesley encountered a similar type of hostility and criticism.

How did Calvinists view the pastoral policy of the 'Arminian' John Wesley? There is much to indicate that those of Reformed persuasion were impressed by Wesley's example and his influence had a significant impact on their own pattern of pastoral care. In fact, John Wesley himself acknowledged his own debt to the Puritans and in particular their teaching on the progressive Christian life. He said, 'It is the "peculiar excellency" of the Puritan divines that they instruct us how to use the faith which God has given, and to go from strength to strength. They lead us by the hand in the paths of righteousness, and show us how, in the various circumstances of life, we may most surely and swiftly grow in grace, and in the knowledge of our Lord Jesus Christ.'[10]

John Wesley's friend and colleague, William Grimshaw

(1708-1763) minister of the Anglican church in Haworth, Yorkshire, was clearly persuaded of the great benefits of the class meeting. Speaking of the pastoral guidance he gave to those who responded to his gospel preaching, he says, 'After a season I joined people, such as were truly seeking, or had found the Lord, in society, for meetings and exercises. These meetings are held once a week, about two hours, and are called classes, consisting of about ten or twelve members each. We have much of the Lord's presence among them, and greatly in consequence must such meetings conduce to Christian edification.'[11]

Henry Venn, vicar of Huddersfield from 1759 to 1771 was similarly influenced. 'He preached on Sundays; he preached on Thursdays in Church. During the week he held class meetings throughout his wide parish. For these he appointed class leaders, who led in prayer when he was not present. A text was discussed at each meeting which began and ended with prayer.'[12]

Further commendation of Wesley's pastoral method was the birth and growth of 'the experience meeting' among the Welsh Calvinistic Methodists. The class meeting and the experience meeting had much in common in both form and purpose. Both were products of the Evangelical Awakening in the eighteenth century. A most useful insight into the spiritual value of the meetings in Wales can be gained from the small book *The Experience Meeting* by William Williams,[13] — author of the hymn 'Guide me, O Thou great Jehovah.' His book has been translated from Welsh into English by Mrs D.M. Lloyd-Jones. Her husband explains why he urged his wife to undertake the task of translation. He observes that the 'experimental' or 'experiential' aspect of the Christian life has been seriously neglected during the present century. After identifying the causes which have given rise to this neglect he goes on to say, 'All this has greatly impoverished the spiritual life of both the individual Christian and the churches, and led to coldness, barrenness, and loss of power. The great need of the hour is a return to the emphases of the Evangelical Awakening.'[14]

Of the book he says, 'I would particularly urge ministers and pastors to read it, not only because it will prove to be an invaluable help in what is now called counselling of individuals, but also because I would press upon them the importance of introducing such meetings into the life of their churches. Much untold blessing would follow.'[15]

We cannot conclude our remarks about the pastoral aspect of John Wesley's ministry without saying something about the life and ministry of George Whitefield who was mightily used of God in the work of gospel preaching in the United Kingdom and the United States. The second volume of Arnold Dallimore's two-part work on the life and times of George Whitefield has recently been published. This major work fully documents the Herculean labours of this evangelist aflame for God. We are also given a detailed insight into the relationship between John Wesley and George Whitefield. Certainly, Dallimore has not hesitated to paint in the 'warts' of John Wesley's character. To say that, at times, the relationship between the two men became strained would be something of an understatement. Whitefield held with increasing firmness to the Calvinist position, whereas John Wesley was firmly committed to the Arminian viewpoint. It would have been surprising if there had been no friction between these two brethren because of their differing, but sincerely held doctrinal views. Better that these two men of God did not seek a truce of silence on their doctrinal distinctives, than paper over these issues with a cosmetic unity concealing their differences. When two men of God hold their doctrinal convictions with firmness, and even tenacity, this does not necessarily involve a diminishing of the Christian love between them. The apostle Paul tells us, 'When Peter came to Antioch, I opposed him to his face, because he was in the wrong' (Gal. 2:11). This action did not produce a rift between them. Indeed, when Peter wrote the last chapter of his second letter he spoke of 'our beloved brother Paul' (2 Peter 3:15).

It remains to be seen whether there will be any come-back on what Dallimore has written. No doubt many will feel that justice has been done to Whitefield by the publication of this book. Probably others will spring to the defence of Wesley. Perhaps some will plead for a more even distribution of the 'warts' between these two mighty, but fallible, men of God. It is of the utmost importance that we keep in true perspective the matters over which Whitefield and Wesley differed. Newspapers often try to boost sales by exposing some scandal of 'the famous' that has been previously hushed up. Christian believers need to be very careful about their response to an exposure of the 'sins of the saints'.

While we have no right to disguise or diminish blemishes of

Growing together

character and differences of doctrine, we ought to counterbalance this with some most heartening facts. Subsequent to their differences over the Calvinist-Arminian issue, God continued to use both men mightily. There was a measure of continued co-operation between the two men in the work of the gospel. Letters which passed between them show their concern for each other and their concern that their sincerely held differences should not jeapordize their 'love in the Lord' for each other. Before Whitefield's death in 1770 he asked that, should he die overseas, then he wished to have John Wesley preach the funeral sermon. Whitefield died at Newburyport, Massachusetts, U.S.A. on 30 September 1770. This news reached Wesley by 10 November. As requested, he preached the funeral sermon on Sunday, 18 November. In Whitefield's will the following bequest was included: 'I leave a mourning ring to my honoured and dear friends and disinterested fellow labourers, the Rev. Messrs John and Charles Wesley, in token of my indissoluble union with them, in heart and Christian affection, notwithstanding our difference in judgement about some particular points of doctrine. Grace be with all them, of whatever denomination, that love our Lord Jesus, our common Lord, in sincerity.'[16]

Our discussion of the relationship between Whitefield and Wesley may appear to be a digression from our subject, and to have no direct bearing upon it. Our digresion, if it is that, has been more necessary than we realize. A commonly held impression is that in the nurture of young believers where Wesley had demonstrated his great pastoral and administrative gifts, Whitefield had been spiritually careless and unwise. Whitefield is purported to have said about Wesley's work: 'My brother Wesley acted wisely. The souls that were awakened under his ministry he joined in class, and thus preserved the fruit of his labour. This I neglected, and my people are as a rope of sand.'[17]

The authenticity of this confession of neglect is open to doubt. There is a good reason for challenging it. It does not fit the facts as we now know them. It is all too easy to assume that because these men had their doctrinal differences their practices would diverge also. That assumption need not necessarily follow. In fact, the truth is that, both in open-air preaching and in the forming of a number of societies for the pastoral care of new converts, it was Whitefield who pioneered the way.

In the second volume of Dallimore's biography of Whitefield he devotes an entire chapter to the matter of 'Organizing the Work'. In that chapter we discover that, far from being neglectful, Whitefield is most positive and practical in his policy for the operation of these societies: 'The public were invited to the services of the Tabernacle, but Society members were received only after strict examination as to their spiritual state and were given tickets of admission which required renewal every three months — this also on the basis of satisfactory manner of life. The Society was divided into bands and classes, each under the direction of a leader who was known also as a Visitor.

'The *Minute Book* of the Tabernacle reveals that the Society conducted two schools — one for boys and one for girls — maintained a Book Room and operated an organization for the relief of the poor. It also had a workshop — apparently a small manufactory that provided employment for some of the needy and earned a revenue that assisted these other endeavours. There was a kind of small employment exchange — a means of contact between prospective employers and persons seeking employment.'[18]

How many evangelical urban churches today would show such an active concern for spiritual growth *and* for the secular employment of people who are young Christian converts? Certainly, the 'rope of sand' confession of pastoral neglect is wholly contradictory to the evidence we have examined.

As we conclude our look at the 'class meeting' we need to identify the particular benefits of such a meeting for the spiritual nurture of working-class people who are just beginning the Christian life.

1. It can give to the working man a sense of belonging. Here again we can see the solidarity factor appearing. If in his daily work he seems to be nothing more than a cog in an impersonal industrial machine, then his membership of the class meeting places him among people who know his name, people to whom he belongs, people who will miss him if he is away, people to whom he matters.

2. It aims to provide a strong focus on the experiential aspect of our faith. A working man often finds it hard to absorb a great deal of the content of a solid expository sermon. He is not at his

best when seeking to grapple with the intellectual aspects of Christian truth. But he is far more at home when he is dealing with the concrete issues of daily life. It is then that he really 'opens up' and 'comes into his own'.
3. It provides a 'family' in which all its members can show unjudging acceptance towards one another. All the members of this group will accept one another 'just as they are'. Where this kind of 'acceptance' is given and received, any member of the group need feel no embarrassment at opening his mouth. Nobody will 'look down' on him either for what he says or the way he says it.
4. It can provide a very necessary and regular source of spiritual encouragement. The lone Christian at the factory bench may feel very exposed and vulnerable. He may find it really tough going trying to maintain a consistent witness before his workmates. At times he will feel it is easier to quit than fight on. The regular class meeting should provide an opportunity to share news of the battle, to get spiritual wounds tended and healed, to get spiritual morale lifted up, to check and repair 'the weapons of our warfare'. Hearing of one another's victories and defeats should provide inspiration for the continuing battle.
5. It gives working people an opportunity to develop their spiritual potential, to become articulate in their faith, to accept responsibility and generally to improve their usefulness for God.
6. It is able to provide a very efficient system of pastoral care.

An all-round teaching ministry

What is an all-round teaching ministry? What distinguishes it from any other kind of teaching ministry? The term all-round has been coined in order to draw attention to the need for wholeness and balance of methods in a thoroughly biblical teaching ministry. It is possible to have a ministry which is a biblical teaching ministry only up to a point. Our views on the way in which believers should be taught may be too narrowly defined. If the beginning, middle and ending of a pastor's teaching ministry is expository sermons, then he is deficient in his understanding of biblical methods of teaching. Full marks for the preaching to which he is committed; no marks at all for other aspects of a teaching ministry which he has omitted. Where a teaching ministry lacks balance and completeness, the method he does use is likely to benefit certain groups or categories of people more than others. Where this happens certain believers may acquire a taste for one method of teaching and at the same time a distaste for other methods of teaching. That problem is not hypothetical but real. I would contend that only an all-round teaching ministry will enable all believers in a local church — working-class, middle-class, or of whatever social mix — to grow towards full spiritual maturity in Jesus Christ. In considering what we judge to be essential aspects of an all-round teaching ministry, we will look first at the teaching ministry of the apostle Paul.

Paul's example: Acts 20:17-35

At the beginning of chapter 6, we made a comparison between various audiences to which Paul spoke and saw how this affected the approach and content of his addresses. The speech recorded in Acts 20:17-35 is addressed to yet another kind of audience. Here he is speaking solely to Christians and, more particularly, to those who were mature Christian leaders charged with the pastoral care of God's flock at Ephesus. We will now identify those features of Paul's ministry at Ephesus which indicate that it was an all-round teaching ministry.

1. *All aspects of truth were expounded.*   Paul claimed, 'You know that I have not hesitated to preach anything that would be helpful to you ...' (v.20); 'I have not hesitated to proclaim the whole will of God' (v.27). The word 'hesitated', which appears in both of the verses we have mentioned, comes from the Greek verb which means 'to suppress' or 'conceal'. There is a suggestion in the way Paul has expressed his claim that there can be pressures to hold back or suppress certain aspects of Christian truth. Believers are not guaranteed by their regeneration an automatic submission to all of God's truth. It is James who tells his readers that they should 'humbly accept the word planted in you' (James 1:21). Resistance to truth can come from people we would least expect. Jonathan Edwards (1703-1758), an American contemporary of Whitefield and Wesley, tells us that in his early childhood his mind was full of objections to divine sovereignty. A.M. Toplady (1740-1778) says that after his conversion 'there was not a more haughty and violent free-willer

within the compass of the four seas'. Truth has the habit of taking us down a peg or two ... or more! Paul was not a man to be swayed by opposition. Regardless of the consequences, he taught the truth, the whole truth and nothing but the truth.

2. *All sources of opposition were identified.* One of the requirements for appointment to the office of elder which Paul indicates in his letter to Titus is an ability to 'hold firmly to the trustworthy message as it has been taught, so that he can encourage others by sound doctrine and refute those who oppose it' (Titus 1:9). Elders must expound truth *and* refute error. Teaching which seeks to instruct and to warn is not always popular. The church leader who regularly sounds strong notes of warning may be regarded as a pessimist, a doctrinal hypochondriac or just narrow and uncharitable in his views about those who do not share his convictions. Was the apostle a pessimist rather than a realist? Was he unnecessarily fearful for the future of the Ephesian believers? He tells the elders at the church: 'I know that after I leave, savage wolves will come in among you and will not spare the flock. Even from your own number men will arise and distort the truth in order to draw away disciples after them. So be on your guard. Remember that for three years I never stopped warning each of you night and day with tears' (Acts 20:29-31). Did the warnings prove necessary? Did the threats materialize? Read Revelation 2:1-7. Attacks upon the church came from *outside* and from inside as well. At some points the adversary was resisted, but at other points he had infiltrated. The Ephesian church was urged to repent.

3. *All kinds of people were instructed.* 'I have declared to both Jews and Greeks that they must turn to God in repentance and have faith in our Lord Jesus (v.21). Paul did not have his 'favourites'. There is no suggestion that he tried to cultivate an 'inner spiritual elite'. He did not give preference to his fellow-countrymen the Jews. Nor did he neglect them in spite of their repeated opposition (v.19). The apostle's conscience was clear. He declared to the elders that he had completed the task the Lord had assigned to him: 'I declare to you today that I am innocent of the blood of *all* men' (v.26).

4. *All places of opportunity were employed.* Where did Paul do his teaching? He says that he 'taught ... publicly and from house to house' (v.20). Paul preached in the synagogue for the first three months of his stay in Ephesus. When opposition forced him to

leave the synagogue he then moved elsewhere. 'He took the disciples with him and had discussions daily in the lecture hall of Tyrannus' (Acts 19:9). The expression 'from house to house' suggests more than the use of a few Christian homes in a locality, but rather a systematic approach to evangelistic preaching and pastoral instruction. When Paul says, 'For three years I never stopped warning each of you night and day with tears', the depth of his pastoral concern and the intensity of his spiritual zeal are nothing less than astonishing.

5. *All modes of speaking were used.* Paul's ministry to the Ephesian church would well qualify for the description 'all-round'. We have already seen that the *content* of his teaching was 'all-round': he spoke 'the whole will of God' (v.27). The *manner* of his teaching at Ephesus also exhibits the same characteristics. If we look through the whole of Acts 19 together with the first verse of chapter 20 and then verses 13 to 35, we find that no fewer than *nine different 'speaking' verbs* are used to describe Paul's evangelistic and pastoral ministry. A list of these verbs as they are translated in the Amplified Bible will help us to appreciate another aspect of the 'all-roundness' of Paul's Ephesian ministry.

Table II
Verbs used to describe Paul's ministry

A. *Acts 19:8:* Paul ... *spoke boldly* there for three months.
B. *Acts 19:8: persuading and arguing and pleading* about the kingdom of God.
C. *Acts 19:9: holding discussions* in the lecture room of Tyrannus. (This is the same verb as in B. above.)
D. *Acts 20:1:* Paul sent for the disciples and *warned and consoled and urged and encouraged* them.
E. *Acts 20:20:* I ... *taught* you ... publicly and from house to house.
F. *Acts 20:21: constantly and earnestly I bore testimony* to both Jews and Greeks.
G. *Acts 20:25: proclaiming* the kingdom.
H. *Acts 20:26: I testify and protest* to you.
I. *Acts 20:27:* I never shrank or kept back or fell short from *declaring* to you the whole purpose and plan and counsel of God. (The same verb is used in verse 20 where it is translated *telling.*)
J. *Acts 20:31: to admonish and advise and exhort* you.

Growing together

The five features of Paul's ministry at Ephesus explain why we have used the term 'all-round' to describe its wholeness and balance. A more narrow approach to his ministry would have resulted in more limited benefits to the believers at Ephesus. We shall now indicate aspects of an all-round teaching ministry today which we believe are in line with the biblical example set by Paul.

Expository preaching

What is expository preaching? Put simply, it means 'explaining preaching'. Expository preaching has as its chief concern the 'setting forth in detail', 'explaining and interpreting' God's Word.

In an earlier chapter we made reference to the ministry of Ezra who returned to Jerusalem with Nehemiah. It was Ezra's task to read and teach from the Book of the Law. His helpers in this task were the Levites. Theirs was an expository preaching ministry. What did it involve? 'They read from the Book of the Law of God, making it clear and giving the meaning so that the people could understand what was being read' (Neh. 8:8).

In the New Testament we read of Paul's reminder to Timothy concerning the nature of the biblical and expository preaching ministry to which he was called: 'Study to be eager and do your utmost to present yourself to God approved (tested by trial), a workman who has no cause to be ashamed, correctly analysing and accurately dividing — rightly handling and skilfully teaching — the Word of Truth.' (2 Tim. 2:15, Amplified Bible).

What is it that makes expository preaching so important? It is because a preacher's first and foremost duty is to tell people what 'God has spoken'. It is that above all else which the preacher must make as clear as possible. Expository preaching is the only preaching which will direct us back to God's authoritative and infallible disclosure of Himself which is given through the Holy Scriptures in their entirety. The words of the Westminster Shorter Catechism, Question 3 are appropriate at this point. 'What do the Scriptures principally teach? The Scriptures principally teach what man is to believe concerning God, and what duty God requires of man.' It is the preacher's task to make plain what God requires and to instruct how this can be achieved.

In an earlier chapter we drew attention to the fact that

throughout the years of this century so far there has been a progressive decline in the general level of Bible knowledge in society. We made reference to R.B. Kuiper's estimate that, 'The general populace is well-nigh abysmally ignorant of Bible history and Bible doctrine, as well as Bible ethics.' Some indication of this disturbing decline in Bible knowledge can be measured when we compare the view of expository preaching held by Dr W.G.T. Shedd (1820-1894) with that of Dr D. Martyn Lloyd-Jones (1899-1981), probably the foremost Bible expositor of this century.

Dr Shedd was Professor of Biblical Literature and then Professor of Systematic Theology at Union Theological Seminary, New York. In his book *Homiletics and Pastoral Theology* (published in 1867), he says, 'The expository sermon should be *occasionally* employed. There is somewhat less call for this variety than there was before the establishment of Sabbath Schools and Bible classes. Were it not that these have taken the exposition of Scripture into their own charge, one very considerable part of the modern preacher's duty, as it was of the Christian Fathers and the Reformers, would be to expound the Bible. Under the present arrangements of the Christian Church, however, the ministry is relieved from this duty as to considerable extent. But it is not wholly relieved from it. It is the duty of the preacher *occasionally* to lay out his best strength in the production of an elaborate expository sermon, which shall not only do the work of a sermon but which shall also serve as a sort of guide and model for the teacher of the Sabbath school and the Bible class.'[19]

Move the clock forward approximately one hundred years, and we find that in his book *Preaching and Preachers* (1971) Dr Lloyd-Jones says, 'As you start preparing your sermon you must begin with the exposition of your passage or single verse. This is essential, that is vital; as I have said, *all preaching must be expository.* ... We are always to give the impression, and it may be more important than anything we say, that what we are saying comes out of the Bible, and always comes out of it. That is the origin of our message, this is where we have received it.'[20]

The obvious lesson we are to learn from these two contrasting views on expository preaching is not difficult to define. As our 'post-Christian' society becomes progressively more ignorant of the content of the Word of God, so the need for expository preaching becomes progressively more important. There can be no substitute for it.

There is so much more that could be said on the topic of expository preaching and particularly as it is directed to deal with the spiritual needs of the working man. Our earlier consideration of 'Plain Speaking' is clearly relevant at this point. This is not really the place to develop a more detailed discussion on this vital subject. But there is one further thing that must be said.

The term 'expository preaching' places proper emphasis on the way the Scriptures are to be handled in order to discover *what* they are teaching. This kind of preaching always begins by answering the question: 'What exactly does the Scripture mean in the portion being studied?' However, if the preacher stops at that point then he has not preached in a biblical and truly expository way. Biblical expository preaching comprises *explanation* and *application*. Those who come to hear expository preaching want to know *what* Scripture means and *how* this is to affect the way they live.

Dr Lloyd-Jones comments on a common misunderstanding: 'A sermon is not a running commentary on, or a mere exposition of, the meaning of a verse or a passage or a paragraph. I emphasize this because there are many today who have become interested in what they regard as expository preaching but who show very clearly that they do not know what is meant by expository preaching. They think that it just means making a series of comments, or a running commentary, on a paragraph or a passage or a statement. They take a passage verse by verse; and they make their comments on the first, they go on to the next verse, and do the same with that, then the next verse, and do the same with that, then the next, and so on. When they have gone through the passage in this way they imagine they have preached a sermon. But they have not; all they have done is to make a series of comments on a passage. I would suggest that far from having preached a sermon such preachers have only preached the introduction to a sermon!

This, in other words, raises the whole question of the relationship of exposition to the sermon. My basic contention is that the essential characteristic of a sermon is that it has a definite form, and that it is this form that makes a sermon. It is based upon exposition, but it is this turned or moulded into a message which has this characteristic form.'[21]

Shared experience

What we have already considered earlier in this chapter, under the section 'A lesson from John Wesley: the importance of the group' is much the same material that should be examined in relation to the topic of 'shared experience'. A summary of those particular benefits to be gained through the 'Experience Meeting', as William Williams saw them, explains their potential for aiding spiritual growth. These meetings were profitable and edifying because

'1. First of all, ... they are a means of keeping up this same warmth and liveliness that was ours at the beginning: as iron sharpeneth iron, so a man sharpeneth the countenance of his friend.

'2. In the second place, this kind of fellowship is profitable to unravel the various nets and hidden snares woven by Satan to catch the simple believer on his own ground.

'3. Thirdly, these special fellowship meetings are good at forestalling contentions, suspicions, prejudices, discords, jealousies and all uncharitableness.

'4. In the fourth place we may say that such a gathering together is profitable in order that we may look after and watch over each other's lives, lest any should fall into loose living and turn the grace of God into lasciviousness.

'5. In the fifth place, these fellowship meetings give us the opportunity of bearing one another's burdens.

'6. In the sixth place, this kind of meeting is profitable because it gives us the opportunity to declare the work of God on our souls, and to praise His name for it.

'7. But, lastly, these fellowship meetings are profitable for strengthening ourselves against all our spiritual enemies, and for praying together as one man against them all.'[22]

Catechetical teaching

Catechizing as a method of teaching scriptural truth seems to have fallen into a large measure of disuse. The word 'catechetical' derives from the Greek verb *katecheo* which means 'to instruct orally, to inform'. The term 'catechism' is normally used to describe a series of questions and answers comprising a systematic arrangement of Christian teaching. Throughout the history of the Christian church there appear to have been three purposes for which catechisms have been used: instruction, confession and preparation for confirmation.

A number of reasons may be suggested why catechetical teaching is not in vogue at the present time. Along with the decline of Bible knowledge in society generally, there is also a decline of interest in precise doctrinal formulations. In order to further the cause of unity among the churches and to maintain the spirit of co-operation, doctrinal collisions have studiously to be avoided. Added to this, the arrival of printing has in certain respects encouraged a mental laziness. For many churches doctrinal 'Statements of Faith' have been carefully formulated and then carelessly forgotten. They have been treated much like insurance policies — seldom thought about in day-to-day life, and only referred to in a time of crisis. Reference to what has been written has only been regarded as necessary where orthodoxy is threatened. But sound doctrine is better stored in the human mind and heart than merely recorded on paper. God intended that it should provide edification rather than be consulted in the occasional periods of doctrinal crisis. Learning by rote is not fashionable practice nowadays. Many find it difficult to grasp formulations of biblical truth in conceptual rather than concrete terms, and these would create certain problems of 'spiritual digestion' for young working-class Christians in particular.

How shall we assess the value and importance of catechetical teaching? In order to avoid being unduly influenced by the prevailing fashion in methods of biblical instruction, we shall make a brief and general survey of the influence and impact of catechetical teaching throughout the history of the church. Then we shall be in a better position to say whether this form of teaching can be regarded as optional or essential in the pursuit of an all-round teaching ministry.

The catechetical method of instruction was prominent in the Jewish educational system at the time of our Lord. We are told that from His earliest years Jesus 'grew in wisdom and stature, and in favour with God and men' (Luke 2:52). The instruction He received through the catechetical method will have contributed greatly to His advance towards spiritual manhood. It is clear that this style of teaching operated on the principle that the pupil does not possess what he has received until he is able to verbalize his knowledge in his own terms. There can be no accurate indication of satisfactory progress in the learning process until this response has been achieved.

By the end of the apostolic age the influence of catechizing continued to grow rapidly. In a paper on the *Spiritual Nurture of Children* Terence Aldridge says, 'The successful use of this approach of interlocutory teaching is the mainspring of the rapid extension of the church during the ante-Nicene age. Writes Schaff: "It is a remarkable fact, that after the days of the Apostles no names of great missionaries are mentioned till the opening of the Middle Ages ... There are no missionary institutions, no organized efforts in the ante-Nicene age; yet in less than three hundred years from the death of St John the whole of the population of the Roman Empire, which then represented the civilized world, was nominally Christianized." '[23]

By the time of the Reformation — a time for the recovery of sound doctrine — the importance and influence of catechetical teaching is again evident. 'The term "catechism" itself seems to be without primitive precedent, and evidently not until the Reformation was it used to mean specifically the documents setting out instruction by the responsive method — though it could and did mean simply any manual of instruction. These latter became particularly popular with the rise of printing in the latter half of the fifteenth century.

'At the Reformation the term was employed by Luther to describe his *Kleiner Katechismus* (1529) and this meaning attaches to virtually all Protestant and Reformed use of the word thereafter. Luther's Catechism was based upon the Ten Commandments, the Creed, the Lord's Prayer, and the sacraments and these became the staple components of Reformed instruction. *Catechizing in this responsive method was a great instrument of reformation of the common people throughout Europe.*'[24]

So far our survey of the influence of catechizing has been historical and universal. The name particularly linked with catechizing in a local situation is that of Richard Baxter (1615-1691). Baxter sought to pioneer a recovery of the catechetical method in his teaching ministry as vicar of Kidderminster from 1647-1661. By diligent application to public preaching and by an outstanding programme of personal catechizing, his ministry transformed the inhabitants of his parish. It was Baxter's aim and achievement to upgrade the practice of personal catechizing from a preliminary discipline for children to a permanent ingredient in pastoral care for all ages.

In his book *The Reformed Pastor*, Baxter powerfully argued for ministers to show holy zeal in the performance of their duties and, in particular, he placed special emphasis upon the benefits to be gained from personal catechizing. He wrote, 'The most godly people, therefore, in your congregations, will find it worth their labour to learn the very words of a catechism. If, then, you would safely edify them, be diligent in this work. It will make our public preaching better understood and regarded. When you have instructed them in the principles, they will better understand all you say. They will perceive what you drive at, when they are once acquainted with the main points. This prepares their minds, and opens a way to their hearts; whereas, without this, you may lose the most of your labour; and the more pains you take in accurate preparation, the less good you may do. As you would not, therefore, lose your public labour, see that you be faithful in this private work.'[25]

What place should catechetical instruction have within the overall pattern of teaching ministry? How should it be handled? What benefits does it bring? Should we preach methodically through a catechism or is another method to be preferred? Richard Baxter treated this as a 'private work' which had many beneficial repercussions for his 'public labour' of preaching. This is much the view of Dr Lloyd-Jones who has reservations about preaching through a catechism because it tends to 'an over-intellectual attitude to the truth'. This is not to suggest that he views catechisms with disfavour. In his opinion catechetical instruction should take place in a different context. He says, 'It is not that I do not believe in teaching people the Catechism. I do. But my view is that this should be done at another time and in a different way. I would place this under the heading of instruction and deal with it in a series of lectures. But, still better, it seems to me, is to tell the people to read and study the Catechism for themselves and then consider it together in discussion groups.

'The function of a catechism ... is to safeguard the correctness of the preaching, and to safeguard the interpretations of the people as they read their Bibles. As that is the main function of creeds and catechisms, it is surely wrong therefore to just preach constantly year after year on the Catechism, instead of preaching directly from the Scripture itself, with the Scriptures always open before you, and the minds of the people directed to that rather than to men's understanding of it.'[26]

To be honest, I cannot claim to speak from long experience in practising what I am advocating. However, like Baxter, I am persuaded of the great value of this method of instruction. Just as a paediatrician wants to see the limbs of a child grow straight and strong so that the developing body will function correctly and efficiently, so a pastor wants to see the 'doctrinal limbs' of a believer's faith grow straight and strong so that the developing Christian life will function correctly and efficiently. The surest way this spiritual goal can be achieved is by the patient method of catechetical instruction. It also provides an ideal opportunity to turn a 'deformed' faith into a 'Reformed' faith! It may be that some Christians have reservations about the use of a catechism. Is it just turning Christians into doctrinal 'memory machines'? Handled in the wrong way, it may certainly give that impression. But with a little initiative and imagination catechetical teaching need not be a 'dry-as-dust' spiritual exercise. There are ways of making it relevant, memorable and enjoyable.

A place for questions

Our teaching Master was a Master Teacher. He knew the value of actively involving His pupils in the learning process. It is not surprising, therefore, that Jesus employed and encouraged the use of 'questions and answers' to impart many aspects of His teaching. There were times when Jesus took up and used the questions put to Him; at other times He Himself put the questions to His hearers. On a number of occasions He skilfully used a question to counter a challenge or query which had been put to Him. The range of situations in which questions arose and provided teaching opportunities was very varied. We will mention a few of them.

Much of Jesus' teaching was given in answer to the questions of the puzzled disciples. His words on rewards in heaven, in Matthew's account of the incident, were a direct answer to Peter's question: 'We have left everything to follow you! What then will there be for us?' (Matt. 19:27.) The paralysing effects of unbelief and lack of prayer and fasting were pointed out by Jesus to His disciples only when they asked why they could not cast out the demon from the demon-possessed boy (Matt. 17:19).

When Jesus asked questions it was on occasions to test the spiritual understanding of His hearers. The crucial question, which was put to the disciples at a turning-point in the ministry of Christ, was 'Who do people say the Son of Man is?' (Matt. 16:13.) Where questions were put to Him by critics, not with a genuine purpose of gaining knowledge but with the hope of trapping Him by what He said, Jesus skilfully employed the use of counter-question to foil the attack. 'Jesus entered the temple courts, and, while he was teaching, the chief priests and the elders of the people came to him. "By what authority are you doing these things?" they asked. "And who gave you this authority?" Jesus replied, "I will also ask you one question. If you answer me, I will tell you by what authority I am doing these things. John's baptism — where did it come from? Was it from heaven, or from men?" ' (Matt. 21:23-25.) Or, for another example, 'Then some Pharisees and teachers of the law came to Jesus from Jerusalem and asked, "Why do your disciples break the tradition of the elders? They don't wash their hands before they eat!" Jesus replied, "And why do you break the command of God for the sake of your tradition?" ' (Matt. 15:1-3.)

Another way in which Jesus was able to resist the criticisms of His opponents was to expose their ignorance of Scripture. He would frame questions which would begin with the words: 'Have you not read ...?' He found it incredible that the religious leaders of the day should often display such blindness to the meaning of their own Scriptures as to fail to apply these to the situation in hand. If they were so anxious to accuse the disciples of committing sin just because they plucked ears of corn on the sabbath, had they never read what David did in similar circumstances? (Mark 2:25.)

At times Jesus used the art of asking questions in order to challenge His hearers to think through the topic on which He was giving instruction. The technique of raising questions, so that people had to find answers for themselves rather than having them imposed upon them, was not used solely to confound the critics. It was also used more positively in order to draw out responses to His truth. In particular, this kind of question could expose the faith possessed by the person to whom He was speaking: 'As Jesus went on from there, two blind men followed him, calling out, "Have mercy on us, Son of David!" When he had gone indoors the blind men came to him, and he asked them, "Do you believe that I am able to do this?"' (Matt. 9:27,28.) In similar vein, Jesus asked rhetorical questions. Thought was provoked, the point was made, but an answer was unnecessary. 'You are the salt of the earth. But if the salt loses its saltiness, how can it be made salty again?' (Matt. 5:13.) 'If you love those who love you, what reward will you get? Are not even the tax collectors doing that?' (Matt. 5:46.) 'What good will it be for a man if he gains the whole world, yet forfeits his soul? Or what can a man give in exchange for his soul?' (Matt. 16:26.)

Teaching situations cannot be exercised properly without an element of question and answer. Teacher and pupils need to know what has been learnt and what has been either misunderstood or forgotten. Also, teachers need to discover whether their pupils have grasped, not only the content of the teaching, but also its significance. In the best learning situations the pupils should be encouraged to ask questions, and any teacher failing to give such opportunity is failing as a teacher.

We have already seen how Richard Baxter (1615-1691) placed great emphasis on teaching in private as well as in the public services of the church. Baxter's experience of the advantages to be gained from catechetical teaching also influenced other aspects of his teaching ministry. He saw the immense value of giving the members of his flock opportunity to raise any queries and problems that they might have in connection with the sermons he preached. Writing in his *Autobiography*, he describes his weekly routine of preaching and further instruction: 'I preached before the wars twice each Lord's day: but after the war but once, and once every Thursday, besides occasional sermons. Every Thursday evening my neighbours that were more desirous and had opportunity met at my house, and there one of them repeated the sermon, and afterwards they proposed what doubts any of them had about the sermon, or any other case of conscience, and I resolved their doubts; and last of all I caused sometimes one and sometimes another of them to pray (to exercise them) ... And once a week also some of the younger sort ... met among a few, more privately, where they spent three hours in prayer together; every Saturday night they met at some of their houses to repeat the sermon of the last Lord's day, and to pray and prepare themselves for the following day.'[27]

The benefits of two-way teaching

The hallmark of expository preaching should be its divine authority: 'Thus says the Lord'. God has spoken through His written Word; God now speaks through the preached Word. Ideally, every sermon should be a divine monologue. By contrast, the other aspects of an all-round teaching ministry — shared experience, catechetical teaching and place for questions — give opportunity for dialogue. In these forms of teaching the learners are required to be audibly active. There is a two-way exchange of thoughts. There are benefits to be gained from these forms of teaching which would not be present where the teaching method is restricted to expository preaching alone. We will summarize these benefits so that we may better assess what place and emphasis they deserve in a teaching ministry.

1. *Learning stimulated.* If people are encouraged to ask questions, that will tend to stimulate their learning. If they are discouraged from asking questions, that will tend to stifle the learning process. There is more than an element of truth in the claim that 'When a person stops asking questions he stops learning.' People often listen in a totally different way when they know that they (or others) will be able later to raise questions; if they know that no such opportunity will be given, they may tend, consciously or subconsciously, to 'switch off' during the sermon.

2. *Understanding improved.* When the individual believer is actively and audibly involved in the learning process, he or she will be helped to understand and retain what is taught. It is very clear that the Jewish educational system in the time of our Lord operated on the principle that the pupil does not possess what he has received until he is able to verbalize this knowledge in his own terms. How many of our church members would be able, with confidence and yet with humility, to give a reason for the hope that they have? Can they, with simplicity and with accuracy, put into their own words the doctrines they have been taught? How will we know about this unless opportunity is given to encourage and to help believers speak about their faith?

3. *Assimilation aided.* These methods of teaching do not require of those being taught the sustained concentration that is necessary to follow an expository sermon. The uninterrupted discourse demands of those who hear it a mental discipline of

which not all are capable. By the question-and-answer method the truths of Scripture can be assimilated in more manageable pieces. Some Christians are able to digest a meaty and lengthy expository sermon and derive great spiritual nourishment from it. But not all believers have that ability. In connection with the 'indigenous church' principle we looked at earlier, we referred to the missionary Dr John L. Nevius. Speaking of the progress of the gospel work at Shan-Tung in China towards the end of the nineteenth century, and more particularly about the teaching of young believers, he said, 'From the first, we emphasize teaching rather than preaching. I here use the word 'preaching' in its specific sense of logical and more or less elaborate dissertation. We should remember that continuous discourse is something which is almost unknown in China. Even educated Chinamen follow it with difficulty. A carefully prepared sermon from a trained native preacher or a foreign missionary, such a sermon as would be admirably suited to an intelligent educated Christian congregation, is out of place in a new station.'[28]

4. *Progress monitored.* Questions asked and answers given are an indication to the pastor of the progress of the learning. The pace of the teaching is thereby conveniently adjusted to suit the pace of the learning.

5. *Application guided.* The gap between theory and practice, between doctrine and life, can most easily be bridged by the question and answer pattern of teaching. Even when a pastor has carefully expounded a biblical doctrine he may still leave unanswered questions: 'Now I begin to grasp the doctrine. But *exactly* what must I do in *my* situation *tomorrow* in the light of it?' Only when individual believers have opportunity to ask very specific questions will the vital practical advice be forthcoming.

6. *Misunderstanding detected.* A listener's close attention to what is being taught or discussed is, in itself, no guarantee that a correct understanding has been achieved. Even an occasional and spontaneous 'Praise the Lord' from a heart warmed by the teaching does not necessarily give proof that the truth has been properly grasped. Jesus warned His disciples of 'the yeast of the Pharisees and Sadducees'. Discussion among the twelve followed and Jesus overheard what they were saying. The disciples said, 'It is because we didn't bring any bread.' Jesus intervened: 'You of little faith, why are you talking among yourselves about having no bread? Do you still not understand?' (Matt. 16:5-9.)

Growing together

The misunderstanding of the disciples was detected because the topic was discussed.

7. *Objections answered.* 'How can a man be born when he is old?' (John 3:4.) So asked the puzzled Nicodemus. To him there was a clash between biology and theology. It was an objection that needed to be answered. 'Where is this "coming" he promised? Ever since our fathers died, everything goes on as it has since the beginning of creation' (2 Peter 3:4). The challenge of the critic needs to be countered. 'Shall we go on sinning so that grace may increase?' (Rom. 6:1.) The charge is that grace permits a slack attitude to sin. It is a genuine objection to the gospel of God's free grace. The question is understandable. It requires an answer that is both logical and biblical.

8. *Ignorance exposed.* Some of the questions asked will inevitably go beyond the range of the immediate topic being studied. At the time these issues may seem to digress and detract. But they can also prove a valuable clue to other areas of biblical truth in which the church may require systematic instruction.

9. *Crises averted.* Not every question will be the product of an enquiring mind seeking to grasp God's truth. Some questions may signify a real heart-cry for pastoral help. They may expose personal problems that were not immediately evident in general pastoral observation. Comments made in a group discussion may serve as an 'early warning system' of an impending personal crisis. If the signals are 'picked up' then prevention will be better than cure.

10. *Fellowship deepened.* The early Christians 'devoted themselves to the apostles' teaching and to the fellowship, to the breaking of bread and to prayer' (Acts 2:42). The public exposition of Scripture, though important in itself, may give to those who hear it little or no sense of *fellowship* in learning. The question-and-answer pattern, by encouraging participation, will give some evident and beneficial expression of fellowship in learning.

As we conclude this summary of the benefits of two-way teaching, it must be emphasized, in order to avoid misunderstanding, that the participatory methods of instruction are to be a *supplement* to expository preaching and *not* a substitute for it. These methods, we have argued, are biblical and essential if we are to achieve that all-round teaching ministry which we believe is desirable for every fellowship of believers.

8.
Building an indigenous church

Persuading and helping Christians to live locally

Where have all the Christians gone? That is the question we asked at the end of chapter 2. At that point in our study we were concerned to draw attention to the historical evidence for the massive and continuing exodus of Christians from inner-city areas. The tide has flowed in that direction for two hundred years. Can we really expect to halt or reverse the flow? If we attempt to tackle the problem are we not inevitably going to find ourselves in the position of King Canute — only in reverse? There are three questions we need to ask. Why do they go? Why should they stay? How can they stay? We must face these issues with realism and a sensitive conscience.

Why do they go?

Why is it that so many Christians have abandoned the inner city in order to live in the suburbs or beyond? There are a variety of reasons. As far as I know, local estate agents do not describe the inner city as a 'desirable residential area'. There are certain features of the urban environment which are 'less desirable' (even 'undesirable') compared with what exists in another type of area. In our brief survey in chapter 2 of conditions in the inner city today we identified some of those features which may provoke the urban dweller to consider a move to a new location.

Private housing, good educational and recreational facilities, good jobs, gardens, parks, woods, trees, clean air, quietness are all in short supply in the inner city. The only commodity which is not in short supply is ... people! And, ultimately, it is what the people are like, rather than what the environment is like, that will determine the 'quality of life' in any community. This is not to ignore or minimize those Scriptures which tell us of the good things that God has provided for our enjoyment. It is important for the Christian constantly to be reminded that 'everything God created is good, and nothing is to be rejected if it is received with thanksgiving ...' (1 Tim. 4:4). But these many blessings also bring their own responsibilities. 'Keep your lives free from the love of money and be content with what you have,' says the writer to the Jewish Christians (Heb. 13:5). Paul reminds us that 'Godliness with contentment is great gain' (1 Tim. 6:6).

People matter more than things. The urban dweller matters more than the urban environment. Also, it would be quite wrong to imagine that the suburban dweller has all the advantages and the urban dweller has all the problems. There is an earthiness, a warmth, a frankness, a humour, a resilience, a natural generosity, which the urban dweller possesses that is not nearly so much in evidence in other areas. In particular, the resilience shown is remarkable when we pause to consider the kind of forces and pressures which bear upon the urban dweller. Bishop David Sheppard comments, 'People who live in the working-class areas ... experience the weight of great impersonal pressures upon them. These can stop a man from making the choices he wants to, and can eventually rob him of the confidence that he can make decisions at all. It is a testimony to the toughness and adaptability of the human spirit that we can list as working-class characteristics endurance, expressiveness, humour, openness, solidarity, compassion, as well as the bad things which confront us in working-class life in the big city.'[1]

These 'urban assets' — features of working-class character — are all the more precious because they are measured in terms of living people and not lifeless possessions. Nevertheless, when the urban Christian faces realistically his obligation to 'love his neighbour as himself' he soon realizes that our urban resources of Christian love are in rather short supply. There just is not enough to go round! There are too many urban people and too few urban Christians. So we cannot afford a 'believer-drain' to the suburbs. The crucial question we must now face is 'Does the

Christian have the right to choose where he will live?'

When God established His covenant with Abraham, the father of the faithful, He gave specific instructions concerning *where* His servant was to live. 'The Lord had said to Abram, "Leave your country, your people and your father's household and *go to the land I will show you*" '(Gen. 12:1). Many years later when God redeemed His people from cruel slavery in Egypt He gave them a land to be their own. He determined *where* they would live. A study of the prophets of the Old Testament and a survey of the missionary journeys in the book of Acts reveal an oft-repeated instruction to God's servants: 'Go where I tell you.' Where is God directing urban Christians today? We can now move on to look at our next question.

Why should they stay?

There are two ways of approaching the matter of where God wants us to live. One approach is to assume that we may make plans to move to the place of our choice. If the plans fail to materialize, we could take that as God's indication that we should stay where we are. In other words, we take it as a right that we may move to the place of our choice *unless* God, through circumstances, 'blocks' our path and shows us that we must stay where we are. The other approach is to assume that we must stay until God prompts us to move and 'opens doors' that we may do so. I am more than inclined to the view that the latter is a safer and more biblical approach.

In this respect, it is instructive to read the whole of Genesis 12 which we have just mentioned. Abraham set out for Canaan at God's command and God blessed him for his obedience (Gen. 12:1-9). But when Abraham decided to travel down to Egypt because of famine in Canaan, he did this on his own initiative. Abraham deceived the Pharaoh concerning Sarah, his wife, and, as a result, God brought trouble to the household of Pharaoh. Abraham's deception was discovered and his action was rebuked by the Pharaoh (Gen. 12:10-20). He learned the hard way that God must determine *where* He wants His people to be.

It would be wrong to suggest that God wants all Christians in the inner city to stay where they are and never to consider a move. But I do believe that no Christian should leave the inner city without considering fully the spiritual issues involved.

Building an indigenous church 225

There are, no doubt, Christians who pray a prayer for guidance which begins, 'Lord, I will go anywhere you want me to ... except for ...'. That was Jonah's attitude and he lived to regret it. We should learn from his mistake. There are a number of factors to weigh up.

1. *God's values.* God so loved the world. He said so, and He proved it (John 3:16). Christians claim to be the 'children of God', and so they are (1 John 3:1). Because they are members of this family, they ought to reflect the same love and the same sense of values as their heavenly Father. God is far more concerned with a crowded bus queue than a glowing sunset, a noisy market-place than a starry galaxy, a towering tenement than a snow-capped mountain, a bustling city than a sequestered retreat. God is far more concerned with people than with anything else that He has created. 'The heavens declare the glory of God; the skies proclaim the work of his hands' (Ps. 19:1). We tend to associate the presence and power of God with the glory of the heavens and the beauty of the countryside. But God's highest creation is more in evidence in the bustling din of a city rush-hour than in the relaxing peace of a rural landscape. 'So God created man in his own image, in the image of God he created him' (Gen. 1:27). This is the summit of God's creative achievements. This is God's marvel of miniaturization. God made man small, weak and utterly dependent on His Maker and yet, amazingly, capable of enjoying a meaningful companionship and communion with the One who made him. One sinner, made in the image of his Creator, means more to God than a million stars! People matter more to God than all the rest of creation put together.

I have a Christian friend who has said that he would rather retire to a place like Birmingham than to a quiet little cottage in the country. When questioned why his 'retirement dream' runs counter to what most others seem to prefer, he calmly points out that he believes God is more concerned about 'people' than about 'places', and more concerned about re-creating beauty of character than merely admiring beauty of nature. People matter to God more than we realize. He has proved it by sending His Son to us. Do we, His children, reflect the same values as our heavenly Father?

2. *The example of Jesus.* When Jesus Christ came down to earth from heaven He 'moved' from a 'very desirable residential area'

to live in a 'very *undesirable* residential area'. When Jesus left behind the holy splendour of His Father's house, He moved to live on an earth tainted by sin and peopled only by sinners. He was born in the primitive and unhygienic surroundings of a cattle-shed. He grew up in the simple home of a carpenter's family. He lived in a neighbourhood which had gained a bad reputation: 'Can any good thing come out of Nazareth?' 'With the poor and mean and lowly, lived on earth our Saviour holy.' The Lord of glory did not cling to the divine privileges which were His by right. He did not turn aside from a world repellent and ugly from the disfigurement of sin. He stooped down and 'pitched his tent' (John 1:14) among us for thirty-three years. And all this He did for us. His example must be our guide. 'Each of you should look not only to your own interests, but also to the interests of others. Your attitude should be the same as that of Christ Jesus' (Phil. 2:4,5).

3. *Reaching others.* Every Christian has a responsibility to spread the gospel. No true believer is exempt from this duty. The point at which a Christian should take up this task is obviously among those who are nearest to him.

The conversion of Matthew is an object-lesson in this respect. While Matthew was busy in his tax-collecting work, Jesus Christ called him to immediate and unquestioning discipleship. Matthew took his opportunity: he 'left everything, and followed' Christ. Matthew was graciously called out by the Lord from among that despised category in Jewish society — the tax collectors. After his call to discipleship he was immediately concerned to introduce his former colleagues (and possibly crooks) to the Saviour (Luke 5:29). Who was the person best equipped to talk to those tax-collectors about faith in Jesus Christ? Matthew, of course. He could speak 'on their wavelength' and understand how they 'ticked' and what it would cost them to leave all and follow Christ. What better proof that Jesus could transform the lives of even bent tax-collectors than the living evidence in the person of Matthew?

'You couldn't be a Christian in my job,' says one sceptical working-class enquirer. 'Sunday and Monday are like two different worlds and it's hard to fit the two together.' 'It wouldn't work for me either,' says another who feels the same way. A carefully reasoned biblical answer may leave the sceptics unconvinced. The shining example of a Christian comrade in the same work situation, who proves Christ's power to live as he should, is a more convincing proof than any amount of reasoned argument. The best ambassadors of the gospel to working-class men are other working-class men whom the Lord has saved. If Matthew had not introduced his tax-collector colleagues to the Saviour, who would have done so? If working-class Christians are not willing to stay in working-class communities in order to introduce friends and neighbours to the Saviour, who will?

4. *Weighing the issues.* When the apostle Paul spoke to the Philippian believers of his personal feelings concerning his possible imminent death, he did not conceal what he himself would prefer. To these loyal friends in Christ he was open and frank and really bared his heart. He said, 'If I am to go on living in the body, this will mean fruitful labour for me. Yet what shall I choose? I do not know! I am torn between the two: I have a desire to depart and be with Christ, which is better by far; but it is more necessary for you that I remain in the body. Convinced of this, I know that I will ... continue with all of you for your progress and joy in the faith' (Phil. 1: 22-25). In saying this, what was the apostle doing? He was really applying in his own life the principle he was about to urge on others: 'Each of you should look not only to your own interests, but also to the interests of others' (Phil. 2:4).

Paul did not banish from his mind any tendency even to think upon his own interests. He was quite open in saying that he would prefer to be 'with Christ' straight away and he gave the reason why. There was nothing wrong in that desire; it was quite spiritual and proper. He was legitimately considering his own interests and not pretending that they did not exist. But it did not stop there. More than counterbalancing his personal desires were the spiritual needs of the Philippian Christians. Paul, like his Saviour, and like his colleague Timothy (Phil. 2:20), gave the higher priority to the needs of others.

It is not wrong for a Christian in an inner-city area to consider the advantages of moving out to another situation. We do not have to shut our eyes to the benefits to be gained and pretend they are not there. But we must also seek to obtain an unbiased assessment of the reasons why we may need to stay in the inner city. When Paul was weighing up his situation, he confessed, 'I am torn between two.' If the inner-city Christian does not share a similar feeling when considering a move then there may be something wrong with that Christian's life. If he sees no attraction or benefit in moving out, that would be strange. If he does not appreciate any powerful reasons why he should stay, that would be sad. It is to be hoped that most inner-city Christians will come to the conclusion reached by Paul: 'I am torn between the two: I desire to depart, ... but it is more necessary ... that I remain ...' (Phil. 1: 23,24).

'In all your ways acknowledge him, and he will direct your paths' (Prov. 3:6).

How can they stay?

In what ways should a Christian tackle the problem of finding a suitable home in an urban area? It is important to pray about it continually. It is also important for that Christian to show practical resourcefulness.

1. *Individual initiative.* A strong and sure sense of God's call to remain in an urban area does not necessarily guarantee an easy and immediately successful search for the suitable accommodation when it is needed. There will not be a telegram from heaven with the address of God's provision printed on it! The measure of a Christian's diligence in the search for accommodation will, in part, reflect whether continued residence in the inner city is being approached with half-hearted resignation or whole-hearted consecration. The accommodation columns of the local paper will need to be carefully studied. The noticeboards in local newsagents should be checked regularly. Applications for a tenancy through the local authority or through a local housing association should be considered. Christian friends must be urged to keep their eyes and ears open. Watch and pray so that you might enter into the right accommodation!

2. *Christian involvement in housing associations.* If we believe it is important to secure suitable accommodation for a missionary who is ready to serve God overseas, then logically there is no reason why we should be any less methodical and thorough in our efforts to obtain suitable accommodation for a missionary who is ready to serve God in an urban area of the home missionfield. The missionary to a tribe in Papua, New Guinea, will not arrive at his destination with a do-it-yourself house-building kit! If it is all-important that an overseas tribe should hear the gospel of Christ in order to be saved, then no effort should be spared to

Building an indigenous church

have the missionary suitably housed among the people to whom he is called. Accordingly, a missionary society will apply its administrative skills and Christian dedication to the need in question. Similarly, a number of Christians to whom God has given a concern and a vision for bringing the gospel to the inner city have taken very practical steps to aid the fulfilment of that vision. The opportunities offered through housing associations for helping Christians to live and serve in urban situations have been explored by a number of Christians.

Housing associations are voluntary organizations providing homes for rent and not for profit. Each association is run by a committee of people who know and care about housing. They usually have their own staff to manage the property. Some associations improve old houses; some build new homes. Some build special homes for the handicapped or sheltered housing for the elderly. Local authorities encourage housing associations because they make a valuable contribution to meeting the never-ending housing needs, which are particularly acute in urban areas. The local authorities make money available for these ventures, but before the associations can have any public money they must be registered with the Housing Corporation. The Corporation (set up by the government) checks that associations do their work well and makes sure that they use the tax-payers' money properly.

The funds made available by local government for this type of housing provision are obviously not for the exclusive benefit of Christians and churches, but there are legitimate benefits which can bring real help to the work of the gospel. If Christians serve on the management committee of a housing association, then they are in a position to know what properties are available. Also, by virtue of their position as members of the management committee, they have certain rights to nominate persons to be considered for the grant of tenancies.

A common form of housing association in urban areas is one which seeks to acquire old, run-down properties in order to improve and modernize them, and then make them available for letting. It is through this kind of venture that a growing number of Christians, and especially young couples, have been able to stay and continue their work for God in urban situations.

A less common but more ambitious venture is one which seeks a total redevelopment of its church site and premises. Many urban churches have vast old decaying church premises. A handful of members fight valiantly to cope with the deterioration of the fabric. It is a losing and depressing battle. But all may not be lost. What may seem to be a major liability may yet prove to be a major asset. Land is scarce in the inner city. Therefore its value is high. A church which has a large site area may discover that its work could be continued within a comparatively small part of its present site. If the area not required by the church could be made available to help meet housing needs the value of the land could go a long way towards paying for the building of more suitable church premises.

I am not able to say whether this kind of opportunity exists in many urban situations, or whether it is the rare exception. Of course, it is one thing to say that the opportunity exists, it is another thing for a small church membership to commit itself to the demands and upheavals of such a scheme. However, I do know that this kind of project has been attempted and achieved. St Mark's Church, Old Ford, Bow, in east London is an example of this. The value of this kind of scheme is very obvious when the scale of the transformation is considered. In place of the old St Mark's church, church hall and vicarage, there now stands a new church centre, plus accommodation for *thirty-two families*.

Ted Roberts, the vicar who piloted the scheme, tells the story of this project in his book *Housing and Ministry*. One paragraph from his book conveniently summarizes the financial structure of the venture and also the benefits which were envisaged. He says, 'The church was represented in the development by a Housing Association which we created ourselves for the purpose ... Once officially recognized and registered, the Housing Association was able to borrow money from the local authority to finance the acquisition of the site and the building of the flats. In return the Greater London Council gains the right to nominate 70% of the tenants; this right expires after 15 years. This means in effect that we are building homes with money borrowed from the G.L.C. In addition to the mortgage from the council, we receive government subsidies which enable us to reduce the rents we would have otherwise to charge. We are free to nominate our own tenants for the remaining 30% which means that we have a few flats to offer to people who would not normally qualify for a council flat but have something to give to the community, for example, teachers, social workers, and young couples from the church who would otherwise have to move out of the area. This last group is important because young Christian couples must be able to settle in the district if a strong church is to be built in the inner city.'[2]

I can well understand a small church being frightened off such a project. The upheaval may seem to be a burden beyond their strength or skill to carry. They are faced with an unenviable choice. If the church turns away from the feared administrative millstone of bringing into being a new church building, how long can it survive with the ever-growing burden of a decaying old building? I think I would prefer to climb on to a life-raft that is floating rather than cling to a ship that is sinking. Our Lord's second advent may not come soon enough to prevent our having to make this difficult choice!

Strictly speaking, we have deviated from our main topic, getting Christians housed in the inner city. But the problems of deteriorating fabric will not go away if we choose to ignore them. Whether the St Mark's scheme is one which could be repeated at the present time, I do not know. That project took place in the early seventies. Economic conditions have changed since then. It may be that government legislation has altered too.

3. *Church house conversion project.* A housing association is an officially registered and recognized agency for the provision of housing units. It attracts local government funds and naturally has to be administered in accordance with definite rules and regulations. The project we are now suggesting is a much more modest scheme and its operation may be wholly within the work of a local church. Quite simply, it is a project in which a local church seeks to acquire a second house similar to, or possibly larger than, the house it already has for a manse. It may be possible to obtain a large old property, and have it modernized and converted into a number of residential units which could prove a useful base from which to look for more suitable accommodation when the time is convenient.

Where does the money come from? If inner-city churches usually have crippling maintenance costs on old and decaying buildings, how can they be expected to consider seriously this kind of scheme? Inner-city churches may be impoverished, but their God is not! Did not James, our Lord's brother, say that at times we 'don't have because we don't ask'? Is it altogether out of the question that a thrifty church member might be 'called home' leaving a most useful legacy to the church? The provision of a legacy and the availability of a suitable property may be God's green light for the church to proceed with such a project. It is sound spiritual sense and good biblical stewardship to explain to church members the vital importance of Christian homes in the neighbourhood and how this need ought to be borne in mind when a will is being made. I would think that every Christian ought to be a good steward of all that the Lord has entrusted to him in life and at his death, in the bequests of his will.

Are these housing schemes really necessary and are they realistic? I have not the slightest hesitation in affirming their necessity. We do not expect to evangelize pagans in another country by remaining at a distance from them. The missionary must live among the people whom he is called to evangelize. Pagans need to *hear* the words a Christian missionary speaks and to *see* the life he lives. They must be consistent. What is true of the overseas mission-field is equally true of our own urban mission-field. The Christian home, as an instrument of witness and evangelism, is of the utmost importance in the inner city. There is no substitute for it.

Are these schemes realistic? From personal knowledge and experience I can confirm that they are viable. They have all happened in a number of urban situations known to me. Our own experience is that of the church house conversion project. There is very little private housing in the immediate neighbourhood of our church — just a little way south of London's Elephant and Castle area. In our search for a suitable manse, we were unable to obtain any help from the local authority because waiting lists are always long in an area where there is continuing redevelopment. However, at the right time and in the right place we were able to acquire a derelict vicarage only three hundred yards away from our church premises. This property, which had been severely vandalized during the years it had stood empty, was then converted from being a large battered shell into 'Whitefield House' — a small residential centre comprising a manse, one other flat, four bed-sitting rooms, and a basement for use in the work of the church. Certainly this provision is a concrete example that our God 'is able to do immeasurably more than all we ask or imagine'

(Eph. 3:20,21). That is true not only of the kind of property that we acquired; it was equally true of the funds that were provided to pay for its purchase and conversion.

Corinth, culture and class

What is culture?

This is where we must begin because the term 'culture' has more than one meaning. Dr E.A. Nida says, 'For many people, culture (especially when pronounced with a super-sophisticated air) means music, art, and good manners. This is not, however, the anthropologist's definition of culture. For him, culture is all learned behaviour which is socially acquired, that is, the material and non-material traits which are passed on from one generation to another. They are both transmittable and accumulative, and they are cultural in the sense that they are transmitted by a society, not by genes.'[3]

In the context of our particular study the culture with which we are concerned is *all learned behaviour which is socially acquired.* This means that the range of topics which can be included under the subject of culture is very considerable, although certain features of any culture will be more prominent than others. The language that is spoken; how family life is organized; how marriages take place (arranged or personal choice); the size and structure of the typical family unit (extended or nuclear); the relationship between husband and wife in terms of status and authority; standards of morality within the community; methods of punishment; the organization of community life; religious beliefs and rites; styles of dress; occupations pursued; methods of education; superstitions; mental mechanisms (concrete or conceptual thinking); attitudes to authority, to history, to tradition and to other social groups — all these and more fall within the definition of culture.

Assessing the relative importance of various cultural features, Nida says, 'Canoes, huts, clothing, weapons, domesticated animals and farm crops are all material parts of culture; but equally important — and usually much more prized — are titles, rank, prestige, family connections, and religious beliefs.

The features of a culture which tend to give it a distinctive quality, or ethos, are far more likely to be the non-material than the material.'[4]

Because religious belief and religious behaviour are a part of culture, any attempt to change the religion will also bring about a change in the culture. The same applies to morality. Culture is not amoral. It is bound to have its own accepted standards of right and wrong, good and bad. Where certain culturally accepted practices are immoral according to the law of God, a realignment of the moral standard with the law of God automatically brings cultural change as well. Wrong conclusions may be drawn where there is an attempt to consider either religion or morality isolated from their cultural context. Cultural patterns are never totally static. There will always be a certain amount of interaction between the various facets of the culture and neither religion nor morality can be insulated from the effects of this normal cultural process.

'Test everything. Hold on to the good. Avoid every kind of evil' (1 Thess. 5:21,22). This New Testament injunction must include the matter of 'culture'. There is no such thing as a perfect culture; nor is there a culture which is totally corrupt. In any culture there will be certain features which are 'good' and should be retained. Certain other features will be 'evil' and must be avoided. A third group of aspects of a culture will be those which can be regarded as spiritually and morally neutral. What is acceptable in this category may be determined by the custom of the social group or the personal preference of the individual. An example of this category would be styles of dress. There is no one particular portion or chapter in the New Testament to which we can turn for a clear and comprehensive statement on the subject of culture. It will, therefore, prove helpful to our study if we work patiently through a cultural exercise in relation to a New Testament urban church. As we draw together various terms, categories, principles and tests we shall be better equipped to examine later our present urban situations within a biblical framework of thought.

Culture in a New Testament urban church.

Corinth was the commercial metropolis of Greece. Situated on the Isthmus of Greece, about fifty miles west of Athens, it was one of the largest, richest and most important cities of the

Roman Empire. Its population has been put at 400,000, although other estimates show a considerable variation from this figure. Corinth stood on the principal trade route of the empire. Understandably, it was a very cosmopolitan city. It was a city where 'Greeks, Latins, Syrians, Asiatics, Egyptians, and Jews, bought and sold, laboured and revelled, quarrelled and hob-nobbed, in the city and its ports, as nowhere else in Greece'.[5] Corinth's commercial importance was matched only by its moral decadence. Old Corinth had been a byword for licentiousness. The cosmopolitan hotchpotch of commercial transients ensured that new Corinth retained its unsavoury reputation. It was a 'renowned and voluptuous city, where the vices of East and West met'. Our next step is to examine a number of features of Corinthian culture to see how the church at Corinth reacted to its environment. For our purpose this need be only a sampling rather than a comprehensive survey.

Testing the phenomena

1. *Unity.* A city as racially cosmopolitan and as morally corrupt as Corinth would almost inevitably be troubled by tensions and frictions between the various ethnic groups. Unfortunately, the quarrels of society in general were also mirrored in the life of the Corinthian church. Paul's immediate task in his first Corinthian letter was to attack the evils of division and party factions which were destroying the unity of the church. Why did the tensions and troubles break out? It is possible to detect some issues. Did the high-principled former God-fearers in the church show a critical intolerance towards some of those Christians who had once been among the riff-raff of Corinthian society? (1 Cor. 6:9-11.) As the church became progressively Gentile in its overall membership, did the 'I am of Cephas' group look back nostalgically to earlier days when the Jews had a greater influence? Did these Jews resent Gentile intolerance of their narrow Jewish nationalism?

Paul's references to some of the believers engaged in litigation and attending private banquets point to free men, and men of means. Did the small number of 'upper-class' Christians view with patronizing condescension the much larger group of believers from the lower social strata? (1 Cor. 1:26f.) Were there differences over preferences of preaching style? Paul's preaching had a studied simplicity (1 Cor. 2:2-4). That of Apollos was probably highly rhetorical (Acts 18:24,27f.). Paul strongly condemned these divisions. The believers at Corinth were urged to heal their relationships and to display a unity in Christ over against the disunity of their cultural environment.

2. *Morality.* Venus was the principal deity of Corinth. Her temple was one of the most magnificent buildings in the city. In it a thousand priestesses, public prostitutes, were kept at public expense. They were always available for those who wished to indulge their carnal lusts in the worship of their principal deity.

With such a system of sin accepted as a normal part of Corinthian life, we can understand the kind of problems this posed for the Corinthian church. Regrettably, one professing Christian brother had committed incest. 'A man has his father's wife' (1 Cor. 5:1). A sin denounced even by the ungodly called for extreme disciplinary measures. Paul indicated what these were to be (1 Cor. 5:5). At various other points in the same letter Paul gave instruction on the biblical view of sexual morality. It is obvious that the incestuous offender was not the only one in the church to feel the corrupting pressures that surrounded them. Paul climaxed his teaching on this subject by presenting a clear argument which provided a powerful incentive to avoid all sexual impurity. 'Do you not know that your body is a temple of the Holy Spirit, who is in you, whom you have received from God? You are not your own; you were bought at a price, Therefore honour God with your body' (1 Cor. 6:19,20).

3. *Family life.* An atmosphere of lust and licentiousness in society led to broken laws, broken hearts and broken homes. Fragmented families were a feature of Corinthian culture. So great was the moral confusion in Corinth that the believers actually sent a message to Paul requesting instruction concerning Christian family life. Paul readily acceded to their request (1. Cor. 7:1-40). He was specific in his teaching about the right use of God's gift of sex. He recognized that this powerful and God-given desire had to be harnessed and used for the enrichment of a permanent relationship, but only within the married state. His first instructions gave guidance to the Christian husband and wife. He then moved on to deal with the marriage in which one partner had become a Christian subsequent to the event of marriage. Paul considered the various reactions that could be expected from the unbelieving partner

and advised accordingly. Instruction for the unmarried and widows was also given. Paul was well aware of the unhelpful sights and sounds that the believers would encounter in Corinth. His detailed and practical counsel was designed to enable the Christian to extinguish every fiery dart of sexual temptation and to build his family life according to the Word of God.

4. *Christian worship.* 'The ideal of the Corinthian was the reckless development of the individual. The merchant who made his gain by all and every means, the man of pleasure surrendering himself to every lust, the athlete steeled to every bodily exercise and proud in his physical strength, are the true Corinthian types: in a word the man who recognized no superior law but his own desires.'[6] A people who praised selfish individualism and fostered competitive attitudes, rather than those which were communal and compassionate, unavoidably degenerated into an anarchic flux of social disorder. God's order for the most intimate of human relationships was ignored and this in turn gave rise to a harvest of other disorders in society in general. A rotten root yielded rotten fruit. 'Every man for himself' was an utterly pagan philosophy.

The disease of selfish individualism had infected the church at Corinth and this spiritual malady was most obvious in their times of worship. Paul prescribed God's remedy for this disorder (1 Cor. 11:1-14:40) and repeatedly stated and demonstrated that God is a God of order. The most serious evidence of disorder in worship was apparent in the way they kept the Lord's Supper. 'When you come together, it is not the Lord's Supper you eat, for as you eat, each of you goes ahead without waiting for anybody else. One remains hungry, another gets drunk' (1 Cor. 11:20,21). God's disapproval of this blatant mockery of true fellowship had provoked the Lord to respond with severe disciplinary action (1 Cor. 11:30). Paul established that the rule for all aspects of Chrstian worship must be 'Everything should be done in a fitting and orderly way' (1 Cor. 14:40).

In the four aspects of culture examined, we have observed that accepted practice in Corinthian society ran counter to biblical standards. Consequently, the believers at Corinth were required to dissociate themselves from these particular features of local behaviour. In the case of Corinth there was much, *but not all*, which was at variance with Scripture. No culture is totally corrupt. But it would be fair to describe Corinthian culture as predominantly pagan. In order to demonstrate that there were 'good' aspects of Corinthian culture we shall briefly mention three examples of this.

1. *Evangelistic method.* Paul's preaching at Corinth commenced in the synagogue. It was not long before Jews hostile to his preaching forced him to abandon his gospel work there. 'Then Paul left the synagogue and went next door to the house of Titius Justus, a worshipper of God. Crispus, the synagogue ruler, and his entire household believed in the Lord, and many of the Corinthians who heard him believed and were baptised' (Acts 18:7,8). In certain respects it might have seemed risky, if not provocative, for Paul to establish his evangelistic base so near to the place of the earlier opposition. But Paul knew what he was doing. He was employing accepted Greek cultural custom familiar to the people of Corinth. After his ejection from the synagogue, 'In the following months he was evidently understood by the Corinthian population to be one of those lecturers on philosophy and morals, so common in the Greek world, who often travelled, and settled in new cities where there seemed a good opening for a teacher'.[7]

2. *Athletic analogy.* It is clear from a number of Paul's letters that he took more than a passing interest in the sporting contests which were popular in his day (1 Cor. 9:24-27). He saw himself as God's athlete. The event for which he was entered demanded total dedication. Peak fitness could only be achieved by strict training. His entire energies were directed towards winning the victor's crown. A casual or careless approach to the Christian contest was utterly unthinkable. Paul dreaded the thought of disqualification. But what exactly did disqualification (being a 'castaway', A.V.) mean when applied to the Christian life? Is there a suggestion that a believer can be 'saved' and then 'lost'?

'Next to the Olympic games, the Isthmian games held at Corinth every three years were the most highly acclaimed athletic contests of the first century. To compete, an athlete had to have Greek citizenship. Paul saw in the games an excellent analogy to the Christian life. To him, life was like a race. To compete a person had to be a regenerated Christian. The reward for running was not heavenly citizenship, but the praise of the Saviour at the judgement seat of Christ ... An Olympic athlete who won a race did not lose his Greek citizenship if he was subsequently disqualified: however, he did lose the honour and forfeited his wreath crown. Christians, like Paul, should not want to lose the opportunity to serve Christ and the subsequent praise at the judgement seat of Christ' (cf. 3:14-15).[8]

3. *Women at worship.* It was customary in Greek and Eastern cities for women to cover their heads in public, except women of immoral character. Christian women at Corinth needed to be discreet in the way that they conducted themselves. It appears that some women, taking advantage of their new-found liberty in Christ, decided they were now entitled to discard their veils in church meetings. This horrified those of a more modest type. Paul condemned this practice which gave offence to other believers.

Although Paul reasoned powerfully that women should have their heads covered, he argued his case from spiritual principles rather than social customs. It is in accord with God's order in creation (1 Cor. 11:3). The head covering worn by the women was intended to signify an inner disposition of submission. It was also necessary 'because of the angels' (1 Cor. 11:10).

Although Paul made no explicit reference to social custom, he was well aware of the spiritual damage to the work of the gospel which would ensue if Christian women defied local custom. Paul made sure that no 'liberated' Christian woman could charge him with making a particular fuss about nothing at Corinth. The apostle said, 'If anyone wants to be contentious about this, we have no other practice — nor do the churches of God' (1 Cor. 11:16). The need for Christian women to conform to accepted social practice is quite obvious. The gospel itself carries its own 'offence'. Christians are not to add to that offence by ignoring or condemning every social convention. When the gospel comes to people who have not heard it before, it should progressively purify local culture, not destroy it!

Steering the church

The church leaders at Corinth were described by Paul as 'steersmen'. This we gather from what he says in 1 Corinthians 12:28 where the gifts of leadership which certain men possess are described as gifts of 'administration' or 'governments'.[9] This conclusion is drawn from the fact that nowhere in his Corinthian letters does Paul speak of elders or deacons, which became the more standard descriptions of church leaders in his later letters (1 Tim. 3:1-10; Titus 1:6-9; Phil. 1:1). Some believe that the term is more suited to describe the work of deacons, while others are more inclined to link it with the work of elders because it clearly involves direction. The word is used in Acts 27:11 to describe the activity of the steersman of a ship. He is the man to pilot his vessel through the hidden dangers of shoals and rocks and bring her safe to port. Likewise, the 'steersmen' of the Corinthian church had the spiritual responsibility of piloting the Corinthian believers safely through the particular hazards of the local culture.

When we think of the church leaders as 'steersmen' we can visualize the spiritual skills that are required for their task. The responsibility for testing the culture and steering the believers rested with these men. By what criteria is any culture to be spiritually tested? From our experience in assessing Corinthian culture it should be possible for us to devise a framework of tests which we can apply to our contemporary urban situation.

Some cultural criteria

1. *Is there a biblically correct distinction between Christian conduct and cultural practice?* For example, 'One does not expect to find women sitting in church with pipes in their mouths, nor men with hats on their heads. But that is exactly what one finds in some of the churches in the San Blas Islands along the Caribbean coast of eastern Panama. Many San Blas women take up pipe smoking as they get older and the men regard the wearing of hats inside a community building as quite proper.'[10] We know Paul's directives for the women at worship in Corinth, but what would the biblical requirement be here?

2. *Does the Bible expressly forbid the practice which is being considered?* 'We assume that it is unnatural for a man to wish to loan his wife to guests, but Eskimo men have been doing just this for centuries and they do not seem to suffer from jealousy. They are expected to share their wives with certain men, and they in turn have the same privilege.'[11]

3. *If the practice is not forbidden by Scripture, is it a trait to be encouraged or curbed?* 'The Eskimo society is what could be called distinctly individualistic, for the primary reliance is on the individual, and he is relatively free to work out his own problems either on a small family basis or in voluntary groupings.'[12] There are, no doubt, historical and social reasons to explain the Eskimo's

'excessive individualism'. Biblical teaching on family and community relationships point to a need for the trait of 'individualism' to be curbed.

4. *Would the forbidding or the encouraging of a particular practice cause unnecessary offence to local custom?* Paul's decision to have Timothy submit to circumcision may seem to run contrary to the decision taken by the Council of Jerusalem concerning the entry of Christian Gentiles into the membership of the church (see Acts 15:28-29). But Timothy's case was exceptional. It was Timothy's mixed parentage that made Paul decide to circumcise him before taking him along as a travel companion. In the eyes of the Jews, Timothy was a Gentile because he was the uncircumcised son of a Greek. In Gentile eyes, however, he was practically a Jew, having been brought up in his mother's religion. Paul, therefore, regularized Timothy's status in Jewish eyes by the act of circumcision. In this case, from Paul's point of view, the step was taken not as a religious rite, but rather as a sign of cultural identification. Paul wisely showed himself ready to 'conciliate Jewish susceptibilities'. He had no wish to give offence to accepted custom (Acts 16:1-5. See also Matt. 17:27, but contrast Gal. 2:3.)

5. *Is the church unnecessarily discarding aspects of local cultural practice in favour of a non-indigenous cultural practice?* 'One of the very thrilling things in South Thailand in the Malay-speaking church is that the missionaries do not seem to have translated any Western hymns, and the small congregation sings verses of the Bible in their own indigenous music which sounds uncommonly like the call from the minaret with which all are familiar. The musical *form* is national, but the *content* is thoroughly biblical. With this we may contrast the amusing American habit of importing both a piano and an organ as the only proper way of accompanying a singing congregation.'[13]

6. *Is the practice being considered likely to promote unity or provoke division in the church?* The decision of the Council of Jerusalem concerning the conditions for Gentile entry into membership of the Christian church was both spiritually unifying and culturally discreet. Gentile believers were not expected to become converts to Jewish culture as well. They were not required to keep the Jewish ceremonial law, but were asked to abstain from food sacrificed to idols, from blood, from the meat of strangled animals and from sexual immorality (Acts 15:28,29).

7. *In what particular ways can the life and witness of a local church reflect the indigenous culture?* The planting and the progress of the church at Philippi provides us with a very useful biblical example of the way in which a local church is able to reflect the indigenous culture.

The first opponents of the gospel at Philippi complained to the magistrates of 'cultural interference' on the part of Paul and Silas. 'These men are Jews, and are throwing our city into an uproar by advocating *customs* unlawful for *us Romans* to accept or practise' (Acts 16:20,21). By alleging a threat to their Roman colonial privileges, these enemies of the gospel provoked a hostile reaction to Paul and Silas, which led to arrest and imprisonment. After an eventful night (during which the jailor and his household were converted), Paul was able, in a limited way, to turn the tables on his opponents by informing his captors that they were guilty of infringing the rights of two Roman citizens: 'They beat us publicly without a trial, even though we are Roman citizens' (Acts 16:37). A shock wave hit the authorities when they realized what they had done. Paul and Silas were courteously asked to leave the city (Acts 16:39).

Philippi was 'a Roman colony and the leading city of that district of Macedonia' (Acts 16:12). Her citizens knew it and were proud of their status and privileges. 'Us Romans' (Acts 16:21), as they proudly described themselves, were entitled to use Roman law locally, enjoyed certain tax concessions, were granted particular rights in relation to the ownership and transfer of land, as well as other benefits in connection with local administration. These features of Philippian culture were not forgotten by Paul when he wrote to these believers some years later. Using the 'citizenship analogy', Paul urged his friends to conduct themselves 'in a manner worthy of the gospel of Christ' (Phil. 1:27). More accurately, they were to let their life as citizens be worthy of the gospel of Christ. Later in the same letter, he reminded the Philippians that their 'citizenship is in heaven' (Phil. 3:20). They were nothing less than a 'colony of heaven' (Moffat) on earth. None could enjoy higher status or privilege than that. Necessarily, the great privilege carried with it equally great responsibility (Phil. 3:20,21). Thus the colony status of Philippi and the benefits of Roman citizenship provided Paul with a convenient means of cultural identification, as well as a useful framework of thought on which to present his teaching about the Christian's heavenly citizenship.

8. *If the local community is multi-racial and multi-cultural is this reflected in the composition of the church membership?*

9. *If the social or racial composition of the church membership is changing, are the church's 'steersmen' pursuing the appropriate cultural course to take account of this change?*

10. *Does the church's leadership reflect the social and racial composition of the church membership?*

11. *If a minority social or racial group in the local church is growing to become the majority group, are the church's leaders willing to 'dilute their power' by actively encouraging the training and appointment of new leaders from the expanding group?*

12. *Are the church's leaders prepared actively to foster, in the life of the church, a growing reflection of the expanding group's culture, even if this goes against their own personal cultural preferences?*

Questions 8 to 12 are not so straightforward as the first seven questions. However, their application to a local church situation may have a more crucial relevance to the matter of indigenous culture than the earlier questions. In order to make these questions come alive in our own situation we have a most useful biblical precedent by means of which we can illustrate the issues involved.

As the Christian gospel continued to spread throughout various cities of the Roman Empire, this encouraging progress raised certain anxieties in the minds of the more conservative Jewish Christians. Before long there would be more Gentile Christians than Jewish Christians in the world. The Jewish Christians feared that the influx of so many Gentile believers would bring about a weakening of Christian moral standards, and the evidence in Paul's Corinthian correspondence shows that their misgivings were not unfounded.

Although this provoked concern in the more conservative Jewish Christians generally, in a particularly unenviable position were those Jews who shared in the leadership of the church at Corinth. That there were Jews in positions of leadership in the early days at Corinth cannot seriously be doubted. Paul commenced his evangelism at Corinth in the synagogue. The first Corinthian converts were Jews, and a number of them were influential people (Acts 18:7,8). In addition, their spiritual heritage, familiarity with the Scriptures and general moral standards gave them a significant advantage over more recently converted Gentiles, when appointments to positions of leadership were being considered. As the church grew in numbers and the membership became predominantly Gentile, Jews who held positions of leadership were faced with increasingly difficult decisions. Humanly speaking, it would have been understandable if the Jewish leaders and Jewish members had attempted to preserve their particularly Jewish influence as long as possible. Were these leaders not striving to maintain spiritual standards, rather than just impose cultural preferences? Such distinctions are not always easy to define. Inevitably subjective factors are involved. Was the 'I follow Cephas' party at Corinth really engaged in a battle to halt the church's slide towards corrupt pagan behaviour? How did their leaders attempt to face up to hard spiritual facts? Did they come to recognize that a predominantly Gentile church had a right to expect that its life should reflect a predominantly Gentile culture? Whatever those Jewish leaders might have desired for reasons of personal preference, they were nevertheless under spiritual obligation to allow and encourage the church increasingly to reflect Gentile culture.

Culture in a contemporary urban church

Our examination of indigenous culture and the way it affected the New Testament church at Corinth should help us as we now come to look at our urban situation today. The emphasis in that particular study was very much on the ways in which the Corinthian Christians needed to dissociate themselves from the corrupt features of their moral environment, while at the same time reflecting in their church life good and wholesome features of Corinthian life. Our task now is to look at features of British culture as they are reflected in the two social groups which we call 'working class' and 'middle class'. It would be reasonably accurate to speak of the working-class culture as 'urban', and the middle-class culture as 'suburban'. Just in case a reader is under the impression that such cultural distinctions are more imaginary than real we will now look at a table of working-class views and attitudes and how, on the same issues, middle-class views and attitudes have a significantly different outlook.

Table III

	Working-class perspective	**Middle-class perspective**
General beliefs	The social order is divided into 'us' and 'them': those who do not have authority and those who do.	The social order is a hierarchy of differentially rewarded positions, a ladder containing many rungs.
	The division between 'us' and 'them' is virtually fixed, at least from the point of view of one man's life chances.	It is possible for individuals to move from one to another.
	What happens to you depends on a lot of luck; otherwise you have to learn to put up with things.	Those who have ability and initiative can overcome obstacles and create their own opportunities. Where a man ends up depends on what he makes of himself.
General values	'We' ought to stick together and get what we can as a group. You may as well enjoy yourself while you can instead of trying to make yourself a 'cut above the rest'.	Every man ought to make the most of his own capabilities and be responsible for his own welfare. You cannot expect to get anywhere in the world if you squander your time and money. 'Getting on' means making sacrifices.
Attitudes on more specific issues	*On the best job for a son* 'A trade in his hands'; 'A good steady job'.	'As good a start as you can give him'; 'A job that leads somewhere'.
	Towards people needing social assistance 'They have been unlucky.' 'They never had a chance.' 'It could happen to any of us.'	'Many of them had the same opportunities as others who have managed well enough.'

On trade unions

'Trade unions are the only means workers have of protecting themselves and of improving their standard of living.'

'They are a burden on those who are trying to help themselves.'

'Trade unions have too much power in the country.'
'The unions put the interests of a section before the interests of the nation as a whole.'[14]

Testing the phenomena

At various points in the book so far we have had opportunity to look at some of the facets of working-class culture. In the second chapter we made a brief survey of life in a typical inner-city area. The working man's mental processes, his solidarity and his superstitions have already received our attention. Our plan now will be to select a representative number of features of working-class culture, in order to see how far they can and should be reflected in the life of a contemporary urban church. A comprehensive examination of working-class culture is not possible in this present study, nor is it necessary. There is no such thing as a standard description of British working-class culture. The more dominant features will be common to most, if not all, working-class communities; whereas there will inevitably be some regional variations, for example, 'the North' compared with 'the South'.

1. *Solidarity.* This is without question the most evident feature of working-class culture. This contrast between urban and suburban culture is indicated in the general values in the table of class attitudes at Table 3. 'In any discussion of working-class attitudes much is said about the group-sense, that feeling of being not so much an individual with "a way to make" as one of a group whose members are all roughly level and likely to remain so ... Certainly working-class people have a strong sense of being members of a group, and just as certainly that sense involves the assumption that it is important to be friendly, co-operative, neighbourly. "We are all in the same boat"; "it's no use fighting

one another"; but "in unity is strength" ... The sense of a group warmth exercises a powerful hold, and continues to be missed when individuals have moved, financially and probably geographically, out of the working classes.'[15]

This most prominent of all working-class characteristics not only contrasts with the suburban middle-class individualism, it also accords with the New Testament teaching on the nature of the local church. Paul's use of the body analogy to explain the nature of a local church demonstrates the importance of solidarity. The family analogy has its limitations. A family can fragment and yet its individual members will survive. The parts of a human body can only survive as they continue to live within the body. Detachment from the body means the death of that particular member of the body. Solidarity in the local church is imperative for spiritual birth, growth and survival.

This 'group warmth' (to use Hoggart's term) needs to be experienced and expressed at every opportunity in the day-to-day life of the local church. Group activities for Bible study, prayer, fellowship, recreation, etc., are essential if working-class people are to *feel* thoroughly 'at home' in the life of the church. We have also studied the 'group' and its particular suitability for evangelism in the urban areas. A regular church outing, a church week-end away, or a church holiday can all be used to develop and harness the *felt* solidarity for the pursuit of spiritual goals.

For those Christians who have a built-in traditional British reserve, and who mistakenly believe that 'I keep myself to myself' is a Christian virtue, there needs to be reassessment and readjustment. From his wealth of knowledge of various cultures throughout the world, E.A. Nida observes that 'Our incurably individualistic temperaments make us half blind to people as a part of a society. Collectivism in any form becomes for some a mark of Satan.'[16]

Thinking more particularly of culture in the United States, Nida also says that 'Rather than selecting to emphasize social responsibility and community living, we have laid stress on "rugged individualism" and a pattern of dog-eat-dog economic competition, which is no doubt efficient in bringing people more gadgets at less expense, but also brings incomparably more suffering at incalculably greater cost.'[17]

The Scriptures not only teach us that we are members of a

body — the local church, they also teach that we are 'members one of another' (Rom. 12:5). And that means solidarity!

2. *Plain speaking.* 'Calling a spade a spade' is a feature of working-class speech. The language of the inner city lacks finesse, but not vigour. From rhyming slang to the patter of the barrow boys it has a cutting edge blunted elsewhere. The working man says what he thinks and shows what he feels. By contrast, the middle-class suburban dweller will generally speak with more restraint and more courtesy. Where the suburban dweller makes a measured, rational and polite defence of his lack of interest in the Christian faith he may, by choice of words and skill in speaking, foil any attempt to probe further his need to consider the spiritual issues of life. By the manner of his speaking he may appear to wrap himself in a 'crust of courtesy', which proves impossible to penetrate.

This problem of communication is much less in evidence in an urban area: 'Working-class speech and manners in conversation are more abrupt, less provided with emollient phrases than those of other groups: their arguments are often conducted in so rude a way that a stranger might well think that after this, at the worst, fighting would follow, and at best a permanent ending of relations ... Neither the phrasing nor the rhythms of working-class speech have the easing and modified quality which, in varying degrees, is characteristic of other classes. The pattern of their speech follows more closely the pattern of emotions they are feeling at the time ...'[18]

It must be admitted that 'plain speaking' pushed too far can lead to unnecessary and unspiritual coarseness, rudeness and insensitivity. Properly controlled, this aspect of working-class culture can be turned to advantage. Where Christian witness is involved, frankness of expression can pierce the armour of apathy or courtesy.

3. *Family life.* Family life in the inner urban areas has undergone some major changes over the period since the Second World War. In the pre-war years the urban communities knew much poverty and hardship before the advent of slum clearance. In the immediate post-war years the family and community links, which were deepened through the dangers and comradeship of war, remained intact. In spite of poor housing and overcrowding, there were certain qualities in urban family life which were not nearly so evident in the middle-class suburban

communities.

'The most closely-knit type of community is to be found in the lower income groups. This is particularly noticeable in the old urban areas, like Bethnal Green, where families have lived for generations. Peter Townsend found that those he interviewed had "an average of thirteen relatives within a mile and they saw three-quarters of all their children, both married and unmarried, once a week, as many as a third of them every day". There was usually a strong link between mother and daughter, the grandmother being asked for advice on how to run the home and care for the children, and called upon in any emergency. She would look after the children if the mother went to work, and it was usually she who would bring up an illegitimate child. Similarly, the sense of neighbourliness was strong, perhaps because families had to live close together in rooms or cottages, often sharing essential amenities and being intimately aware of what was going on in other families around. Quarrels and feuds might exist, but in time of difficulty it was the neighbours who could be depended upon.'[19]

In many respects urban family life has experienced some major upheavals in the last thirty years. Slum clearance and redevelopment schemes have destroyed the close-knit communities which were once common. The moral conditions in these areas have also contributed to an increasing breakdown of family life. In the mid-seventies the national percentage of illegitimate births was 9%. In our own inner urban area the figure was 21%. The number of one-parent families in the community is still rising. Inner urban areas now have about one family in three which is a one-parent family. Where both parents work, often 'unsocial hours', this places further strains on the family life. There is no way of avoiding the fact that the increasing breakdown of family life is an ominous trend which must eventually undermine the stability of our community and national life. Urban areas today need the kind of teaching Paul gave to the Corinthian believers concerning married life and God's plan for the family unit. Christian families should be like rocks, on and around which a God-fearing community is built. Their strength and stability should be signs of hope amid the shifting sands of our collapsed moral standards.

4. *Natural generosity.* 'There is a generosity, a willingness to help with time and skills, which is lacking in more individualistic

areas. There is a community flavour, a spirit which eliminates the pallid isolation of the suburbs ... There is a love of trading, buying and selling, wheeling and dealing. Street markets are an ineradicable part of the inner-city panorama. There is the tremendous resilience in the face of hardship and disaster whether it emanates from natural disasters or the slings and arrows of outrageous authorities.'[20]

When someone is ill or in trouble, neighbours are quick to rally round to help in any way they can. Several years ago our church vestry was gutted by fire. It was caused by an electrical fault and, thankfully, the remainder of the church building suffered very little damage. Within a few days of the fire, the street traders in 'East Lane market', in which the church stands, presented us with a gift of over £25 which they had collected among themselves to help with the cost of repairs. More recently the market traders organized a collection among their customers for the young policeman from Catford, in South London, who suffered the loss of a hand through handling a parcel bomb. The sum they sent was well in excess of a thousand pounds!

So far in our study we have identified features of working-class culture which ought to be reflected in the life of a church in an urban community. There are, of course, other aspects of working-class culture, which would not be appropriate in the life of the church and these we must avoid. Two examples will illustrate the point.

1. *Non-commitment.* 'One aspect of working-class styles especially important for participation in church life is the widespread resistance to *any* kind of major involvement in voluntary associations, trades unions included. With every step up the status scale active participation in voluntary associations of every kind increases.'[21]

There is something of an enigma here which it is not easy to explain, particularly the working man's attitude to involvement in trade union activities. An attitude of non-commitment to voluntary associations appears to run counter to the cultural phenomenon of solidarity. Why is this so? It is perhaps significant that Roger Lloyd entitles Part One of his book *The Riddle of the Artisan.* It seems that, in part, the key to this issue turns on 'what' or 'who' is trying to gain the working man's allegiance and commitment. Commitment usually involves

Building an indigenous church

loyalty to 'other people' and 'the cause' with which those people are associated. Where there is a call for commitment to those who are included in the category of 'us' (the neighbours, workmates, members of the local tenants' association, etc.), then an attitude of *solidarity* is encouraged. But where there is a call for commitment to those who are included in the category of 'them' (the government, the employers, the church) then an attitude of *suspicion* is provoked. The government, the employers, and the church all have 'power' of authority and control and are suspected of using that power for their own ends, and often at the expense of 'the workers'.

If we reflect on what we have learned about the history of the working classes we shall better understand the attitudes which lie behind this baffling disposition of non-commitment. Roger Lloyd explains this by referring to the intolerable working conditions endured by Liverpool dockers in the early years of this century: 'It cannot be easy for them [the dockers] to give the place in their thoughts which they should to society's need for their work when they remember how little society seemed to mind about the conditions of their work for so many bitter years. It would be strange if a suspicion of all authority and a deeply rooted resentment were not part of the motives that determine the artisan's attitude to life. No doubt it is true that today this attitude is neither reasonable nor reasoned. It is subconscious and the more real for being so.'[22]

2. *Depersonalization.* Christianity holds that in the last analysis it is the person rather than the group or organization that counts and who must receive primary consideration. But one of the devastating effects of our modern social order is the way it *depersonalizes* the individual. A large number of forces in society contribute to this feature of urban culture. Doing a boring and repetitive job on a factory production line; living in a modern high-rise block of flats which has an appearance more like a military barracks or a massive penitentiary with its rows and rows of cells; lacking any sense of personal ambition or identity; feeling (or not feeling) like a number recorded on some vast filing index for 'the masses' — these and more are the sinister forces of our urban organization which reduce the individual person to a 'unit' in the urban process, a 'cog' in an industrial machine.

In this cultural environment the local churches need to be

committed to a policy of *repersonalization*. Through their emphasis on the individual, developing the potential of the group with its warmth and sense of belonging, and by majoring on the quality of personal relationships, urban churches can help to counter this most unattractive feature of modern urban culture.

Steering the church

The role of the 'steersmen' was explained in our look at Corinth and its culture. The 'steersmen' of today's urban churches should aim to apply to their own situations the cultural criteria which we developed earlier in the chapter. To that general approach we need to add some further practical points.

1. It is important that church leaders should possess a clear grasp of the biblical principles involved in the issue of culture. Leaders must be able to define clearly and explain simply what the Scriptures have to say on this topic. This is particularly important for at least two reasons. The first is that there is a need to 'dig' into biblical facts in order to expose and expound the teaching. It is not there on the surface of Scripture staring us in the face! The second reason is that the topic often generates heat in discussion. Some Christians are particularly sensitive when words such as 'class' or 'culture' are used. A good dose of confused thinking added to a similar quantity of personal prejudice is an ideal mixture for verbal dynamite!

2. In the discussion on culture we are to understand that one culture is *different from* another culture. We are *not* saying that one culture is superior to, or inferior to another culture. We must be sure to *believe* it as well as say it. It is not merely a diplomatic comment without substance which can be used as a ploy to defuse any militancy.

3. In our examination of culture and the way it affected the local church at Corinth, we saw that there were particular cultural principles which needed to be applied where the church had different social and racial groups within its membership. The leaders of the church at Corinth had to face some difficult decisions in order to steer the Corinthian church correctly. As the church became predominantly Gentile in its membership, the Jews among the church leaders were required to encourage the development and appointment of new Gentile leaders. In addition to this they were required to allow and encourage the

Building an indigenous church

church progressively to reflect Gentile culture in its life and witness. If this policy had not been followed then the church's witness in Corinth would have been undermined. Nowhere in the New Testament do we read that in response to the Christian gospel the new believer must repent of his sin *and* repent of his culture!

The contemporary parallel with the Corinthian situation can easily be appreciated if we substitute the term 'middle class' for the word 'Jew' and the term 'working class' for the word 'Gentile'. It is more than probable that in many established urban churches today, the leadership will be wholly or mainly middle class. Although these leaders will see their duty as primarily spiritual, their influence will, whether they realize it or not, spill over into the realm of the cultural. If the church is evangelizing as it should, then in time the membership should become predominantly working class. As that trend continues the church leaders will need to encourage the training and appointment of new leaders from the predominant social group.

The leaders must also encourage the church progressively to reflect working-class culture in its life and witness. That obligation may well run counter to some of their personal cultural preferences, but it must not be avoided. If a local church adopts a culture which is not indigenous, then it may appear to their non-Christian neighbours that repentance from sin *and* a turning from local culture are all part of a proper response to the Christian gospel. In addition, a local church which is spiritually and culturally isolated within the community it professes to serve will find that it has added to its problems in evangelism, and has widened the gap between the local Christians and their non-Christian neighbours.

4. Any attempt to move a local church in a new direction culturally could well provoke suspicion and hostility from existing church members. This is where wisdom, and patience and tact are very necessary. The initial action should be to explain the issues clearly, and then to attempt to get the church, at least, to face in the right direction culturally. But we should not be surprised if there is an obvious measure of reluctance to do this. 'It is a well-known fact that those who have changed sides are very intolerant of members of their original group. Consequently, a middle-class church in a working-class area made up of those who have gone up in the world can be very

intolerant of those around with working-class standards.'[23]

The rate of progress in the right direction will largely be determined by the church leaders' ability to lead. How far and how fast will the flock follow? Any suggestions of a 'cultural revolution' could prove counter-productive. People might suspect the church leaders to be more influenced by Chairman Mao than the apostle Paul! A simple and spiritual policy might be 'Start from where you are: move at the speed you can.'

5. Is the matter of culture important or irrelevant? The answer must be 'It depends on who is asking the question.' To many present church members and officers the topic may seem to be 'a lot of fuss about nothing'. 'We've managed to get on all right so far without dabbling in this culture thing. Why start digging it up just now?' Such might be the remarks of a Christian of some years' standing. The crucial question is this: 'How do we know that what is regarded as trivial by a person "on the inside" of the Christian faith is similarly viewed by people "on the outside"?' What to us is trivial may be entirely different to an outsider. It is neither courteous nor Christian to dismiss the matter with the wave of a hand: 'I'm not going to get tangled up in this 'culture' issue. I just want to get on spreading the gospel: no more and no less!'

In his major work *An Introduction to the Science of Missions*, J.H. Bavinck answers the objection we have just anticipated. He says, 'It is possible to have the best intentions and to ignore the cultural possessions of a people, and to preach the gospel pure and simple, without any application to their specific characteristics. History has shown that such a procedure is (also) questionable, for in such instances the missionary supposes that he is simply preaching the gospel in its purity, whereas in fact he is unconsciously propagating his own Western way of thought. Here again theology can offer a corrective criticism, since such a method does not take seriously enough the people to whom one speaks. God, in contrast, takes us, and those to whom we speak, very seriously, and as His ministers we ought to do the same. Abstract, disembodied and history-less sinners do not exist; only very concrete sinners exist, whose sinful life is determined and characterized by all sorts of cultural and historical factors; by poverty, hunger, superstition, traditions, chronic illnesses, tribal morality, and thousands of other things. I must bring the gospel of God's grace in Jesus Christ to the whole man, in his concrete existence, in his everyday environment. It is obviously then a great error on my part if I do not take a person's culture and history seriously.'[24]

We conclude our consideration of the topic of culture with a comment from Dr E.A. Nida. He says, 'If a person is no longer hampered by his cultural pride and by failure to identify himself completely with those to whom he goes with the words of life, he can more fully carry out his divinely ordained mission, in which the message and the man, the Word and the witness, combine to make known the will of God.'[25]

Right about race?

It had not been my intention to introduce this topic into our study. This is not because I rate the subject as unimportant. In fact, the reverse is the case. Such is the importance of this matter, that I believe that it is highly desirable that any theoretical discussion of the issues involved should be realistically supported from adequate experience. I cannot claim to have this level of first-hand experience. This explains my original intention. However, I have had a change of mind. It has only recently occurred to me that the way we have conducted our examination of the Christian responsibility to a *social* class in British society has also produced for us a framework of thinking which can be applied to a *racial* category as well. We are now in a position to take a selection of the principles we have evolved in connection with our 'working-class' study, and to apply them to the subject of race. Our limited objective will be to formulate what we consider to be some of the right questions. That ought to give readers and writer alike clues where to look for the right answers.

On the topic of race and the issues it raises, the following are among the key questions that need to be asked:

1. What do we know about the people who form the racial groups for whom we are concerned? Has there been any attempt to learn more about them from a study of their history or sociology? Is the need to understand their culture clearly recognized? Is there an awareness of the differences between the various ethnic cultures — West Indian, Asian, African, etc.? We need to know

what they think, and *how* they think if we are to communicate effectively to them. (See chapter 3, 'Battle for the mind'.)

2. How do they view the Christian church in this country? How are 'the church' and church-going viewed in their countries of origin?

3. Dimensions of deprivation. In what ways do working-class communities and 'black' communities share a common urban deprivation? Housing, education and employment are just three areas of life in which the more obvious forms of social disadvantages are experienced. Powerlessness, with all its ramifications, is also shared in common with the working classes. (See chapter 2.)

4. Do we practise 'racial discrimination' in our evangelism? If a local church is situated in a multi-racial community, does it pattern its evangelistic outreach bearing in mind the various ethnic groups which comprise the local community? Or is the local church guilty of favouritism because it directs its major gospel endeavours to a minority group in the community who seem to show a more sympathetic attitude towards the gospel? (See chapter 4.)

5. Salvation and solidarity: the influence of 'the group'. What is the social structure of the standard family unit? Is it a nuclear family, or an extended family? We speak of racial solidarity. Is there a family solidarity? How does their racial solidarity compare or contrast with 'working-class' solidarity? In what ways should such knowledge have a bearing on the forms of evangelism that we use? (See chapter 5.)

6. How important is the small 'group' as a context for the spiritual nurture of new converts? Is this form of teaching method important for the continuing spiritual growth of the whole church family?

7. If a local church congregation is multi-racial, in what ways can and should its worship reflect a multi-cultural influence?

8. Does the church's leadership reflect the racial composition of the church membership? Is this seen as a necessary 'biblical goal' towards which the local church ought to work? (See chapter 8.)

9. Has the local church been adequately instructed in what the Scriptures have to say about 'race'? Have the weeds of ignorance, prejudice and fear been successfully uprooted? Has the good seed of God's Word and its teaching on race been correctly expounded and practically applied?

10. In what ways can Christians work for social justice in the deprived local communities?

Home-grown leaders

The doctrine of the Christian ministry is a subject of great importance. It has a very direct bearing on the spiritual health and usefulness of a local church. One section of a single chapter in the book restricts very much the scope of what we can look at in the present context. An examination of the terminology used in the New Testament, a consideration of the qualifications, duties, training and appointment of church leaders are all topics of great interest, but they must be excluded from the scope of our present study. For an adequate treatment of the biblical doctrine of the Christian ministry, specialist theological works should be consulted.[26]

The application of the New Testament teaching to urban situations in particular will mean that we ought to focus on two clear principles which we derive from the New Testament. First, we need to see why the leaders should be 'from within' the local churches they serve, and secondly, why there should be a number of leaders sharing the work as a team, rather than the solitary 'multi-gifted' 'professional' pastor. Although the New Testament uses a variety of terms to describe the leaders of local churches, there is good evidence to show that the terms 'elder', 'bishop', 'pastor' and 'leader' are virtually synonymous. In the context of this study that is how we will regard the terms. After a discussion on the training of Christian leaders, our main exercise will be to demonstrate the benefits a church derives from having a team of spiritual leaders, rather than the traditional 'lone' pastor.

The New Testament knows nothing of a 'one-pastor' church where the leader is imported into the local situation for a number of years and then moves on to another local church. In the early church, men were *selected from* a local church, *trained within* that local church, and then called to the *service of that local church*. An apprentice-trained, non-mobile, indigenous team of local church leaders may be new to our thinking, but it is possible to show that this policy is soundly biblical and eminently practical. Here are some of the reasons.

1. Based upon the evidence available to us, we can claim that this was the common pattern of leadership in the local churches of the New Testament period (Acts 14:23; 20:17; Phil. 1:1).

2. Local training enables the local congregation to take much more seriously their duty to assess a potential leader's personal spiritual maturity and domestic godliness, as well as spiritual gift. The present pattern of a mobile ministry makes it difficult, if not impossible, to get to know 'the man himself' and not only his gift which is evident in the conduct of worship and preaching (1 Tim. 3:1-7; Titus 1:5-9). In certain respects, the settlement of a minister in a particular pastorate is something like a marriage. After due consideration, followed by proposal and acceptance, pastor and people come together in a new relationship. But there is a glaring weakness in the preparation for this particular kind of marriage — there is no provision for a *realistic* courtship!

3. Where an elder has been trained and appointed in a local situation, the respect and esteem which Scripture requires believers to show towards their leaders is earned and not just demanded by virtue of the office to which the man has been appointed (1 Thess. 5:12; Heb. 13:17).

4. Jesus said, 'I am the good shepherd; I know my sheep and my sheep know me' (John 10:14). Local leaders are able to apply their teaching and pastoral care to a people they already know. It should meet their particular needs and condition. Where a pastor has been 'called into' a local situation both sheep and shepherd will take some time to get to know each other before there can be teaching and pastoral counsel based upon intimate knowledge and understanding of the individual needs of the members of the local flock.

5. Local selection and training makes possible a much greater flexibility in terms of field of selection, and duration and style of training. A local apprenticeship allows the scheme of training to take into account a man's individual abilities, his past experience, his rate of learning, his domestic circumstances. It should enable working-class churches to have working-class leaders. The pace and level of teaching and training can be flexible enough to suit their particular requirements and abilities.

6. By focusing the training within the local situation, both for the full-time elder and for those who pursue other secular

occupations, it is possible to work to overcome the artificial and unbiblical distinction between 'clergy' and 'laity', 'minister' and 'laymen'. The New Testament knows nothing of a hierarchical government *over* a number of churches. In addition, within the local church there is parity of leadership. The full-time elder does not hold a status above those church leaders who serve with him in the team of elders.

It is important to realize that the pattern of local church leadership we are advocating not only involves a return to what we claim is the New Testament pattern; it is, in many respects, a return to the pattern of ministry which was in force in the early industrial period following in the wake of the Evangelical Awakening of the eighteenth century. Regrettably, various social and spiritual influences were operating to carry the churches away from that pattern of ministry. In the early years of the nineteenth century, churches were generally 'outward-looking' and ministers were chiefly involved in equipping and mobilizing the believers to carry the gospel forward on a wide front. But with the passing of the years the evangelistic zeal cooled. There was a trend towards ministerial professionalism. Ministers became 'specialists' in particular areas of teaching and pastoral work. Ordinary church members found their scope for Christian service more limited, yet they were apparently ready to accept these changed roles without protest. This in turn led to 'introverted evangelism' which served to accentuate further the gulf between the local churches and their non-Christian working-class neighbours, as we discussed more fully in chapter 2. This is much the pattern of ministry we have inherited from our forefathers. We must now reverse the trend of the mid-nineteenth century and return to a biblical order.

If this pattern of local church leadership is more in line with the New Testament practice than that which we currently employ, then we ought to do something about it. Right biblical views of local church leadership are not optional extras. However, I would not be surprised to see resistance to this kind of change. Churches may well prefer to stay as they are. And so might some pastors! To train local men to do the kind of work that he, as pastor, has till now regarded as his own particular responsibility may seem to him to pave the way for his own redundancy! In order to dispel fear, caution or prejudice, we now move to consider the positive benefits of having an indigenous team of elders.

Plurality of indigenous leaders

I must confess that I am puzzled. Why is it that some Christians, who regard the Scriptures as fully authoritative on the subject of salvation, appear to regard them as less than authoritative on the matter of local church government? It must be admitted that there are aspects of this doctrine which provoke debate and controversy. The need for a plurality of leaders in the local church, however, does not seem to be a matter in question. The following Scriptures all point to a plurality of elders in local churches: Acts 14:23; 11:30; 20:17; James 5:14; 1 Peter 5:1, and there are others.

The reasons why a number of elders are appointed to serve in one church is quite simply that the work is more than one elder can do. His time, his gifts, his knowledge, his experience are all limited. He is not a spiritual superman! Moses found his task of leading God's people was more than he could cope with single-handed. He said to the Lord, 'I cannot carry all these people by myself; the burden is too heavy for me' (Num. 11:14). God's solution for Moses' dilemma was the appointment of an eldership to share in the task of leadership. God said, 'They will help you carry the burden of the people so that you will not have to carry it alone' (Num. 11:17). It is true that the flock Moses led was considerably larger than even the most numerically prosperous of our urban churches today, but the principle remains the same. Leading God's people is a responsibility that no man should be called to bear on his own. He needs fellowship in leadership.

According to New Testament practice the elders selected *from* a local church were appointed *for* that local church. The New Testament pattern of pastoral leadership among the churches did not envisage 'imported' elders who would serve for a number of years, few or many, and then move on to another local church. This inherited pattern is a departure from the New Testament norm. But is it really necessary that the elders should be indigenous? Provided that they have the biblical qualifications is that not all that really matters?

Apart from the fact that it is the biblical pattern that a local church should have indigenous leaders, there is also a further important reason in the case of local churches situated in

Building an indigenous church

working-class communities. In our sociological study much earlier in the book we looked at certain features of urban life. The topic of 'Power and the professionals' is of particular relevance to the issue we are now considering although it may not immediately be obvious why this is so. We must explain. Within the structure of urban local government, the positions of power and influence would, as in other communities, be held by men who are professionally qualified and adequately experienced in their own particular skills. But people possessing their kind of status and earning their kind of salary would almost certainly not live within the community which is the particular concern of their daily occupation. They would be residents from the 'commuter belt'. Their daily decisions in the course of their work would have a direct bearing on the quality of life in the urban area, but they themselves would not be directly affected by their own decisions. Understandably, residents in the urban community who fail to have their grievances heard, their requests dealt with, or necessary amenities provided, will find it all too easy to say, 'It's all right for them. They don't have to live here.' Power over the affairs of the community is seen to be in the hands of people who are not part of that community, and that can be resented.

If the 'power structure' in the community is also mirrored in the leadership of the local church there can be a 'gap' between those who do the leading and those who are led. It is still common for a pastor and some, if not all, of his elders and deacons to live where there is suitable private housing some miles away from the church premises. They journey into the urban area, render their Christian service within the life of the church, and then journey home again. Many urban churches still rely very much on commuting leaders. Without their service it is probable that a good number of these churches would be unable to continue their work. But there are major disadvantages. These leaders are not part of the local community and their Christian lives are not *seen* by the people who most need to *see* what a genuine Christian life is like. In their responsibility to live consistent Christian lives, they may not come up against the same kind of problems that believers might face in an urban area. A response to certain teachings and exhortations from the leaders might be 'It's all right for you. You don't have to live here!'

In order to bring salvation to us, Jesus exchanged the 'sapphire-paved courts for stable floor'. He left the glory of heaven to be born and grow up in a carpenter's family. He is able to sympathize with our weaknesses because he has been tempted in every way, just as we are. He has been identified with us. No one could say of Jesus, 'It's all right for him. He hasn't had to live here.' He has! He became like us, in human flesh, so that he could 'pitch his tent' (John 1:14) among us, and then die for us. Because of this we can with great confidence approach Him with our fears and failings and know that He will understand. For the same kind of reasons, local churches in urban areas need an indigenous leadership, people who share a common life with the people they lead.

'You couldn't be a Christian and live in this block,' said Ron and Lil to me one evening. Lil openly confessed that part of her problem was that she could not help hating some of her neighbours who lived in that block. I knew what she meant. They lived in a decaying tenement long overdue for demolition. Among their neighbours were more than a fair share of the community's crooks, layabouts and scroungers. I had no easy answers. I did not live where they lived. For Ron and Lil being a real Christian was a non-starter in that kind of environment. A sympathetic and realistic answer to their objection needed to come from one who was more fully identified with them. It is highly unlikely that God will expect leaders of urban churches today to live in condemned slum tenements. But at least they need to be part of the local urban community.

Diversity of spiritual gifts

Although the qualifications for elders are quite specific, men appointed to this ministry will still exhibit a variety of gifts. All elders will share in the teaching; all elders will share in the pastoral oversight. But some men will be more gifted teachers than others; some men will be more gifted in pastoral care than others. Some elders will be gifted preachers, while others will not. Not only do skills differ, but so also does experience. Senior elders will provide inspiration and example not only to the flock in general, but also to their more recently appointed colleagues in the eldership.

We have already shown that New Testament churches knew nothing of the 'omni-gifted' pastor. But is the biblical alternative realistic? All elders are to have ability to teach. This is according to the qualifications set out in 1 Timothy 3:2. But is that not expecting too much? It depends what we have as our idea of a biblical teaching ministry. If we regard the full-time pastor as a man 'professionally' qualified and gifted to do his job, it may mean that we view the elders who serve with him as 'amateurs' doing their best in terms of sincerity and enthusiasm but lacking the gifts and skills of the 'professional'. We need deliberately to turn away from the inherited pattern of pastoral ministry and turn to what we have called an 'all-round teaching ministry', as we considered it in detail in chapter 7. There we saw a much greater variety of teaching roles demanding a greater variety of teaching gifts. One elder may have little gift for public preaching, but he may be excellent in catechetical instruction. Another elder may find it hard going to prepare and deliver a detailed discourse on a controversial doctrine, but he may find great opportunity for his gifts in leading 'an experience meeting'.

A specific distinction in gifts and teaching roles is explicitly stated in 1 Timothy 5:17. There Paul makes reference to those whose daily work is 'preaching and teaching'. Such men are what we usually call 'full-time' pastors or elders. They are entitled by their calling to be supported financially by the church they serve. Apart from the blessings of fellowship in leadership, there are other good reasons why a full-time pastor needs to have a team of godly elders working with him. The full-time pastor is in the privileged position of being able to devote himself wholly to the work of the ministry. But in so doing he will to some extent be shielded from the sharp edge of hostility or ridicule, temptation or persecution that members of his flock may encounter in the pursuit of their daily work. The elders who continue their secular employment, while at the same time exercising pastoral oversight in the church, will be able to make sure that the full-time elder does relate his teaching to the realities of the working world today, and not just to the 'working world' as he sees it from his somewhat sheltered position.

Continuity of biblical teaching

We have already highlighted some of the defects of the pattern of pastoral ministry that we have inherited. A further defect concerns the problem of discontinuity in teaching. Between the going of one pastor and the coming of the next, the church will be without its own qualified and recognized teacher. During the interregnum deacons do their best to maintain the teaching of the church by a careful choice of visiting preachers and perhaps, on occasions, by taking some part in the pulpit ministry themselves. These efforts, though commendable, present a pattern which is less than biblical. Where a local church has an eldership, the responsibility for continuity of teaching rests with a number of men and not with one individual pastor. Although Timothy was 'imported' into a New Testament pastoral situation, it is clear that the apostle Paul wanted this young preacher to make proper provision for continuity of teaching. Paul instructed Timothy, 'The things you have heard me say in the presence of many witnesses entrust to reliable men who will also be qualified to teach others' (2 Tim. 2:2). A plurality of elders within a local church is the biblical pattern for preserving continuity of teaching. This spiritual objective should be our goal, whether or not we continue to seek 'imported' full-time pastors.

A reservoir of corporate wisdom

When King David died, his son Solomon came to the throne. Upon him was placed the awesome responsibility of leading God's people in God's ways. Aware of his own inadequacy for the task, he prayed to God that he might be equipped with divine wisdom. It was a prayer that greatly pleased the Lord: ' "Now, O Lord my God, you have made your servant king in place of my father David. But I am only a little child and do not know how to carry out my duties. Your servant is here among the people you have chosen, a great people, too numerous to count or number. So give your servant a discerning heart to govern your people and to distinguish between right and wrong, for who is able to govern this great people of yours?"

'The Lord was pleased that Solomon had asked for this. So God said to him, "Since you have asked for this and not for long life or wealth for yourself, nor have asked for the death of your enemies but for discernment in administering justice, I will do what you have asked. I will give you a wise and discerning heart, so that there will never have been anyone like you, nor will there ever be" '(1 Kings 3:7-12).

Building an indigenous church

If Solomon was acutely aware of his need for divine wisdom in order to lead God's people aright, surely the need for the same kind of divine enabling should be recognized by those who are called to lead God's people today. The task of the elders in a local church is not just to be ever increasing in Bible knowledge so that they can impart this knowledge to those whom they lead. Knowledge is very important, but it is not to be equated with wisdom. Wisdom goes beyond knowledge. Knowledge may comprise an accumulation of facts, and points to an intellectual skill and discipline. Wisdom has application in a moral dimension. Knowledge may be largely a mental relationship with 'facts'. Wisdom is concerned about a heart relationship with people. 'The fear of the Lord is the beginning of wisdom, and knowledge of the Holy One is understanding' (Prov. 9:10). This reverential and submissive relationship with God Himself brings with it the necessary 'relationship skills' we shall need to show towards our fellow men. 'I, wisdom, dwell together with prudence; I possess knowledge and discretion' (Prov. 8:12). In his New Testament letter, James expands that description of divine wisdom. He says, 'The wisdom that comes from heaven is first of all pure; then peace-loving, considerate, submissive, full of mercy and good fruit, impartial and sincere' (James 3:17). Heavenly wisdom is not to be viewed as the sum of human wisdom multiplied many times over. 'Has not God made foolish the wisdom of the world?' (1 Cor. 1:20.) 'For the foolishness of God is wiser than man's wisdom' (1 Cor.1:25.) The wisdom of God is altogether different from the wisdom of this world, both in quantity and in quality. 'Oh, the depth of the riches of the wisdom and knowledge of God! How unsearchable his judgements, and his paths beyond tracing out!' (Rom. 11:33.)

To whom is this wisdom available? On what conditions is it to be received? 'If *any of you* lacks wisdom, he should ask God, who gives generously to all without finding fault; and it will be given to him' (James 1:5.) It is interesting to note that the seven men appointed for the daily distribution of food among the widows in the church at Jerusalem were required to be men who were 'full of the Spirit and wisdom' (Acts 6:1-7). It was some measure of indiscretion or inefficiency on the part of the apostles which precipitated the selection of these seven men for their administrative task. The Grecian widows had complained of neglect. Appropriate action was required to deal with the grievance and prevent its recurrence. The men appointed for this task had to be men who commanded the confidence of the people. They had to be men competent in administration and also qualified to deal wisely with a situation in which there were such delicate human susceptibilities to consider. If the spiritual asset of wisdom was necessary for those engaged in 'deacon' work, it is certainly no less necessary for those who are charged with the oversight of the flock of Christ.

In his pastoral and preaching work does an elder need to share with his fellow elders matters requiring discernment and decision? If he has sought wisdom from the Lord, is there any need to consult fellow elders? If he feels the need to do so, does it point to a weakness — indecision and uncertainty — in a man who should be a leader of God's people? Some verses from the Book of Proverbs (part of the 'Wisdom Literature' of the Old Testament) provide an answer to our question: 'The way of a fool seems right to him, but a wise man listens to advice' (Prov. 12:15). 'Instruct a wise man and he will be wiser still' (Prov. 9:9). 'Plans fail for lack of counsel, but with many advisers they succeed' (Prov. 15:22). Certainly there is indecision in an elder if he never makes any decisions without consulting his colleagues. On the other hand, the verses from the Book of Proverbs point to the fact that an evidence of a person's spiritual wisdom is, in the first place, his readiness to listen to advice rather than his ability to give it. Every under-shepherd will know of those difficult and delicate pastoral issues in which he greatly values the counsel and encouragement of colleagues who have mature spiritual discernment. As an under-shepherd expresses his pastoral care in a particular situation, it is not always easy for him to discern whether he is being biblically firm or unwisely harsh, whether his approach demonstrates spiritual gentleness or unspiritual compromise. A good leader must be neither arrogant nor impetuous. He must be humble enough to seek and receive advice. He must be sensible enough to think before he speaks and not speak before he thinks! In that case, every leader needs to pray the words of Solomon: 'So give your servant a discerning heart to govern your people and to distinguish between right and wrong.'

Preservation of spiritual unity

We have already discussed in detail the place and the potential of the Christian home in the day-to-day life of a local church. We saw that the home has a vital role to play in the matter of evangelism. The small group of people meeting in a Christian home provides the working man with a 'family' to which he can belong, which meets regularly, where every member matters, where people are missed if they are not there, where every member can receive and give, where no issues of status or rank intrude, where there is a realistic opportunity for members of the group to get to know all other members of the group, where friendships deepen, and where joys and sorrows can be shared. We have also seen that the Wesleyan class meeting and the Welsh Calvinistic Methodist's 'experience meeting' proved to be most useful instruments for the developing and monitoring of spiritual growth.

This range of benefits gained through group gatherings clearly made a major contribution to the spiritual life and health of the New Testament churches. The early church did not have church buildings in which they could meet. Necessarily, their homes assumed a greater importance in their daily Christian life and witness than is the case today. Further, it is possible to identify certain aspects of the life of a local church which may be more conveniently expressed and cultivated in the informal home setting rather than in the formal setting of services and meetings in a church building. The words 'one another' which occur in a number of New Testament exhortations point to the kind of spiritual interchange which promotes and deepens the experience of Christian fellowship. We shall mention just two examples, but there are others as well. 'Let the word of Christ dwell in you richly as you teach and admonish *one another* with all wisdom, and as you sing psalms, hymns and spiritual songs with gratitude in your hearts to God' (Col. 3:16). 'Let us consider how we may spur *one another* on towards love and good deeds. Let us not give up meeting together, as some are in the habit of doing, but let us encourage *one another* — and all the more as you see the Day approaching' (Heb. 10:24,25).

Although the advantages of using the Christian home in the daily life and witness of the church far outweigh any disadvantages which we may experience, we ought to consider where and when our adversary might choose to disrupt and damage the spiritual progress of these groups. It not infrequently happens that some who share in the home group gatherings prefer the informal atmosphere of these meetings to the formal services in the church building. Where there is inadequate supervision of these home gatherings there can be a trend which transfers first loyalty to the home group and away from the church family as a whole. Some groups may then become, by design or accident, splinter groups or pressure groups, creating a divisive spirit in the church. Remember Corinth! There were quarrels among the various groups or cliques that had formed there. One group said, ' "I follow Paul"; another, "I follow Apollos"; another, "I follow Cephas"; still another, "I follow Christ"' (1 Cor. 1:12). Paul did not mince his words in condemning this unspiritual behaviour which dishonoured the name of Christ.

If the seeds of division are being sown in group gatherings, what is the Christian leader to do? He knows that any attempt to place a ban on home meetings would not be the best solution. There is so much spiritual good which can be gained from these groups. What is God's answer for counteracting any divisive tendencies which may occur? It is a team of godly elders. When Paul gathered together the elders of the Ephesian church at Miletus, among the many things which Paul said he gave a clear indication that divisive influences *would* come. He said, 'Even from your own number will men arise and distort the truth in order to draw away disciples after them' (Acts 20:30). This threat to the unity of the Ephesian church could not have been put more plainly. It was the task of the elders to do all within their power to prevent, rather than cure such a spiritual disaster.

If the various groups that meet are under the general supervision of elders this will exert a unifying influence. This is not to say that every time the group meets it must be led by an elder. There will be times when another member of the group, possibly a potential future leader, will conduct the study and discussion. The elder may be present to observe and advise. He is not there to dominate the proceedings, nor to clamp down on free speech. He is not there as a 'spiritual bugging-device' to detect spiritual militants who want to revolutionize the church! He is in the group to provide mature spiritual counsel. He is also there as one to whom God has entrusted authority within the local church. Should it prove necessary, he is there to curb and correct any fragmenting ideas and influences which may appear. As an under-shepherd he is there to see that God's flock is led 'in paths of righteousness, *for his name's sake*'.

Promotion of pastoral efficiency

What level of pastoral care can the members of a local church expect from their pastor? There is no easy answer to that question. The answer *must* begin with the words: 'It all depends ...' It all depends on the number of people in the church membership, the time the pastor has to allocate to the preparation of sermons and Bible studies, his spiritual zeal, his physical energy, the importance he places on the pastoral care of the individual, whether his spiritual gift is more or less in pastoral work than preaching. There are other factors as well. It is probable that in his mind a pastor gives assent to a certain level of pastoral care as the biblical ideal, but at the same time he may confess that with the distribution of his time and energy as it is at present he sees no real way of achieving the ideal in practice. If there is any aspect of church life which demands a plurality of elders, rather than the 'one elder' church it is in the matter of pastoral care.

If the members of a local church were allocated to a number of home group gatherings, as we considered them just now, and if these gatherings were ordered in programme and purpose much as Wesley organized the Methodist class meetings this would provide a very efficient method of pastoral care. It is worth repeating Wesley's 'job description' of the class leader: 'It is the business of a Leader, (1) to see each person in his class, once a week at the least, in order to enquire how their souls prosper; to advise, reprove, comfort, or exhort, as occasion may require; to receive what they are willing to give, toward the relief of the poor. (2) To meet the Minister and Stewards of the society, in order to inform the Minister of any that are sick, or of any that are disorderly and will not be reproved; to pay to the Stewards what they have received of their several classes in the week preceding.'[28]

If 'efficiency' in pastoral care is a desirable and God-honouring achievement it is doubtful whether this can be attained without the aid of some method or plan. It is here that John Wesley gives us an example well worth considering and adapting to suit the needs of our own local church.

Development of Christian maturity

There are three ways in which a team of elders will contribute to the developing maturity of a local church. In their preparation, appointment and exercise of their ministry they will promote spiritual growth in the church. The apostle Paul commends those who aspire to the work of eldership. 'Here is a trustworthy saying: If anyone sets his heart on being an overseer, he desires a noble task' (1 Tim. 3:1). The word Paul uses here, which has been rendered 'sets his heart on', means literally 'to reach forward to', 'to stretch oneself out'. It is more than wishful thinking. It carries the idea of a strong inward aspiration expressing itself in a determined application to achieving the thing desired. As men consciously prepare themselves for this pastoral office by endeavouring to attain those biblical qualifications laid down, they will necessarily advance their own spiritual growth. This in itself will contribute to the developing maturity of the church.

Secondly, the responsibility for ratifying appointments to the office of elder rests with the local church. When the serving elders bring the names of prospective elders to the church meetings for their appointment to be ratified, this must be no mere formality. The church meeting is not designed to be a rubber stamp of decisions already taken by the elders. The clear approval of the entire membership is what is most desirable. When a church meeting ratifies appointments to the office of elder it is saying that these men, now appointed, are recognized to be 'over them in the Lord'; from now on they are men who have the heavy responsibility of 'watching over' the souls committed to their charge.

It may be argued that we cannot expect every member of a local church to understand the requirements of spiritual leadership. Some of the members may still be spiritual infants. Necessarily they will need to look for guidance to those of maturer years. What we are seeking to emphasize here is that according to the New Testament it is a local church, and not a committee of theological experts, which approves the appointment of the elders. They are chosen *from* a local church, *by* that local church, *for* service in that local church. Where the procedure of Scripture is followed it will demand of, and develop in, the local church a greater spiritual maturity. The believers will need to be instructed carefully on this matter so that their action in ratifying the appointment of these men will be meaningful and whole-hearted. In one sense it may seem strange that the whole church should be required to assess and appoint those to whom is committed the rule of pastoral oversight. The workers on the 'shop floor' are not usually asked to approve the appointment of the new Chief Executive! But it is clear that here as elsewhere the Holy Spirit does empower a local assembly of believers to discern those whom God has equipped and called to a particular form of Christian service (See Acts 6:3-6; Acts 13:2).

Thirdly, the exercise of the ministry of elders is specifically designed to promote healthy growth towards spiritual maturity. Elders are the 'pastors and teachers' (Eph. 4:11) in the local church and their ministry is 'to prepare God's people for works of service, so that the body of Christ may be built up until we all reach unity in the faith and in the knowledge of the Son of God and become mature, attaining to the whole measure of the fulness of Christ' (Eph. 4:12,13).

A ministry of mutual encouragement

A shepherd leads his sheep, but who leads the shepherd? A shepherd guards his sheep, but who guards the shepherd? At times, a shepherd needs to restrain his sheep from wandering away. But who will do the same for the shepherd? Every elder or pastor whom Christ has appointed for service in His church is himself in need of pastoral care. A pastor is both shepherd and sheep! The pastor who is the lone elder in a company of believers is vulnerable to Satan's assaults aimed to exploit isolation and to promote discouragement.

When Moses was called by God to hand on his leadership task to Joshua, God explained how the new leader should be treated. 'But your assistant, Joshua son of Nun, will enter it. *Encourage* him, because he will lead Israel to inherit it' (Deut. 1:38). In the New Testament we learn that the Holy Spirit, the divine Paraclete, is by definition 'the Encourager' (John 14:16,26). The Scriptures were given for a similar purpose: 'For everything that was written in the past was written to teach us, so that through endurance and encouragement of the Scriptures we might have hope' (Romans 15:4). The apostle Paul explains to his friends at Corinth the sources of his own encouragement. He says, 'Since through God's mercy we have this ministry, we do not lose heart' (2 Cor. 4:1). Although the immediate outlook for the Christian presents various problems and trials, we can be sure that ultimately God will have the last word, and His purposes will come to pass. 'Therefore we do not lose heart. Though outwardly we are wasting away, yet inwardly we are being renewed day by day. For our light and momentary troubles are achieving for us an eternal glory that far outweighs them all'(2 Cor. 4:16,17).

In one sense, this need for a ministry of mutual encouragement is a matter of simple arithmetic. What one cannot do, a minimum of two can. That is how the author of Ecclesiastes saw it: 'Two are better than one, because they have a good return for their work'; if one falls down, his friend can help him up. But pity the man who falls and has no one to help him up! Also, if two lie down together they will keep warm. But how can one keep warm alone? Though one may be overpowered, two can defend themselves. A cord of three strands is not quickly broken' (Eccl. 4:9-12).

These words of wisdom from 'the Preacher' can most fittingly be applied to the particular needs of leaders of local churches. If the lone pastor does 'fall down', who will help him up? He may fall down through physical fatigue, mental staleness, spiritual indiscipline, criticism, compromise, depression or a host of other trials and temptations, but who will 'restore his soul and lead him in the paths of righteousness'? At times the dangers may be unavoidable, but the cost can be dear. Who would have expected Elijah, the hero of Carmel, to become a whimpering fugitive fearful of the threat of a pagan queen? But Elijah was exhausted, his defences were down, he was caught unprepared, and he stood alone. Satan detonated his fiery darts of depression and discouragement and scored a direct hit. Elijah's pitiful cry, 'I am the only one left,' explains why the valiant prophet had become the crushed coward. It is true that there were still seven thousand in Israel who had not turned to Baal, but they were unaware of Elijah's crisis, and he did not know about them. The lonely prophet was an easy target for the enemy of souls. It is true that Elijah was a prophet and not a pastor, but they face a common enemy and can expect a similar kind of treatment. We are not ignorant of Satan's devices. If all members of a local church need continually to 'spur one another on towards love and good deeds' and to 'encourage one another' (Heb. 10:24,25) then it becomes doubly important for those who lead God's people. Our adversary knows: 'Smite the shepherd and the sheep will be scattered.' He has done it before (Matt. 26:31). He will try to do it again.

9.
Salt where it counts

'You are the salt of the earth' (Matt. 5:13). So said Jesus in His sermon on the mount. Few would challenge the view that Jesus is here describing the effect that Christians ought to have on the society of which they are members.[1] Food has a tendency to decay. This happens naturally. But salt has chemical properties which can arrest the rate of decay. Applied to such food as meat or fish, the salt will act as a preservative. Of course, in a day of refrigerators and freezers we do not appreciate the value of salt and what it can do for our food. A secondary property of salt is its ability to bring out the flavour of the commodity being preserved. It improves the taste, and brings out the best in the food to which it is applied. What salt does for food, Christians must do for society. This is the significance of the analogy Jesus selected. Society has a natural tendency to decay. Not only are people themselves stained and bent by sin, but the environment in which we live is bound up in this corrupting process (Rom. 8:18-23). Christians are to exercise a restraining influence on the advancement of evil. By their holy lives they, along with other instruments of God's common grace — the state, the law, the family, providence, etc. — will slow down the corrupting influence of sin.

The subject which we have begun to examine here is usually described as the Christian's 'involvement' in society. It is evident that this is a very popular subject among Christian authors at the present time. There must be reasons for this. But what are they? There are big changes taking place in society at the present time: and the rate of change is accelerating.

In the introduction to his book *The Christian in Industrial Society*, Sir Frederick Catherwood describes various changes that have come about in our society over the past one hundred years. He says, 'Society has changed out of all recognition since Christianity attained its last peak of power and influence about a hundred years ago. It has changed radically even since the present pattern of theological positions, parties and movements became established round about the turn of the century. The old social pattern centred round the local community. Half the population a century ago was still agricultural and even the industrial population of a particular town would have been, for the most part, more stable than it is today. More likely than not, people would have lived in the same surroundings and among the same neighbours for most of their lives. Today, the majority of the population of Britain are townsmen, and of these the majority live in huge impersonal conurbations, whose millions scarcely know their neighbours or their workmates. They may change their neighbourhood a number of times in a lifetime and their job a good deal more often. This is the age of a society that is increasingly nomadic and atomized and where even the basic unit of society, the family, is in increasing danger of being split up. There have been many instruments of this change, but the greatest single cause must surely be the power of industrialization which has loosened the narrow confines of traditional society.'[2]

How are the Christian and the church to relate to a nation in industrial upheaval, social flux and moral confusion? What does the Scripture say? Christians are not unanimous in their answer. Among the churches there are a wide variety of views concerning the origin, nature and purpose of Scripture. Consequently, a wide variety of remedies are proposed for the ills of our society. If we are to honour God in this aspect of our Christian living we shall need to give careful thought and prayer so that we shall 'rightly handle the word of truth' (2 Tim. 2:15).

The scope and purpose of this final aspect of our study do not permit us to explore the subject in depth. We shall have to leave some of the more complex and controversial issues unconsidered. Although the biblical teaching of the Christian's involvement in society applies to all believers, irrespective of class, there are some particular reasons why working-class

Christians living in working-class communities should take special note.

To justify this claim we shall need to refer to the context in which Jesus introduced His description of Christians as the 'salt of the earth'. At the beginning of the sermon on the mount, Jesus spoke first about the character of the Christian in that series of 'sayings' which we know as 'the beatitudes' (Matt. 5:1-12). Immediately following that, Jesus went on to explain what effects the lives of Christians should have on the society of which they are part. Jesus said, 'You are the salt of the earth. But if the salt loses its saltiness, how can it be made salty again? It is no longer good for anything, except to be thrown out and trampled by men. You are the light of the world. A city on a hill cannot be hidden. Neither do people light a lamp and put it under a bowl. Instead they put it on its stand, and it gives light to everyone in the house. In the same way, let your light shine before men, that they may see your good deeds and praise your Father in heaven' (Matt. 5:13-16).

In the third chapter of this book we looked at the 'battle for the mind'. We examined some of the content and mental processes of the 'working-class mind'. There are two points to be noted from that chapter which have a direct bearing on the topic we are now considering. We discovered that the average working man 'thinks visually', that is, he grasps facts which are presented to him in concrete terms. It does not come easily to him to think in conceptual and abstract terms. What he *sees* with his eyes, or by his imagination, makes an impact on his thinking. Jesus points to the impact that a *visible* Christian life can have on the unbelievers: 'Let your light shine before men, that they may *see* your good deeds and praise your Father in heaven.' Such is the potential of this form of 'visual persuasion' that unbelievers will not only 'sit up and take notice'; they will go so far as to 'praise your Father in heaven'.

We know *how* the working man thinks. We also know *what* he thinks about Christianity. For him Christianity is largely irrelevant. It appears to have little or nothing to do with the ordinary business of day-to-day living. It is assumed that a working man who goes to church on Sunday, and then is at the factory bench on Monday morning, will find himself living in 'two different worlds'. The general impression of 'church' is of a place where people talk a lot of unintelligible and irrelevant *words*, whereas in the factory the next day the working man and his fellow workers are engaged in meaningful and important *deeds* — making 'things', which will continue to improve the material comfort of their living. How will the working man be convinced that being a Christian involves both words and deeds, and leads to relevant and practical actions?

Jesus tells us that if we function correctly as 'salt and light' in society then people will take notice of our *good deeds*. Again, we must say, in keeping with what Jesus claimed, that such is the potential of these *deeds* that not only will people have their ignorance, prejudice and other false notions of Christianity undermined, but they will go so far as to 'praise your Father in heaven'. The relevance of the Christian faith for seven days a week will become plain. Jesus indicates that biblically ordered involvement in society has some most welcome repercussions for the church's work of evangelism. Of course, it needs to be said that good deeds must spring from right motives. The Christian will not be advertising himself through these deeds. Any temptation to seek personal glory is strongly condemned by Jesus in Matthew 6:1. Nor must the Christian do his good deeds primarily as a bridge for more effective evangelism. Good deeds are to be performed because the Bible teaches us that this is the way to 'love our neighbour', as we are required to do. We are to do our good deeds because they bring needed help and pleasure to those towards whom our Christian love is directed. The fact that there is a spin-off for evangelism is a bonus. The opportunities created will need to be explored wisely.

A crucial, and often controversial, issue at the heart of this Christian duty of 'social concern' relates to the ideas of 'separation' and 'involvement'. The older generation of evangelical Christians will no doubt be more familiar with a biblical demand for 'separation' from 'the world'. 'Don't you know that friendship with the world is hatred towards God?' (James 4:4.) Holiness means 'separateness'. In the past this has been worked out by not associating with places and activities which were regarded as 'worldly'. The current generation of evangelical Christians hear a new note. While the call to holiness is still preached, the call to 'involvement' has now become the dominant theme. An active participation in the life of contemporary society is urged and encouraged. But what does this lead the Christian to do? What is required is not entirely clear.

Separation appears to be a contradiction of involvement. Is one of these teachings a misinterpretation of Scripture? Provided that the Scripture is properly interpreted and the exposition reflects a biblical 'balance', then there is no actual conflict between the two teachings. But confusion is always a possibility. The word 'world' is used in *five* different ways in the New Testament. The expositor must be careful to 'rightly handle the word of truth' on this particular point.

Christians are to show in their lives a moral and spiritual separation from society in general (1 John 2:15-17). The quality of their lives is to be marked by a radiant holiness. But this does not justify a physical withdrawal from society in order to preserve an untainted sanctity. Light is of most value in the darkness. Society needs the beauty of holiness to expose and expel the ugliness of sin. That is holiness 'where it counts'! A monastic holiness (if there is such a thing) finds no support in Scripture.

It is true that there are many clear calls to holy living throughout the New Testament, but the force of the 'salt analogy' which Jesus used is a most positive endorsement of a deliberate and deep involvement in the everyday life of contemporary society. The Bible expositor Dr W. Hendriksen says, 'The words of [Matthew] 5:13-16 show both how totally different from the world and yet how closely related to the world believers are. Worldly-mindedness or secularization is here condemned, but so is also aloofness or isolationism. Salt is a blessing when it remains truly salt; light, as long as it is really light. But salt must be sprinkled over, better still, rubbed into, the meat. Light must be allowed to shine into the darkness. It must not be put under cover.'[3]

In the ethical sections of their letters the apostles give clear instruction on the way the Christian is to put aside specific sins. They also explain how some basic human relationships are to be patterned biblically. The Christian is to be a responsible member of the family (Eph. 5:22-6:4; Col. 3:18-21; 1 Peter 3:1-7). He is to be a conscientious workman (Eph. 6:5-9; Col. 3:22-4:1; 1 Peter 2:18-25). He is also to be a loyal citizen of the state (Rom. 13:1-7; 1 Peter 2:13-17). The strong condemnation of social evils such as injustice, oppression and exploitation, though prominent in the preaching of the Old Testament prophets (e.g. Isa. 1:16-18; 58:6-10; Jer. 7:5-7; Ezek. 34:2-6,

15,16; Amos 5:10-15; 8:4-7; Zech. 7:9-10; Mal. 3:5) may at first *appear* not to be a major concern of authors of the New Testament letters. But we must be careful what conclusions we draw from an attempt to compare the ministries of the Old Testament prophets with those of Jesus Christ and the apostles. The New Testament presents to us a very different historical and soteriological context from the one in which the prophets exercised their ministries. Social concern is clearly evident in the life and teaching of Jesus (e.g. Matt. 5:13-16; 5:43-48; 6:2-4; 22:15-22; 23:23, 24; 25:31-46; Luke 10:25-37). It is Peter who tells us that Jesus '*went around doing good* and healing all who were under the power of the devil' (Acts 10:38). Social responsibility also has its place in the writings of the apostle Paul (e.g. 1 Cor. 16:1-4; Gal. 6:10; Eph. 4:28; 1 Tim. 2:1,2; 1 Tim. 5:1-16).

A word of caution is appropriate at this point. It concerns the weight of emphasis we should give to the matter of social concern when it is set within the overall framework of the full-orbed Christian life. There are those Christians who set Jesus and Paul over against each other on the matter of social concern. Our Lord lived a perfect life in all His relationships and, it is argued, we should model our concern on His supreme example. There is an implication here that Paul majors on 'spiritual' relationships and consequently the social aspect of Christian living receives relatively less emphasis in his writings. Again we must watch our reasoning. We can go astray here. It would have been most strange if the ministry of Paul had been a 'carbon copy' of the ministry of Jesus. Jesus lived a perfect life, but Paul did not. Jesus died for sinners, but Paul did not. Jesus never wrote a book, but Paul wrote many. Of course their ministries were different!

It must also be stressed that the frequency with which a topic is mentioned in Holy Scripture is not necessarily an indication of its importance. In only one of the fourteen letters Paul wrote is there any mention of the Lord's Supper. The letter to the Romans, the most doctrinally systematic and comprehensive of all Paul's letters, makes no reference at all to the Lord's Supper. We do not thereby conclude that the Lord's Supper is relatively unimportant, particularly in view of the fact that we have evidence that the early church kept this ordinance as a weekly celebration (Acts 20:7). The relative importance of the Lord's Supper, social concern, or any other aspect of the Christian life ought to be determined by the *didactic* portions of Scripture rather than those which are only *descriptive*. Our conduct should be governed chiefly by New Testament *principle* rather than the frequency of reference to New Testament *practice*.

If we believe that our authority for social involvement must come more from the writings of the New Testament than from the examples of the Old Testament prophets, then the letter of James provides us with an adequate biblical basis for our Christian duty of social concern. This short letter is full of instructions and exhortations regarding the Christian's role in society. Interestingly, it has been noted that many of the topics which Jesus touched upon in His sermon on the mount also find an echo in the letter of James, who was a younger brother of our Lord. For some believers the letter to James is a neglected book. For others it is a controversial book, particularly with reference to what James says about 'faith' and 'works'. Before we seek to open up some portions of the letter dealing with social responsibility, it may be helpful to remind ourselves of the nature of the Scripture which we are handling. The letters which Paul wrote were 'God-breathed' (2 Tim. 3:16) by the Holy Spirit. So also was the letter of James. But his one letter is not in any way less God-breathed than are the many letters of Paul. This means that there cannot be any conflict between the writings of James and Paul. There may be *apparent* conflicts but they are not *real*. Careful exposition (2 Tim. 2:15) will resolve the conflict. There cannot be any real contradictions in Scripture. *All* Scripture is God-breathed, and the Holy Spirit does not contradict Himself.

A friend of the lonely

'Religion that God our Father accepts as pure and faultless is this: to look after orphans and widows in their distress and to keep oneself from being polluted by the world' (James 1:27).

No doubt we would not expect Paul to put it that way! But James does. So what does he mean? James is concerned for the practical outworking of the Christian faith in daily living. He is concerned that Christians should not give the impression to others that their religion is a lot of talk and little action.

Salt where it counts

Christians should not merely store up Bible knowledge in their minds. All that is taken in should later be worked out. Christianity which is not practical is not Christianity at all. James translates the principle of 'good works' into a concrete example when he mentions that Christians should 'look after orphans and widows in their distress'. James points to the need for Christians to have a compassionate concern for the individual, and particularly for those whom others might overlook.

The reference to orphans and widows draws our attention to God's concern for those who are 'lonely' — not just 'being on their own', but perhaps feeling unwanted, and feeling that they 'do not belong' to any other person or people. The orphan once belonged to parents, but now he no longer belongs in the way that he did. The widow once belonged to a husband, but now she no longer belongs in the way that she did. It is interesting to note that in the last chapter of the letter to the Hebrews (immediately prior to the first chapter of James) the writer there urges, 'Do not forget to entertain strangers ... Remember those in prison ...' (Heb. 13:2,3). It is significant that both Hebrews and James were written primarily to Christian Jews. The example of compassionate care that James cites has roots deep in the teaching of the Old Testament with which the readers of the letters would be familiar.

God is very concerned for the lonely, those who 'do not belong', those who are particularly vulnerable to the schemes of the unscrupulous. The psalmist tells us, 'A father to the fatherless, a defender of widows, is God in his holy dwelling. God sets the lonely in families ...' (Psalm 68:5,6). The author of Ecclesiastes makes a simple but very practical observation: 'Two are better than one, because they have a good return for their work: if one falls down, his friend can help him up. But pity the man who falls and has no-one to help him up. Also, if two lie down together, they will keep warm. But how can one keep warm alone? Though one may be overpowered, two can defend themselves. A cord of three strands is not quickly broken' (Eccles. 4:9-12).

Because the lonely person is exposed and vulnerable, God has warned those who might be tempted to exploit this situation: 'Do not ill-treat an alien or oppress him, for you were aliens in Egypt. Do not take advantage of a widow or an orphan. If you do and they cry out to me, I will certainly hear their cry. My anger will be aroused, and I will kill you with the sword; your wives will become widows and your children fatherless' (Exod. 22:21-24). It is clear that the early church took these teachings and warnings seriously. Acts 6:1-6 shows us an early improvement of the administrative machinery designed to help the care of widows. Paul gives Timothy some specific instruction concerning the care of widows (1 Tim. 5:1-16).

Although inner-city areas today are teeming with people, paradoxically, this is also where we find very many lonely people. Why do urban areas contain so many lonely people? There are a number of reasons.

Where slum-clearance schemes have taken place, not only have decaying properties been bulldozed out of existence; the community life — that framework of social relationships — has also been destroyed. Former residents in the old terraced houses are rehoused in a new block of flats. But the neighbours in the new flats are often not the neighbours who lived in the old street. There is no secret for 'instant community'. It will take years to grow. Senior citizens are those who find it hardest to adapt to the new situation. Change is not welcome. Old neighbours are deeply missed. The disappearance of the extended family now means that an elderly parent may live a lonely life after losing a partner. A home help, meals on wheels and visits by a social worker are welcome benefits of the Welfare State. But they are no substitute for 'belonging' to a family.

A more recent and rapidly developing feature of lonely living in the inner city is the one-parent family. In urban areas as many as one family in three are now one-parent families. The single parent has no one with whom burdens and responsibilities can be shared. A young mother, unmarried or separated, finds her life very much tied to the needs of her child. She cannot take time off from her parental duties. She may well become physically fatigued and emotionally exhausted. Depression and despair are not uncommon.

Add to these features the 'increasingly nomadic and atomized' condition of society in general, and we may find that we have just touched the tip of the iceberg of urban loneliness. Kathleen Heasman pinpoints the problems of the urbanized society. She says, 'These four types of communities, the older urban areas, the newer housing estates, the new towns and the

Salt where it counts

middle-class suburbs are typical of the sort of surroundings in which most people live. They all lack the fertilizing influence of constant personal mixing with other social groups, classes, occupations or interests which naturally occurred in the village, the market town or the provincial city in the past, and which are rarely found today. Instead there tends to grow up a largely impersonal society which has its own small group of relationships but which forms few close attachments outside. People have little time to make strong social relationships for they are rooted up or move themselves on every few years to what is thought to be great material comfort, but which in fact tends to lead to loneliness, a loss of identity and a greater inner emptiness and lack of purpose.'[4]

Where do we begin to face up to social needs of this dimension? There is no easy answer. We must practise hospitality. We are to do it eagerly rather than reluctantly (1 Peter 4:9; Heb. 13:2,3). Christians must take the time and trouble to be good neighbours. If we are too busy running church activities to find time to be neighbourly, then we are too busy. One particular way in which Christians can help in meeting this kind of need is by participating in the activities of a tenants' association. This would, in a very natural way, bring Christians into contact with fellow residents of a block of flats. An active role in the affairs of the association will provide an opportunity for 'good works', for developing personal relationships, for natural Christian testimony, and eventually an opportunity to introduce neighbours to what should be God's ideal community — the local church.

A defender of the powerless

'My brothers, as believers in our glorious Lord Jesus Christ, don't show favouritism. Suppose a man comes into your meeting wearing a gold ring and fine clothes, and a poor man in shabby clothes also comes in. If you show special attention to the man wearing fine clothes and say, "Here's a good seat for you," but say to the poor man, "You stand there," or, "Sit on the floor by my feet," have you not discriminated among yourselves and become judges with evil thoughts? Listen, my dear brothers:

Has not God chosen those who are poor in the eyes of the world to be rich in faith and to inherit the kingdom he promised to those who love him? But you have insulted the poor. Is it not the rich who are exploiting you? Are they not the ones who are dragging you into court? Are they not the ones who are slandering the noble name of him to whom you belong?' (James 2:1-7.)

When we worship God He is not only concerned with what we think about Him, He is also concerned with what we think about other people. He is aware of the way we view and treat our fellow Christians (Matt. 5:23,24). He is also aware of the way we respond to 'strangers' who may come into our Christian assemblies. James illustrates this point. If two strangers come into our meeting and one is welcomed with courtesy to the point of flattery, and the other is made to feel unwanted almost to the point of appearing to be a nuisance, then the most serious sin of favouritism has infected that Christian assembly.

Would genuine Christians really behave in this manner? I fear it may be more common than we imagine. The difference in the treatment these two men received had nothing to do with the purpose for which they entered the Christian assembly. One was warmly welcomed because he was rich.[5] The other was coolly tolerated because he was poor. This is the sin of 'respect of persons'. Literally, it means to 'receive faces', that is to judge men by something external and not by their real character.

When this kind of incident occurs there is a twofold sin. First, we are 'judges with evil thoughts' (Matt. 7:1,2). It is not our place or prerogative to judge. Secondly, the criterion is altogether unchristian. 'The Lord does not look at the things that man looks at. Man looks at the outward appearance, but the Lord looks at the heart' (1 Sam. 16:7). Why then does it happen? It is patently evil. We fall into the trap of flattery. Someone has said that the difference between gossip and flattery is this: gossip is what you say behind a person's back that you would not dare to say to his face, while flattery is what you say to a person's face that you would never say behind his back. How easy it is to make superficial and sinful judgements of people we meet! How often do we try to assess whether the newcomer is likely to prove an asset or liability to the life of our local church? The weeds of discrimination are not easily rooted out once and for all. The roots have an unfortunate habit of growing again.

A closer look at the two men that James describes for us reveals not only a contrast in economic terms, but also in terms of power and influence. The rich man may well be rich *at the expense of the poor* (James 5:4,5). In addition to that, the rich man also uses his superior power and influence *against the poor*. James is astonished that special interest is shown towards the rich man. He asks, 'Is it not the rich who are exploiting you? Are they not the ones who are dragging you into court? Are they not the ones who are slandering the noble name of him to whom you belong?' (James 2:6,7.) The word translated 'exploiting' is a very strong word, and in the only other place where it is found in the New Testament (Acts 10:38) it refers to oppression by the *devil*. Weymouth translates here, 'Yet is it not the rich who grind you down?' It is used in the Septuagint, in Amos 8:4 (oppression of the poor); Jeremiah 7:6 (oppression of the stranger, the fatherless and widows); and in Ezekiel 18:12 (oppression of the poor and needy). The word translated 'dragging' is used elsewhere, as here, of dragging with force and violence, as in Acts 16:19 and 21:30. The harsh and cruel treatment suffered by the poor at the hands of the rich more than explains James's baffled outburst. The two men in the Christian assembly stand not only as two individuals, but also as representatives of two contrasting social groups. When James used the terms 'poor' and 'rich', he was referring to social categories with which his readers would be familiar from their Old Testament Scriptures.

How are we to understand the 'poor' to whom James refers? J.A. Motyer, in his commentary on the prophecy of Amos, explains the ideas conveyed in the terms 'poor' and 'needy'. He says, 'The analysis offered here arises out of the usage of the key-words as they occur in the Bible. *Poor* is used 22 times of those of lower social rank, but 16 times of the financially poor; *needy* is rooted in the verb 'to be willing' and is used basically of those who 'go along with' something or someone else — voluntarily or under compulsion. It thus has a 'good' use of those who will to do the will of God and are ready to be bent to His will; its 'bad' use refers to the uninfluential in society, those who are open to be 'leaned on' by the boss-classes, those who are fair game to be cheated because they have no redress, etc. It is used 28 times of those in the lower strata of social influence and importance and only five times of the financially poor as such. It sems best, therefore, to allow *poor* to tend to mean those who are without worldly resources and are therefore fair game to be exploited, and to allow *needy* to tend to mean 'the small man' who can so easily be swallowed by the supermarket, etc. and who may, in given cases, be 'small' because of the lack of capital.'[6]

The rich man who enters the Christian assembly is therefore the representative of a social group which possesses 'power, privilege and prestige'. The poor man represents another group of people who do not possess any of these social assets acquired by the rich. It is, at heart, a contrast between the 'powerful' and the 'powerless'. If we have understood the position aright, then where does God stand on these issues? How does He regard these people? Moses tells us: 'For the Lord your God is God of gods and Lord of lords, the great God, mighty and awesome, who shows no partiality and accepts no bribes. He defends the cause of the fatherless and the widow, and loves the alien, gving him food and clothing' (Deut. 10:17-18). James also tells us that 'God has chosen those who are poor in the eyes of the world to be rich in faith ...' (James 2:5). From the Scriptures we have considered, there appears to be a clear obligation on the part of Christians to identify themselves with the 'poor' or 'powerless'.

When we come to apply these biblical principles to our urban populations today, we find that neither the Christian church nor the working classes start from a position of neutrality. The church is already identified with that social group that possesses 'power, privilege and prestige': the working classes are the major social group to whom, generally, these things are denied. It is important for us to grasp just how firmly the contrast is there.

What sort of things identify the Christian church with those who possess power? To the average outsider there is no distinction between the Church of England and Nonconformity. There is an old joke which speaks of the Anglican church as 'the Conservative party at prayer'. In Britain the general impression is that the government and the church have an alliance by which they maintain each other in power. The officers of the church, the hierarchy as well as the local clergy and ministers, are almost entirely drawn from social groups other than the working classes. They are certainly not manual workers. One of my sons, when still a small boy, explained the position helpfully to a friend: 'My daddy doesn't go out to work!'

That's privilege for you! Large vicarages may well provide financial headaches when it comes to maintenance and heating today. But they still convey an impression of affluence and privilege. The maisonette in which our family lives is one of six residential units which have been created out of what was a redundant Anglican vicarage. The early years of this century were times of poverty and hardship for most local people in our immediate community. The poorer families had to make do with the two or three rooms of one floor of an old terraced house. The local vicar was somewhat less confined. He had to be content with an *eighteen-roomed* vicarage!

How far is it correct to identify the working classes with the 'powerless' of our society? Alan Storkey, in his book, *A Christian Social Perspective*, demonstrates convincingly how from the emergence of the working class as a distinct social group, the 'capitalist' and 'middle classes' have managed to withhold from the working classes the 'power' of control and decision-making: 'Not only in the early nineteenth century did the police, the troops, prison hulks and deportation provide a system of control over a population which showed some signs of political instability. More important is the way in which economic control was exercised. Not surprisingly, one of the common weapons was to create fear by fines, punishment and the threat of dismissal. Sometimes the churches were also used to provide moral backing to ensure obedience. There tended, therefore, to be a continual drive to eliminate responsibility, and thus independent power, from the workforce and keep it in the hands of the controlling group. This had the effect, firstly, of creating patterns of centralized, autocratic, decision-making and, secondly, of alienating the workers who, through fear, were removed as far as possible from responsibility in their jobs into routine work patterns. Employers learned that the best way of maintaining control and domination was to centralize responsibility and keep the workforce dependent.'[7]

This power policy pioneered by the employers was later extended and developed through the agency of the Welfare State: 'As the administrative organs of state developed, they were manned by middle-class servants who set out to provide efficient administrative solutions to social problems. At the same time educated socialists began to develop centralized plans for different areas of social life. The effect of this process was that a vast range of dependence-inducing systems were developed which would bring the working classes to a painless acceptance of the existing order. Thus estates, houses, flats, and even external and internal decorations were delivered in a totally planned form to the passive and grateful tenants. The design of estates reflected the middle-class view of the working-class tenants ... The health service, the legal system and the social services all reflected this class paternalism. Millions of people found themselves dependent on payments by the authorities, and the working classes were thus perpetually in debt to the middle-class socialist state.'[8]

In the latter part of the twentieth century, the trade unions of the working classes have greatly developed their organizational power and industrial 'muscle'. Industrial democracy is seen as a goal to be pursued. Nevertheless, there has yet to come a significant shift of power of control away from the employers to the workers.

'Jobs, education, housing and entertainment are provided, and the individual can make the most of his passive situation. Some face more severe problems when they are in acute need and are also powerless, but most get the recompense due to the passive for staying that way.'[9]

How are we to apply the principles of Christian conduct that we derive from the teaching of James? We have claimed that the Christian, like his heavenly Father, must be a 'defender of the powerless'. Some Christians would claim that a defender of the powerless must inevitably be an 'attacker of the powerful'. They would argue the case for a 'new order' in which there is a new balance of power among the various groups that comprise British society. That is a topic which would demand careful application of the principles we have considered. However, the issues are too complex to permit treatment in our present study. We shall consider an application of this teaching in a way similar to that of James in his letter. Reflecting on the kind of welcome given to the strangers who entered the Christian assembly, James says, 'You have insulted the poor' (James 2:6). How was this insult manifested? The Christians showed far more respect, care and concern for one person than they did for the other. The poor man was despised and dishonoured and all but totally neglected. It is a sin to respect one person and to despise another. That much is agreed. But the principle can be carried a stage further. It is also a sin to treat a *person* as a *thing*. It is a sin for an employer to regard his employees as impersonal units in a production process. But the very nature of an industrialized society and its methods of production tend to make this unwelcome consequence a high probability.

The working man resents the depersonalizing consequences of industrial progress and automation. With mass production and the ever-increasing size of modern trading units, there is a tendency for the working man to be reduced to, and to be treated as, a nameless, characterless cog in a machine. Tasks requiring minimum skill, and often bringing with them monotony and boredom, rob the worker of the opportunity for self-fulfilment and a sense of achievement. No amount of economic improvement can compensate for this loss.

Roger Lloyd contends that 'A government which is omnicompetent, as the government of a Welfare State is bound to claim to be, lies under all the *special temptations of power*, and one of them is to seek to overrule one part of the Christian doctrine of Man while asserting another part of it in its provision of material security for all. To say that every separate person is unique, precious, and sacred in God's sight and therefore must be treated as an end in himself is to assert the preciousness of the variety which exists between different persons. The separateness of human beings is divinely ordained. To treat them as so many units in a collective and to reduce their separate tastes and needs to some administrative statistical average is to do violence to all that the Gospel holds to be true about Man's nature ...'[10]

Sir Frederick Catherwood believes that 'Christians must qualify the desire for greater efficiency by the requirement that those who produce should be treated with dignity and consideration.'[11] In this connection, he adds a further comment which should provoke Christians to honest and sober reflection. He speaks of the 'traditions of organized labour', with reference to earlier Christian influence, and then goes on to say, 'Not all of these can be traced to Christian sources. Many of them stem from a feeling of genuine grievance at the sufferings of the working class. They saw these as arising from a system which appeared to regard labour as a commodity rather than a calling. Indeed *the Church's apparent connivance* in this system of society, which seemed detrimental to the interests of the individual, may be one of the reasons why the masses are outside the Church today.'[12]

A champion of the oppressed

'Now listen, you rich people, weep and wail because of the misery that is coming upon you. Your wealth has rotted, and moths have eaten your clothes. Your gold and silver are corroded. Their corrosion will testify against you and eat your flesh like fire. You have hoarded wealth in the last days. Look! The wages you failed to pay the workmen who mowed your fields are crying out against you. The cries of the harvesters have reached the ears of the Lord Almighty. You have lived on earth in luxury and self-indulgence. You have fattened yourselves in the day of slaughter. You have condemned and murdered innocent men, who were not opposing you' (James 5:1-6)

In these dramatic words James thunders a denunciation of those who cause oppression. The content and manner of his speaking have much in common with the message and ministry of the Old Testament prophet Amos. Oppression occurs where there is an absence of justice. But what is 'justice'? J. Motyer says, 'Justice is correct moral practice in daily personal and social life, and righteousness is the cultivation of correct moral principle (both for self and for society); justice is mainly outward, righteousness inward. Of course, for the Bible righteousness always has the connotation 'right with God', 'what God thinks is right', and therefore when the Lord desires that the outflow of religion should be justice and righteousness, He is calling for the establishment of principles and practices of daily living which conform to His word and law.'[13]

We encounter the evils of injustice and oppression where there has been a departure from 'fair dealing'. Injustice occurs where one party in a financial transaction uses his superior power to extort from the other party more than is his just due. It occurs where traders put up prices to unfair levels ('skimping the measure, boosting the price and cheating with dishonest scales' — Amos 8:5); when landlords charge excessive rents (Isa. 5:8; Amos 2:6,7; 5:11; 8:4,6); where tax collectors swindle taxpayers by making excessive charges for tax collection (Luke 19:8); where employers keep wages low or fail to pay what they promise (James 5:4). The crowning oppression occurs where victims of injustice seek redress from the courts, only to find that the extortioners have already 'bought' the verdict which will acquit them. 'You oppress the righteous and take bribes and you deprive the poor of justice in the courts' (Amos 5:12).

The particular form of oppression which James deals with in his letter concerns the matter of 'work' and the proper relationship between employers and employees. The issues he raises have a very obvious contemporary relevance to matters which are continually in the headlines of daily news. There are three aspects of this topic which require comment. They are work, wages and working conditions.

Work

There is no suggestion in what James writes that there is any default on the part of these agricultural workers. They have 'mowed the fields' as their employers required them to do (James 5:4). The workmen had completed their work.

The most basic question we can ask on this topic is 'Why work?' Is work just a 'necessary evil'? It is becoming increasingly important for Christians to be clear in their understanding of what the Bible teaches about work. Two particular reasons make this imperative. First, in our materialistic society attitudes towards work show an increasing departure from the Bible's teaching. These attitudes are bound to affect adversely industrial efficiency and competitiveness. We need to realize that the 'ordinance of labour' was given by God before the Fall. In the sinless world which God created man was designed by God to do work. That is how God made him. So work is essentially good. In itself it carries no element of penalty for sin. Nevertheless, the entry of sin into the world has seriously affected man's attitude to work. The earth has been cursed because of sin. Man experiences the drudgery of toil. As an unregenerate being, he no longer does his work to the glory of God nor does he seek the help of God. We need to be clear on the biblical doctrine of work.[14]

A second reason for needing scriptural views on work concerns the growing problem of unemployment. In his second letter to the Thessalonian Christians Paul is quite explicit about the Bible's attitude towards the person who refuses to work. 'If a man will not work, he shall not eat' (2 Thess. 3:6-10). That is the rule for the person who is able to work but refuses to do so. But how are we to treat the person who wants to work, but cannot find the necessary employment? How can we help him? What does prolonged unemployment do to the worker? Apart from finance, how does it affect the worker's family? How can the situation be remedied?

High levels of unemployment may become a continuing, rather than passing feature of the industrial scene. Even if 'world recession' is overcome and the economic tide turns, we have yet to face the repercussions of the development of micro-chip technology and its effect on the labour market. Christians need to receive more than the biblical teaching on this subject: they need practical assistance as well. In the present situation a number of churches have become involved in 'job-creation' schemes. This practical action has good evangelical precedent. People brought to an experience of Christian conversion through the preaching of George Whitefield were placed within 'class meetings' to safeguard and provide their nurture in Christ. Assistance in securing necessary employment was provided for these young converts. 'The *Minute Book* of the Tabernacle reveals that the Society ... had a workshop — apparently a small manufactory that provided employment for some of the needy and earned a revenue that assisted these other endeavours [i.e., school, bookroom, poor relief]. There was a kind of small employment exchange — a means of contact between prospective employers and persons seeking employment.'[15]

Wages

'The worker deserves his wages' (Luke 10:7). So said Jesus. According to Scripture the wages due to a worker are to be calculated fairly and to be paid promptly.

We have a common-sense maxim which we apply in the assessment of wage rates. 'A fair day's pay for a fair day's work.' It might be thought that this rule only states what is obvious and universally accepted, but that is not so. The apostle Paul instructed those Colossian believers who were 'masters' to 'provide your slaves with what is right and fair' (Col. 4:1). To us this seems to say nothing new. But to the first readers of the Colossian letter a new concept was being introduced. Although we find no direct attack on the institution of slavery in the New Testament, Paul's insistence on just and fair treatment for slaves was a revolutionary assertion. The concept of justice for slaves was never contemplated in the Roman Empire. But in the course of time it was this demand for justice which undermined the institution and in the end destroyed it.

So much for *what* should be paid. There is another question. *When* should it be paid? When is the worker entitled to receive the remuneration he has earned? Certain requirements of the Mosaic law demanded very prompt payment of wages. The employer was not entitled to gain an unfair hold over his workers by withholding wages already earned: 'Do not defraud your neighbour or rob him. Do not hold back the wages of a hired man *overnight*' (Lev. 19:13). 'Do not take advantage of a hired man who is poor and needy, whether he is a brother Israelite or an alien living in one of your towns. Pay him his wages *each day before sunset*, because he is poor and counting on it. Otherwise he may cry to the Lord against you, and you will be guilty of sin' (Deut. 24: 14,15). It was the failure of some rich employers to pay promptly the wages owed to their agricultural labourers that called forth such a vehement condemnation by James. He makes it plain that there will be no 'cover-up' or 'whitewash'! 'Look! The wages you failed to pay the workmen who mowed your fields are *crying out* against you. The *cries of the harvesters* have reached the ears of the Lord Almighty' (James 5:4). James exposed the evil practice in order to remove the scourge of this oppression.

Working conditions

A further aspect of the failure of the employers to keep their part of a 'fair-dealing' relationship with their employees concerns the conditions under which they worked. James says to these callous employers, 'You have condemned and murdered innocent men, who were not opposing you' (James 5:6). It is not entirely clear what this verse means. There may be a link with James 4:2. But it is certain that the employers were 'money-lovers'. This is indicated by their refusal to part with the wages due to the labourers. It is even more obvious in their lives of 'luxury' and 'self-indulgence' (James 5:5). Where a craving for money exists it acts like an addictive drug. 'Whoever loves money never has money enough; whoever loves wealth is never satisfied with his income' (Eccles. 5:10). This craving manifests itself in an obsession with *things* (that money can buy) and a diminishing sensitivity towards *people* and their personal needs. Such was the insensitivity of the employers to whom James directed his words, that their neglect to provide humane working conditions for their employees led to the death of some of the workmen (James 5:6).

Christians have always been in the forefront of caring for the needs of people. This is what we should expect. Various institutions and agencies, which we now take for granted as a necessary part of the structure of the modern Welfare State, were more often than not pioneered by the 'blood, sweat and toil' of Christians who were moved and motivated by the love of Christ. Schools, hospitals, our legal system, the treatment of offenders, care for the disabled and destitute and more besides — all owe their birth and growth to the compassionate initiative of Christians.[16]

Included in this list of expressions of Christian concern must also be the endeavours of those who toiled and fought for improved working conditions, primarily for the industrial wage-earners. We have come to accept that trade unions and their officers have the power and ability to argue their own case for improved working conditions. A century ago the workers did not wield the 'muscle' that they do today. Although Christians were involved in the inauguration of unions, during the nineteenth century it was still caring crusaders as individuals, rather than organized labour, which secured the major improvements in the working conditions of that period.

The one name above all others associated with the fight to obtain these improvements is that of Lord Shaftesbury (1801-1885). A member of Parliament, Shaftesbury spent his whole life and career in campaigning for the welfare of the deprived and oppressed. 'He championed the cause of the women and children working in mines and collieries, and secured the setting up of a Royal Commission of Inquiry into children's employment in general. It was not, however, until 1864 and 1867 that the parliamentary acts regulated child and female labour, and not until 1875 did the Climbing Boys Acts protect children used as chimney sweeps. He also promoted legislation to protect milliners and dressmakers.'[17]

Are Christians needed in the trade unions today? Some believers may consider that the unions possess more than enough power to campaign effectively for the rights and improvements which they regard as just and necessary today.

Perhaps there are more pressing needs towards which Christians should direct their concern and compassion. But Christians are still needed in the work of the trade unions. While nowadays there may not be the need for another man of influence like Lord Shaftesbury, there is still valuable service that dedicated Christians can do within the world of work. Our nation in general continues to slip further and further away from biblical teaching and standards. Consequently, we may expect that unions will progressively reflect a pagan 'doctrine of man' in their thinking, policies and decisions. Inevitably this will mean that certain proposals made by the unions and their leaders will not be in the best interests of the workers. Without bigotry the Christian should aim to bring influence to modify what is being advocated, so that it will more nearly accord with the biblical doctrine of man and thereby bring greater benefit to his fellow workers.

Christians must not opt out of the complexities and pressures and power struggles which are all part of the contemporary working scene. This is really 'salt where it counts'. It does not take a great deal of salt to flavour a large saucepan of vegetables. It may not take a great number of Christians to bring considerable influence to bear for the good of many hundreds of their fellow workers. But the salt must be *where it counts*; otherwise it serves no useful purpose.

The Christian's ministry of social concern must exhibit both negative and positive aspects. Isaiah urged God's people: 'Stop doing wrong, learn to do right! Seek justice, encourage the oppressed. Defend the cause of the fatherless, plead the case of the widow' (Isa. 1:17). It is interesting to observe the close similarity between the kind of social concern shown by Isaiah and that shown by James. In the New Testament it is James, in particular, who repeatedly stresses that Christianity must be a religion of *deeds*, and not just *words*: 'What good is it my brothers, if a man claims to have faith but has no deeds? Can such faith save him? Suppose a brother or sister is without clothes and daily food. If one of you says to him, "Go, I wish you well; keep warm and well fed," but does nothing about his physical needs, what good is it? In the same way, faith by itself, if it is not accompanied by action, is dead' (James 2:14-17).

This kind of reasoning makes good sense to the working man! But it must be admitted that we tend to pay more attention to attacking the evils than we do to practising good. We can identify evils and make plans to eradicate them. The evil that is being done sounds an alarm in our 'caring conscience'. We are impelled to take remedial action, whereas the good that needs to be done often escapes our notice and fails to disturb our conscience. But James tells us that 'Anyone ... who knows the good he ought to do and doesn't do it, sins' (James 4:17). At the time of attempting to cure a particular evil, we should be considering whether there are ways to reduce or eliminate the possibility of the same thing happening again.

John R.W. Stott, in his exposition of the sermon on the mount, says, 'Too often evangelical Christians have interpreted their social responsibility in terms only of helping the casualties of a sick society, and have done nothing to change structures which cause the casualties. Just as doctors are concerned not only with the treatment of patients but also with preventive medicine and public health, so we should concern ourselves with what might be called preventive social medicine and higher standards of moral hygiene. However small our part may be, we cannot opt out of seeking to create better social structures, which guarantee justice in legislation and law enforcement, the freedom and dignity of the individual, civil rights for minorities and the abolition of social and racial discrimination. We should neither despise these things nor avoid our responsibility for them. They are part of God's purpose for his people.'[18]

When Jesus described Christians as 'salt in society' He added a warning to His instruction: 'You are the salt of the earth. But if the salt loses its saltiness, how can it be made salty again? It is no longer good for anything, except to be thrown out and trampled by men' (Matt. 5:13). Jesus sounds a note of caution. In certain circumstances there is a risk that the salt will lose its saltiness. The consequences of such an occurrence are extremely serious: 'The salt from the marshes and lagoons or from the rocks in the neighbourhood of the Dead Sea easily acquires a stale or alkaline taste, because of its mixture with gypsum. It is then literally "good for nothing" but to be thrown away and trampled underfoot.'[19]

Salt is of value only when it is pure. It if becomes mixed with impurities, its value does not merely drop — it disappears altogether. 'It is no longer good for anything,' says Jesus. When a Christian's life is pure and holy it brings a wholesome influence

Salt where it counts

in society. But should that life become contaminated with worldly thoughts, desires and relationships, then the salt loses its value. The benefits to society cease. But here is the crux: the very involvement of that salt in society places it at risk of being contaminated. When James described his understanding of 'pure and faultless' religion he drew attention to the spiritual risk to which the Christian is exposed: 'Religion that God our Father accepts as pure and faultless is this: to look after orphans and widows in their distress and to keep oneself from being polluted by the world' (James 1:27). Even a fellow worker with Paul found himself unable to avoid contamination. The apostle reluctantly admits, 'Demas, because he loved this world, has deserted me ...' (2 Tim. 4:10). Social involvement will always carry an element of risk. That risk of infection may stem from a number of sources: theological compromise, counterfeit faith, social pressure, moral laxity. The risk is implied in what Jesus prayed for His disciples: 'My prayer is not that you take them out of this world but that you protect them from the evil one' (John 17:15). It is further implied in what Jesus taught His disciples to pray: 'And lead us not into temptation, but deliver us from the evil one' (Matt. 6:13).

In all this, a Christian's expression of social concern is not to be activated merely by a law which touches his conscience, but by a compassion which moves his heart. 'Loving our neighbour' in the way that the Bible teaches will invariably involve some risks. The Good Samaritan realized this (Luke 10:30-37). When he crossed the road to come to the aid of the injured man he was exposing himself to danger. Were the robbers hiding nearby ready to strike again? As he approached that battered body, he could not have known what the cost of 'loving' would involve in terms of time and money. There was also the risk of misunderstanding. If other Samaritan travellers passed by, how would they view their countryman's association with a Jew? Did his willingness to stop and care run the risk of making himself late for an appointment? Could this have brought further misunderstanding and even personal loss? James tells us, 'If you really keep the royal law found in Scripture, "Love your neighbour as yourself," you are doing right' (James 2:8). With this commandment, if we really want to avoid being law-breakers, there will be times when we shall have to be risk-takers! (Acts 15:26; Rom. 16:3,4; Phil. 2:30).

10.
How long till harvest?

'Let us not become weary in doing good, for at the proper time we will reap a harvest if we do not give up' (Gal. 6:9).

Responsibility ... yesterday?

Recently I listened with interest to the speaker on Radio 4's 7.50 a.m. *Thought for the Day* programme. The speaker's topic concerned oil in Nigeria, a country with considerable rich oil deposits. Not long ago an explosion occurred on an offshore drilling rig. There was a major spillage of oil and the repercussions were much greater than were at first feared. Not only were the beaches polluted with oil that had washed ashore, but the whole way of life for many Nigerian fishermen was completely destroyed. The pollution of the sea had killed off masses of the fish upon which those fishermen depended for their livelihood. They had no option but to pack their bags, pull up their roots, and set off in search of a new way of life and a new source of livelihood. Grudgingly we pay the ever-increasing price of petrol and associated oil products. Yet for all that our Western way of life is largely undisturbed by the stream of price rises imposed by the oil exporters. But what of the Nigerian fishermen? What price do they have to pay for the oil that is exported to the West? The catastrophe they have suffered is virtually irreversible. But it is certain that they do not have the industrial or economic muscle to enable them to secure the social justice which is their due. They are people without power.

This incident in Nigeria is just one small illustration of what has been happening since the dawn of the industrial age. The industrialist moves in, establishes his enterprise, exploits the resources, inflicts his environmental scars, makes his 'pile', but leaves the 'locals' to pick up some of the bills. Many thousands of people who derive their income from the industrial enterprises located in urban areas make their exodus to their 'desirable residential areas' at the end of each working day, but leave the urban residents to pay some of the bills. Who shares in the responsibility for the high-density housing in the inner city? If suburban authorities refuse to release more land for the development of new estates, then urban housing densities are kept at an undesirably high level. Residents are condemned to live in a drab concrete wilderness with a paucity of parks and safe play space. What of the fumes of industrial plants and processes? Does the industrial worker have to endure the foul air that wafts across from the factory or refinery so that the works manager can enjoy the fresh air that surrounds his suburban three-bedroomed 'semi'? Whose vehicles clog our streets in the rush-hours and gobble up our parking space for the rest of the day? Why should the urban residents suffer from the 'yellow peril' of miles of restricted or metered parking so that 'white-collar' workers can have convenient access to their place of business? And there is more. 'At the turn of the century a certain George Haw wrote: "... All the strong and prosperous people are running away from the inner belt of London as fast as they can; forgetting it, owning no responsibility for it, leaving it to the weaker, poorer, more weary ones. The manufacturers, their managers, and all the staff who take salaries as distinct from wages, come in the mornings, and go away in the evenings, and admit no responsibility, social or religious, for the crowded districts where their workplaces lie, and their workpeople live." '[1]

Human nature has not changed over the years of the twentieth century. Certainly, the responsibility to 'do something' has existed for a long time. 'Yesterday' goes back one hundred years! But the kind of people who had the ability and power to tackle major urban problems were the very ones who were in the vanguard of the exodus to the suburbs. Over the past decade or two the 'authorities' have been taking urban deprivation much more seriously. Urban Aid, Community Development Projects and various other investigatory projects designed to expose need and advise on use of limited resources have been initiated.[2] These are steps in the right direction. But the present serious economic recession will not only aggravate urban deprivation, it will also curtail the availability of funds directed to meet the escalating need. We need advocates who will plead and persuade concerning urban need. Our case will not easily be won.

Bishop David Sheppard speaks of his experience in London's West Ham: 'A principle, which is still a burning issue, was slowly and grudgingly acknowledged. It was that the inner city's scale of problems are not only of its own making. Those who moved out of West Ham and those who took their living from working in West Ham were as much responsible for what it became as were those who still lived there. Inner-city boroughs need to acknowledge that they do not possess the resources to meet their needs; national resources are needed. Equally, national government (which means all taxpayers) needs to acknowledge that the scale of problems in relation to limited resources cannot be compared with those of a town or small city. The inner city is the responsibility of the whole country.'[3]

If the suburban citizen is reluctant to acknowledge that he is his urban brother's keeper, what of the suburban Christian? His ties with the inner city are civil and spiritual. Do believers who live outside the urban and industrial areas give tangible recognition of their obligations towards their urban Christian brothers? Those denominational bodies which have a long-standing national structure and some degree of centralized government are in a better position to focus attention and resources upon those urban churches most in need of help. An example of an attempt to grapple with the specific needs and problems of inner urban areas was demonstrated by the London Baptist churches in 1965. When C.H. Spurgeon and the other founding fathers of the London Baptist Association met at the Metropolitan Tabernacle on 10 November 1865 to inaugurate the new association, the strength of the London churches was much more at the centre of London. Suburbia was still in its infancy. By 1965 the pattern was reversed. The suburban churches are where the strength is now. Generally, the weaker churches are located in the inner urban areas. As part of their centenary celebrations the London Baptist churches launched a New Century Project to direct attention, finance and more workers to the smaller causes of the inner city.

Evangelical churches which are independent of denominational affiliation will probably find that they are less aware of urban need. There can be a very real tendency for urban and suburban independent evangelical churches to become, by accident rather than design, isolationist. Are there ways in which this unbiblical isolation can be cured? The Philippian believers sent Epaphroditus to help Paul in his work (Phil. 2:25-30). If a suburban church was able to send a man of the character and calibre of Epaphroditus to assist a pastor or to aid the work generally in an urban church this could prove to be a spiritually enriching experience for both churches and an excellent expression of 'partnership in the gospel' (Phil. 1:5). In addition, or as an alternative, a 'twinning' arrangement might be explored, whereby an urban church and a non-urban church seek to forge links by practical expressions of partnership in the gospel according to the particular resources and needs of the two churches involved. An occasional or regular pulpit exchange could contribute to the same general aim.

Reformation ... today?

What is a *Reformed* church? A *Reformed* church is one which numbers itself among those heirs of the Reformation who treasure and adhere to the great evangelical doctrines of Scripture which our forefathers in the faith recovered and re-established in the church of Jesus Christ. Unfortunately, not all churches which are Reformed in name are necessarily Reformed in nature as well. Belief and behaviour *ought* to be consistent. Often they are not. The word 'Reformed' has certain limitations of which we ought to be aware. It can imply something which is not intended. The word 'Reformed' suggests a process which has been completed, a goal that has been achieved. We are there! We have arrived! We are already reformed! But that is not enough. A local church which is true to the New Testament pattern must be both *Reformed* and *reforming*.

If it is failing to be the latter then, strictly speaking, it has no valid claim to be the former. There ought to be an ongoing reforming process in the life of the church. In the context of our present study there are a number of issues which demand further consideration with a view to reformation of thought and practice.

Biblical principles

'Your word is a lamp to my feet and a light for my path' (Ps. 119:105). How can we ensure that the local church of which we are part is pursuing a biblical course? It is of the utmost importance that all the principles and issues with which we have wrestled in this book be thought through carefully, hammered out firmly, expressed clearly, explained simply and defended scripturally. This matter is vital not only because we can only honour God when we adhere to His Word, but also because loyalty to Scripture will hold us firm through the difficulties and disappointments we may encounter ahead of us. As we grapple with the issues we will need to distinguish carefully between Scripture and tradition and culture. We may well be in for some shocks and surprises! How easy will it be to persuade certain church members that a particular long-standing tradition in the life of the fellowship is now a liability rather than an asset? Not all will welcome changes which seek to bring the church's life more in line with the indigenous culture. If changes in thought and practice do not yield the results for which some are looking, how well would we weather any storm of discontent? If we are forced to retrench for a while, how long could we bear the apathy of our neighbours, the criticism of our enemies, the disappointment of our colleagues and, possibly, the loss of confidence on the part of our friends? There is only one way and the apostle Paul spoke from experience when he gave his personal testimony in this respect. 'Since through God's mercy we have this ministry, we do not lose heart. Rather, we have renounced secret and shameful ways; we do not use deception, nor do we distort the word of God. On the contrary, by setting forth the truth plainly we commend ourselves to every man's conscience in the sight of God' (2 Cor. 4:1,2).

One particular example may be useful to illustrate this point. Is the word 'sociology' immediately and instinctively suspect to certain evangelical Christians? Where it appears in Christian discussion, is it treated as though it is bound to be associated with 'another gospel'? But why the prejudice? Why the ignorance? Why the confusion? The training of a missionary for work overseas involves scriptural and related studies together with a study of the history, customs, culture and language of the people among whom he is to serve. He must study the Bible. That we do not question. But it is equally imperative that he study the life and history of the people to whom he is sent. This dual aspect of missionary training we accept quite readily. But the predominantly working-class areas of this country are no less a mission-field than those countries overseas. Most men who pastor churches in working-class areas are not native to these areas. Can we really profess to love an unbeliever, either here or overseas, if we are not particularly interested in his way of life, and how the Christian gospel is to be related to that life in every-day practical terms?

E.R. Wickham says, 'The extent of working-class estrangement is still insufficiently realized inside the churches, partly because *the churches do not ask embarrassing sociological questions*, and as also perhaps because we have grown accustomed to the situation, to smaller numbers of all social groups, and can always produce a handful of artisan swallows to suggest that the summer is with us. It is to deny the hard facts of history; and a sociological comparison of the congregation with the parish, or the churches with the industrial area in which they are set, would show the critical nature of the situation. It would show the almost total exclusion of adult men such as miners, steelworkers, engineers, general factory workers, dockworkers, transport workers, and so on. Nor is there a sufficiently skilful and sympathetic understanding by the churches of the working-class pattern of life, in which faith has to be born and the Christian community grow.'[4]

For the clarity and strength of our personal conviction, for the proof of our evangelical orthodoxy, and for the benefit of those who trust us (and for those who do not!) we need to formulate an adequate biblical theology of 'sociology'. We should expound, say, 1 Corinthians 9:19-23 and show why and how we need to understand people if we are to win them for Jesus Christ.

Worship and culture

Worship is a popular subject of debate among Christians at the present time. The content and form of our traditional ways of worship are being questioned. I believe that to be a good thing. If it drives us back to Scripture only good can come. Naturally, we tend to defend what we consider to be the virtues of the way of worship to which we are accustomed. We may also expose defects in other forms of worship which we have observed. But those who defend themselves against any and every criticism may be the losers in the end. Churches who dismiss worship as a *live issue* of debate may find that their traditional worship has become a *dead letter* in practice. Correctness and coldness in worship can often go together, even where the local church is in other ways biblically orthodox. But why does this happen even where the doctrine is sound? We can suggest some reasons.

Many evangelical Christians measure the blessing and value of a particular service of worship by what they judge to be the quality of the sermon. Their appreciation of the other ingredients of worship is seldom voiced. It is all too easy for a church to lapse into a somewhat mechanical approach to the singing of hymns, the reading of the Scriptures and the prayers. A service in which the minister leads everything and in which the congregation is largely passive (apart from the singing) can easily drift into a routine and a ritual. A company of believers may reject the charge that they regard the hymns, Scripture reading and prayers as 'preliminaries' before the preaching of the Word, but at the same time their practice in worship may deny their claim.

It is important for us to think through this subject carefully. We need to turn what we learn to advantage in our urban working-class churches. A portion of Paul's first letter to the Christians at Corinth is a most suitable Scripture on which to base a consideration of New Testament Christian worship. Three reasons can be given for the choice of this particular Scripture.

1. The first Epistle to the Corinthians is one of the few New Testament letters to contain a major portion of teaching on the subject of worship. Chapters 11 to 14 inclusive could suitably be described as 'Principles and Problems of Christian worship in the Early Church'. The value of this extended portion is increased because the Corinthian believers had run into some major problems. Paul's teaching is, therefore, not a detached study of worship principles, but rather an intellectual and

practical wrestling with the issues as a very necessary expression of pastoral instruction and correction.

2. We have already conducted a limited investigation into the beliefs and behaviour of the Corinthian church when we examined the topic of culture in chapter 8. The Corinthian church was in an urban setting and we were concerned to draw out cultural parallels and principles for guidance in our contemporary urban scene. We contended that it is both right and necessary that a local church should reflect, in its life and witness, the influence of the indigenous culture. We saw that the gospel carries no demand that the unbeliever repent of his sins *and* his culture. Only where cultural practice is in conflict with biblical principles, is it necessary to demand that the new believer dissociate himself from the unchristian features of the indigenous culture.

Our earlier study made limited reference to a number of ways in which this affected the Corinthian church. We are now arguing that the cultural exercise needs to be extended to embrace in more detail the subject of worship. In what ways was it right for the Corinthian church to reflect local culture in its conduct of worship? Does that investigation provide us with a suitable model or form of enquiry into our contemporary urban situations? The practice of worship is the highest activity of which any redeemed human being is capable. That being so, the subject of worship cannot be relegated to a category of secondary issues in local church practice. The fact that the form of worship in urban, suburban, coastal and rural churches shows little if any variation strongly suggests that the matter of worship and culture is a neglected area of Christian thought. If, as seems probable, the practice of worship in our urban churches appears to reflect a culture that is other than urban, then this is an area of Christian living where reformation is required.

3. The current interest in the subject of worship seems to be largely due to the influence of what is popularly called 'the charismatic movement'. This movement, with its particular teachings and practices concerning the work of the Holy Spirit, is having a world-wide influence in churches of all denominations and of none. Once again we discover that the first letter to the Corinthian church contains a major portion of Scripture from which a number of the characteristic charismatic emphases are derived. Personally, I do not share the popular charismatic

views in relation to Spirit-baptism and tongue-speaking. But I do believe that we have something to learn from the 'charismatics' and particularly in relation to the matter of worship. Understandably, we may react and guard against any excesses. But we must not allow this proper spiritual caution to prejudice us against features of worship which are demonstrably biblical. Professor A.A. Hoekema — not a 'charismatic' himself — says, 'In the church we ought to leave room for spontaneity in worship and more opportunity for audience response than we do. I am not pleading for a liturgy of "holy disorder" but I am saying that a church service that is marked by what D. Andrew Blackwood of Princeton Seminary used to call "lameness, sameness, and tameness" will not be very helpful to people. Why should a single individual always be at the centre of the liturgical service? Why should there not be more responses from the audience?'[5]

We ought also to remember that it is the Pentecostal churches who, in the current century, have had relatively more success in reaching the working classes with the gospel where the older denominations have failed.

Church history

Throughout the course of our enquiry we have endeavoured to bring the light of church history to bear on the particular topics where it seemed that help could be gained. But there is a right way and a wrong way to use evidence from the past. How have we used it? Some years ago there appeared in *The Banner of Truth* magazine an article entitled 'The Use and Abuse of Church History'. The writer, J.G. Vos, warned against three faulty attitudes to church history and these he defined as (i) romanticizing the past, (ii) absolutizing the past, and (iii) disdaining the past. For those of Reformed persuasion it is in respect of the first two attitudes that vigilance is required.

Thrilled by the 'good old days' of pulpit power, stirred and challenged by the spiritual might and godliness of men of renown, we may almost allow the glow and glory of more recent history to rival even that of the sacred page. It can happen, and the trap is a subtle one. It is possible for pastors and preachers to have their minds so saturated in church history that they look back to Holy Scripture through spectacles with very thick historical lenses! Their view of Scripture is almost unavoidably and strongly coloured by their appreciation of church history. And herein lies the danger. We are to use the Scripture to test church history. We are not to take what thrills and captivates us in church history and then seek to project that situation back on to the pages of the New Testament. We may read back into Scripture what is not there. At times there may appear to be a very narrow dividing line between the two methods of approach, but the principle here being stressed is an important one. It is a fundamental tenet of evangelical belief that Scripture alone is our norm, and *all* church history must be subject to its test.

The words of J.G. Vos are appropriate here: 'The history of the Christian Church, if rightly regarded and used, can be a great source of strength, wisdom and stability to the serious Christian. On the other hand, Church history wrongly regarded and misused can be a stumbling-block, an occasion of weakness and stagnation.'[6]

R.B. Kuiper expands our understanding of what is involved in pursuing the policy we are advocating: 'History tells us that a church is sure to lose its Christian character if it ceases to be conservative. History also tells us that a church will become extinct if it fails to be progressive ... Let no one think that by this time the church has exhausted Holy Scripture. It has done nothing of the kind. It remains the God-assigned task of the church to explore the Word of God ever more thoroughly and to bring forth from its depths ever greater riches of truth ... It is important that the church distinguish sharply between Scriptural teachings and human traditions, and it must ever stand ready, if need be, to discard the latter, no matter how ancient and firmly established they may be. Still another duty of the church which it may not neglect, but often does, is to apply the teachings of Scripture to the specific problems and peculiar needs of the times.'[7]

Revival ... tomorrow?

'Let us not become weary in doing good, for at the proper time we will reap a harvest if we do not give up' (Gal. 6:9). Harvest does not come speedily, the Scripture warns us. Never is this more true than of the urban harvest for which urban Christians wait. It is a long time coming but, we are assured, when 'the proper time' comes, we will reap a harvest if we do not give up. Our spiritual stamina will be put to the test. How can we be sure of persevering? What will keep us steady and resolute in pursuit of our goal? Above all else, it is to the Scripture that we must turn. 'Everything that was written in the past was written to teach us, so that through endurance and the encouragement of the Scriptures we might have hope' (Rom. 15:4). I find the life and ministry of the prophet Jonah hold encouragement for me in my own urban ministry. This is not the place to preach a sermon, but three brief headings may help us to organize our thoughts and assist our memories.

The city God spared

The ancient city of Nineveh was renowned for three things in particular: its size, its splendour and its sin. In size it was a 'very large city' (Jonah 3:3). It was a world metropolis and capital of a powerful empire. It took three days to go all through it. That journey is reckoned to be about sixty miles. The inner wall of the city was only 7¾ miles in circumference, so that Jonah 3:3 refers not to the city in a limited sense, but to the whole extensive administrative area, covering other towns and teeming with a vast population. The population figure is mentioned as 120,000 people 'who cannot tell their right hand from their left' (Jonah 4:11). Some regard this number as those citizens of an age at which they possess moral awareness, but, in the case of Nineveh, this was coupled with moral ignorance.[8] Another estimate puts the total population of Nineveh in the region of 600,000.

The splendour of Nineveh was widely known in the world of Jonah's day. The city itself lasted for 1500 years. Famed for its beauty, it was considered by many to be the fairest city built since Cain founded Enoch. Militarily, Nineveh seemed impregnable. Its outer ramparts stretched for 60 miles. Its inner walls were 100 feet high. Horse-drawn chariots, three abreast, could ride its battlements. The king's house took twelve years to complete. There was a labour force of 10,000 slaves. The city's parks and public buildings had a world-wide reputation.

However, the sinful reputation of Nineveh matched its size and splendour. The Ninevites were notorious for their cruelty to their enemies. The city's prosperity was gained through a brutal regime of oppression, war and plunder. There was exploitation of the weaker nations, and a wide use of slave labour. Occult practices were rife. Witchcrafts and vice were other corrupting features. Her artistic achievements were fouled by obscenities, her culture by idols, and her beauty by violence. She was called 'city of blood' (Nahum 3:1). No wonder that God said to Jonah, 'Its wickedness has come up before me' (Jonah 1:2). The depravity of Nineveh could not be hidden or silenced. Divine intervention was demanded. But, strangely, unlike the equally corrupt cities of Sodom and Gomorrah (Gen. 19), Nineveh was spared in Jonah's day from enduring the severity of God's holy wrath.

The society God changed

That there was a favourable response to the preaching of Jonah is a marvel in itself. When the prophet Amos prophesied at Bethel he was told in no uncertain terms to go back where he came from (Amos 7:12). It is no small wonder that Jonah, the 'foreigner', was not lynched and ejected from the city upon which he dared to predict imminent doom. But the repentance of the Ninevites was genuine. 'The Ninevites believed God' (Jonah 3:5). The king issued a decree confirming the spontaneous repentance of the people (3:7). The moral demands of repentance were announced: 'Let everyone call urgently on God. Let them give up their evil ways and their violence' (3:8). The depth of their repentance was evident: 'They declared a fast, and ... put on sackcloth' (3:5). The extent of their repentance was total. 'All of them, from the greatest to the least ...' (3:5). The solidarity of their repentance was exceptional: 'Do not let any man or beast, herd or flock, taste anything; do not let them eat or drink. But let man and beast be covered with sackcloth' (3:7,8).

If the response to the preaching of the apostle Peter on the Day of Pentecost was astounding — about 3,000 people were converted (Acts 2:41) — then the response of the Ninevites to the preaching of Jonah was nothing short of stupendous and incredible! 120,000 Ninevites turned to the Lord through the preaching of Jonah. Truly, this was an exceptional demonstration of 'amazing grace'!

The servant God used

To what kind of man did God entrust this important urban ministry? In terms of more recent church history, did God select a man of the spiritual stature of a George Whitefield or a John Wesley? We may be in for a surprise. In no sense could Jonah be included in what we might call the category of the 'supersaints'. In fact, the defects of this very earthy man of God are in no way glossed over. His first response to God's call to an 'urban ministry' was to turn his back on God and run the other way (1:3). No doubt we have our modern Jonahs too! But Jonah learned the hard way. God gave him a second chance, and Jonah went at once to tackle his missionary assignment. When the Ninevites responded to his preaching with a repentance that was unquestionably genuine, Jonah reacted angrily (4:1). Instead of praising God for honouring his obedience and rewarding his labours, Jonah blamed God for the outcome. Jonah strongly disapproved of God's widening the circle of His grace and mercy. To Jonah's way of thinking, Israel's enemies ought to be punished and not pardoned. When Jonah did not get what he wanted, he acted like a spoilt child . He blamed God, went into a sulk, and then asked to die. But God did not leave it there. With firmness and yet with sensitivity, God graciously administered pastoral correction to His petulant prophet. The warts have not been hidden. If Jonah, with his very obvious faults, could be mightily used by God, then God can use us, too.

The urban harvest experienced at Nineveh is probably without historical parallel. When we consider the moral degradation of Nineveh and the spiritual defects of Jonah, then the outcome of the prophet's preaching defies all human explanation. It was a work of God. There are Christians who find that the account of Jonah's experiences within the 'great fish' presents some facts which they find 'hard to swallow'! But why? Is there some sort of intellectual embarrassment about this event? I fail to see why the historicity of the event needs to be questioned. In one sense, it was a miracle. But Jonah is not the only person to have been swallowed by a 'great fish' and yet to have survived.[9] Certainly it was *not* the major miracle recorded in the prophecy of Jonah. When God in a sovereign and supernatural way initiated (1:17), directed (2:1-9) and term-

supernatural way initiated (1:17), directed (2:1-9) and terminated (2:10) Jonah's experiences within the 'great fish', He performed a *minor* miracle. The One who had *created* the fish, and the sea in which it swam, had no problem in *controlling* their activities as well. In my judgement, the *major* miracle of Jonah's ministry was the genuine repentance of the entire city of Nineveh. God's control and use of the great fish showed His power at work in the *physical* realm. God's work in the hearts and lives of the pagan population of Nineveh showed His power at work in the *moral* and spiritual realm. For me, God's work of 'inward transformation' was unquestionably the greater miracle of the two.

Strictly speaking, the work of God that Jonah witnessed was not a revival. Where there had been no previous spiritual birth, there could not be a *re*vival of spiritual life. In our contemporary urban scene, God has already begun His work. But many causes struggle to maintain their existence. As today's 'urban believers' continue to be 'urban battlers' against all that morally disfigures the city and spiritually demoralizes God's servants, we desperately need a new and exceptional intervention by God to revive His people and make them a pure and powerful instrument in His hand. If God could transform pagan Nineveh, can He not do the same for pagan London, Liverpool or Birmingham? If God chose to achieve the transformation of Nineveh through an imperfect human instrument like Jonah, then God can use us, too. We must direct our unceasing prayers to this end.

> 'When He saw the crowds, he had compassion on them, because they were harassed and helpless, like sheep without a shepherd. Then he said to his disciples, "The harvest is plentiful but the workers are few. Ask the Lord of the harvest, therefore, to send out workers into his harvest field"' (Matt. 9:36-38).

> Lord, we are few, but Thou art near,
> Nor short Thine arm, nor deaf Thine ear;
> O rend the heavens, come quickly down,
> And make a thousand hearts Thine own!
>
> William Cowper
> 1731 - 1800

Notes

Chapter 1

1. Roger Lloyd, *The Church and the Artisan Today*, Longmans, 1952, p.54.
2. D.M. Lloyd-Jones, *The Christian and the State in Revolutionary Times*, Westminster Conference, 1975, p.103.
3. Geoffrey B. Wilson, *Romans*, Banner of Truth Trust, 1969, p.21.
4. David Martin, *A Sociology of English Religion*, Heinemann, 1967, p.19.
5. *ibid.*, p.47.
6. *New Society*, 22 March 1979, Supplement on 'Class', p.i.
7. David Martin, *op. cit.*, p.52. See also *On the Other Side*, Scripture Union 1968, p.47.
8. K.A. Busia, *Urban Churches in Britain*, Lutterworth, 1966, p.17.
9. Richard Hoggart, *The Uses of Literacy*, Pelican Books, 1958, p.22. (First published by Chatto & Windus, 1957.)
10. Eric Butterworth & David Weir, *The Sociology of Modern Britain*, Fontana, 1976, p.494.
11. L.G. Tyler, *A Christian Front in Industry*, (pamphlet) Industrial Christian Fellowship, p.11.
12. George Burton, *People Matter more than Things*, Hodder & Stoughton, 1965, p.30.
13. David Martin, *op. cit.*, p.69.

Chapter 2

1. E.R. Wickham, *Church and People in an Industrial City*, Lutterworth, 1957, p.69.
2. *ibid.*, p.119
3. *ibid.*, p.150
4. *ibid.*, p.215
5. Charles Booth, *Life and Labour of the People in London*, Third Series, Religious Influences, Macmillan, 1902, vol. 7, ch.10.
6. E.R. Wickham, *op. cit.*, p.56.
7. Robert Wearmouth, *Methodism and the Common People of the 18th Century*, Epworth Press, 1945, p.263.

8. A.D.Gilbert, *Religion and Society in Industrial England*, Longman, 1976, p.60.
9. Robert Wearmouth, *Methodism and the Working Class Movements of England, 1800-1850*, Epworth Press, 1937, p.223.
10. Kathleen Heasman, *Evangelicals in Action*, Bles, 1962, p.17.
11. Hugh McLeod, *Class and Religion in the late Victorian City*, Groom Helm, 1974, p.17.
12. R.Mudie-Smith, *The Religious Life of London*, Hodder & Stoughton, 1904, p.201.
13. I.Murray, *The Forgotten Spurgeon*, Banner of Truth Trust, 1966, p.15.
14. C.H. Spurgeon, *An All Round Ministry*, Banner of Truth Trust, 1972, p.296.
15. I. Murray, *op. cit.*, p.16.
16. K.S. Inglis, *Churches and the Working Classes in Victorian England*, Routledge & Kegan Paul, 1963, p.176.
17. *ibid.*, p.213.
18. R. Mudie-Smith, *op. cit.*, pp.196-9.
19. London Borough of Southwark, *The Story of Walworth*, p.19:
    'By 1900 it had become one of the most densely populated parts of London...In 1801 there were 14,847 people living in the Parish of St Mary Newington. By 1851 there were 64,816 and by 1901 there were 122,172. This is nearly three times as many people as live here today. The figure in 1971 was only about 45,000.'
20. *ibid.*, p.19.
21. A.D. Gilbert, *op. cit.* p.111.
22. David Martin, *A Sociology of English Religion*, Heinemann, 1967, p.15.
23. Peter Lane, *The Industrial Revolution* Weidenfield and Nicholson, 1978, p.19.
    'In England over 80% of the population lives in towns and cities. Indeed, the whole of the Western world is urbanized in its mode of life, even if a minority still inhabit the countryside. There is also now an unprecedented urban growth in the developing countries creating the radical social and economic changes within them. In 1850, 2.4% of the world's population lived in towns with over 20,000 inhabitants; in 1950 the percentage was 20.9% and it is estimated it will have risen to 45% in the year 2,000, and even 90% in A.D. 2050.
    (*On the Other Side*, Scripture Union, 1966, p.33.)
24. A.D. Gilbert, *op. cit.*, p.80.
25. David Martin, *op. cit.*, p.16.
26. *ibid.*, p.16.
27. A.D. Gilbert, *op. cit.* p.151.
28. *ibid.*, p.158.
29. Kathleen Heasman, *op. cit.*, p.64.
30. A.D. Gilbert, *op. cit.*, p.159.
31. *ibid.*, p.198.
32. *ibid.*, p.181.
33. *ibid.*, p.172.
34. *ibid.*, p.170.
35. *ibid.*, p.182.
36. C.H. Spurgeon. *op. cit.* p.292.
37. Kathleen Heasman, *op. cit.*, p.18.
38. K.S. Inglis, *op. cit.*, p.116.

Notes

39. R. Mudie-Smith, *op. cit.*, p.207.
40. David Martin, *op. cit.*, p.28.
41. E.R. Wickham, *op. cit.*, p.205.
42. *ibid.*, p.213.
43. D. Bartles-Smith & D. Gerrard, *Urban Ghetto*, Lutterworth, 1976, p.13.
44. E. Braund, *The Evangelical Magazine*, July 1972, p.17.
45. E.R. Wickham, *op.cit.* p.139.
46. *ibid.*, p.139.
47. *ibid.*, p.174.
48. *ibid.*, p.175.
49. K.S. Inglis, *op. cit.*, p.62.
50. David Martin, *op. cit.*, p.110
51. E. Braund, *op. cit.*, p.23.
52. R. Greenway, *Calling our Cities to Christ*, Presbyterian & Reformed, U.S.A 1973, p.26.
53. London Borough of Southwark, *Southwark: a London Borough*, p.24.
54. Ted Roberts, *Housing & Ministry*, C.P.A.S., 1975, p.17.
55. Clifford Hill, *Renewal in the Inner City*, (Methodist Home Mission), p.18.

Chapter 3

1. Richard Hoggart, *The Uses of Literacy*, Pelican Books, 1958, p.197.
2. Michael Eastman, *The Christian Graduate*, December 1973, 'Bible reading and non-Bible readers', p.106.
3. James Barr, *The Semantics of Biblical Language*, Oxford University Press, 1961, p.10.
4. *ibid.* p.11.
5. Michael Green, *Evangelism in the Early Church*, Hodder & Stoughton, 1970, p.17.
6. R.V.G. Tasker, *John* — Tyndale New Testament Commentary, IVP 1960, p.27.
7. J.C. Ryle, *Expository Thoughts on the Gospels*, John, vol.1, Wm Hunt & Co., 1865, p.209.
8. *ibid.*, p.212.
9. Richard Hoggart, *op. cit.*, p.201.
10. Gavin Reid, *The Gagging of God*, Hodder & Stoughton, 1969, p.74.
11. *ibid.*, p.100.
12. Roger Lloyd, *The Church and the Artisan Today*, Longmans, 1952, p.23.
13. *ibid.*, p.85.
14. Gavin Reid, *op. cit.*, p.31.
15. James Barr, *op. cit.*, p.12.
16. Andrew Quicke, *Tomorrow's Television*, Lion Publishing, 1976, p.9.
17. *ibid.*, p.148.
18. F.Zweig, *The Worker in an Affluent Society*, Heinemann, 1961, p.110.
19. A.Quicke, *op. cit.*, p.166. Here he is quoting from Malcolm Muggeridge in *Pornography – The Longford Report*, Hodder & Stoughton, 1972.
20. *ibid.*, p.201. He is quoting from the *American Commission on the Causes and Prevention of Violence*.

21. *ibid.*, p.230.
22. *ibid.*, p.166. He quotes further from Malcolm Muggeridge.
23. David Sheppard, *Built as a City*, Hodder & Stoughton, 1974, p.175.
24. *ibid.*, p.125.
25. John Wesley, *Forty-Four Sermons*, Epworth Press, 1944, p.v, Preface.
26. John Thornbury, '*David Brainerd*', Prize-winning Essay in *Five Pioneer Missionaries*, Banner of Truth Trust, 1965, p.71.

Chapter 4 Notes

1. R.S. Greenway, *Apostles to the City*, Baker Book House, U.S.A., 1978, p.71.
2. D. Moberg, *The Great Reversal*, Scripture Union, 1973, p.70.
3. See *Evangelism, Salvation and Social Justice* by Ronald Sider with a 'Response' by John R.W. Stott. (Grove Booklet on Ethics No. 16., 1977.) This booklet contains a brief but most useful discussion of the topics indicated. I would personally identify with the position taken by John Stott (p.21) on the three issues he raises in his 'response', i.e.,
    i. The relation between evangelism and social action.
    ii. The kingdom of God.
    iii. Principalities and powers.
4. Stuart Olyott, 'What is Evangelism?' *Banner of Truth*, July-August 1969, p.2.
5. F.F. Bruce, *The Book of Acts*, New London Commentary, Marshall, Morgan and Scott, 1962, p.216.
6. E.A. Judge, *The Social Pattern of Christian Groups in the First Century*, The Tyndale Press, 1960, p.52. (See also chapter 9 note 5.)
7. *ibid.*, p.35.
8. Richard Baxter, *The Reformed Pastor*, Banner of Truth Trust, 1974, p.184. (First published 1656.)
9. C.H. Spurgeon, *The Early Years*, Banner of Truth Trust, 1962, p.222.
10. I. Murray, 'Three Proven Principles in Evangelism', *Banner of Truth*, February 1977, p.21.
11. *ibid.*, p.21.
12. Michael Green, *Evangelism in the Early Church*, Hodder & Stoughton, 1970, p.202.
13. F.M. Harrison, *John Bunyan*, Banner of Truth Trust, 1964, p.25.
14. J.C. Ryle, *Five Christian Leaders of the Eighteenth Century*, Banner of Truth Trust, 1960, p.20.
15. C.H. Spurgeon, *An All Round Ministry*, Banner of Truth Trust, 1972, p.296. First published 1900.
16. Michael Green, *op. cit.*, p.173.

Chapter 5

1. See the remarkable conversion of William Grimshaw — A. Dallimore *George Whitefield*, vol. 2, Banner of Truth Trust, 1980, p.311.
2. J.C. Ryle, *Five Christian Leaders*, Banner of Truth Trust, 1960, p.20.
3. Quoted by J.C. Ryle, *ibid.*, p.32.
4. John Wesley, *Journal*, Epworth Press, 1903, p.35.

Notes

5. C.H. Spurgeon, *The Soul Winner*, W. Eerdman's Pub.Co., Grand Rapids, 1976, p.93.
6. Richard Baxter, *The Reformed Pastor*, Banner of Truth Trust, 1974, p.70.
7. R.B. Kuiper, *God-centred Evangelism*, Banner of Truth Trust, 1966, p.187.
8. Richard Baxter, *Autobiography*, edited by J.M. Lloyd-Thomas, Dent 1925,p.79.
9. Richard Baxter, *The Reformed Pastor*, pp.196-197.
10. *ibid.* p.43.
11. Richard Baxter, *The Reformed Pastor*, p.196. Where did the catechizing take place — in their homes or his? 'Two days every week my assistant and I myself took fourteen families between us for private catechizing and conference (he going through the parish, and the town coming to me)' *Autobiog.*, p.77.
12. *ibid.*, p.182.
13. Roger Lloyd, *The Church and the Artisan Today*, Longman's, 1952, p.11.
14. F.Zweig, *The Worker in an Affluent Society*, Heinemann, 1961, p.212.
15. E.A. Nida, *Customs, Culture, & Christianity*, The Tyndale Press, 1963, p.178.
16. *East Street Baptist Mission, Walworth, Centenary Booklet, 1859-1959*, centre page.
17. David Sheppard, *Built as a City*, Hodder & Stoughton, 1974, p.14.
18. H. McLeod, *Class and Religion in the late Victorian City*, Groom Helm 1974, p.29.
19. Richard Hoggart, *The Uses of Literacy*, Pelican Books, 1958, p.112.
20. L.E. Elliott-Binns, *Religion in the Victorian Era*, Lutterworth, 1936, p.443.
21. K. Heasman, *Evangelicals in Action*, Bles, 1962, p.69.
22. K.S. Inglis, *Churches and the Working Classes in Victorian England*, Routledge & Kegan Paul, 1963, p.330.
23. E.R. Wickham, *Church & People in an Industrial City*, Lutterworth, 1957, p.176. Wickham quotes Charles Booth's *Life and Labour of the People of London*.
24. *ibid.*, p.155.
25. K.S. Inglis, *op. cit.*, p.331
26. David Sheppard, *op. cit.*, p.50.
27. *ibid.*, p.279.
28. Kathleen Raine, *A Choice of Blake's Verse*, Faber & Faber, 1970, p.99.
29. *ibid.*, p.13.
30. David McLean, *L.S.Lowry*, The Medici Society Ltd., 1978, p.6.
31. 'Widecombe: a Lung for the City', *Evangelical Times*, March 1978, p.1. Several years ago a farm at East Shallowford near Widecombe, Devon, was acquired, in connection with the youth work of Providence House, Battersea. Throughout the year parties of children from a local Battersea school spend two weeks 'living on the farm'. During their stay they become temporarily 'de-urbanized' and are given opportunity to discover and enjoy first-hand the living world which God has made. The article in the *Evangelical Times* concluded, 'The urban mind and image of our society has so permeated many Christians that they too have a real need to have this stripped away by being faced at first hand with the basics of life, death, and survival and by being surrounded by the overwhelming facts of God's creation, which are still with us if we have eyes to see them. The vision and thinking behind this venture are vital for much Christian work in the inner-city areas. This project is not just another "good work"; it exemplifies thorough-going biblical thinking put into practice — and stands as a challenge to Christians in other areas to think and act themselves.'

32. *ibid.*, p.8.
33. *ibid.*, p.8.
34. Francis Schaeffer, *Pollution and the Death of Man – The Christian View of Ecology*, Hodder & Stoughton, 1970, p.40.
35. *ibid.*, p.59.
36. John Murray, *Collected Writings of John Murray*, vol. 1, Banner of Truth Trust, 1976, 'The Significance of the Doctrine of Creation', p.326.
37. Joseph Addison, *Grace Hymns*, Grace Publications Trust, no. 112.
38. C.H. Spurgeon, *The Early Years*, Banner of Truth Trust, 1972, p.222.
39. John Wesley, *Journal*, vol. 2., pp.167,172.
40. A. Skevington Wood, *The Burning Heart*, Paternoster, 1967.
    The list of situations in which John Wesley preached is taken from the information gathered in chapter 11, 'A Convenient Place', p.125f.
    For reference to the scale of his life's work, see p.116.

Chapter 6

1. W.M. Ramsay, *Cities of St Paul*, Hodder & Stoughton, 1907, p.408.
2. *ibid.*, p. 409.
3. F.F. Bruce, *The Book of Acts*, New London Commentary, Marshall, Morgan and Scott, 1962, p.291.
4. W.M. Ramsay, *op, cit.*, p.409.
5. W.M. Ramsay, *Hastings Dictionary of the Bible*, article on 'Lystra', T. & T. Clark, 1900, p.179.
6. J.M. Houston, 'Christian Values in City Life', *The Witness*, May 1969, p.168.
7. Michael Green, *Evangelism in the Early Church*, Hodder & Stoughton, 1970, p.153.
8. John Murray, *The Epistle to the Romans*, New London Commentary, Marshall, Morgan and Scott, 1967, p.40.
9. Thomas Watson, *A Body of Divinity*, Banner of Truth Trust, 1958, p.39.
10. *ibid.*, p.39.
11. F.F. Bruce, *op. cit.*, p.293.
12. Albert Barnes, *Popular Commentary*, New Testament, vol. iii, Acts, Blackie & Son Ltd, p.217.
13. A.D. Gilbert, *Religion and Society in Industrial England*, Longman, 1976, p.135.
14. R. Mudie-Smith, *The Religious Life of London*, Hodder & Stoughton, 1904, p.216.
15. Richard Hoggart, *The Uses of Literacy*, Pelican Books, 1958, p.115.
16. Albert Barnes, *op. cit.*, p.218.
17. W.M. Ramsay, *St Paul the Traveller*, Hodder & Stoughton, 1935, p.119.
18. Richard Hoggart, *op. cit.*, p.102.
19. David Martin, *A Sociology of English Religion*, Heinemann, 1967, p.75.
20. R.F. Wearmouth, *Methodism and the Working-Class Movements of England, 1800-1850*, Epworth Press, 1937, p.6.
21. K.S. Inglis, *Churches and the Working Classes in Victorian England*, Routledge & Kegan Paul, 1963, p.41.

Notes

22. R. Mudie-Smith, *op.cit.*, p.214.
23. David Martin, *op.cit.*, p.70.
24. John Murray, *Collected Writings of John Murray*, vol. 1. 'The Significance of the Doctrine of Creation,' Banner of Truth Trust, 1976, p.326.
25. A.W. Tozer, *The Knowledge of the Holy*, James Clarke & Co. Ltd., 1965, p.10.
26. Francis Schaeffer, *Death in the City*, Inter-Varsity Press, 1969, p.12.
27. *ibid.*, p.79.

Chapter 7

1. J.L. Nevius, *Planting and Development of Missionary Churches*, Presbyterian & Reformed Publishing Co., 1899.
2. J.H. Bavinck, *An Introduction to the Science of Missions*, Presbyterian & Reformed Publishing Co., 1961, p.3.
3. A. Dallimore, *George Whitefield*, vol. 2, Banner of Truth Trust, 1980, p.22.
4. John Wesley, *A Plain Account of the People Called Methodists*, Epworth Press, 1951.
5. *ibid.*, p.6.
6. *ibid.*, p.7.
7. *ibid.*, p.11.
8. *ibid.*, p.8.
9. S.W. Christophers, *Class Meetings in relation to the Design and Success of Methodism*, Wesleyan Conference Office, 1873, p.127.
10. John Wesley, quoted by A.S. Wood in *The Burning Heart*, p.187.
11. J.C. Ryle quotes W. Grimshaw in *Christian Leaders*, C.J. Thynne 1902, p.115.
12. G.C. Cragg, *Grimshaw of Haworth*, The Canterbury Press 1947, p.88.
13. William Williams, *The Experience Meeting*, Evangelical Press, 1973.
14. D.M. Lloyd-Jones, intro. to *The Experience Meeting*, p.6.
15. *ibid.*, p.6.
16. A. Dallimore, *op. cit.*, p.546.
17. Quoted by A. Skevington Wood, *The Burning Heart*, p.188.
18. A. Dallimore, *op. cit.*, p.549.
19. W.G.T. Shedd, *Homiletics and Pastoral Theology*, Banner of Truth Trust, 1965, (first published, 1867) p.137.
20. D.M. Lloyd-Jones, *Preaching and Preachers*, Hodder & Stoughton, 1971, p.75.
21. *ibid.*, p.72.
22. William Williams, *op. cit.*, p.13.
23. T. Aldridge, *The Spiritual Nurture of Children* (paper read at a Carey Conference), Carey Publications 1972, p.36.
24. Colin Buchanan, *The New International Dictionary of the Christian Church*, 'Catechisms', Paternoster Press, 1974, p.199.
25. Richard Baxter, *The Reformed Pastor*, Banner of Truth Trust, 1974, p.177.
26. D.M. Lloyd-Jones, *Preaching and Preachers*, p.187.

27. Richard Baxter, *Autobiography*, ed. J.M. Lloyd Thomas, Dent, 1925, p.77.
28. J.L. Nevius, *op. cit.*, p.36.

Chapter 8
1. David Sheppard, *Built as a City*, Hodder & Stoughton, 1974, p.34.
2. Ted. Roberts, *Housing & Ministry*, Church Pastoral Aid Society, 1975, p.37.
3. E.A. Nida, *Customs, Culture & Christianity*, Tyndale Press, 1963, p.28.
4. *ibid.*, p.42.
5. James Moffat, *1 Corinthians*, Moffatt New Testament Commentary, Hodder & Stoughton, 1943, p.xvii. Quoted by Leon Morris in his *1 Corinthians*, Tyndale Press, 1958, p.16.
6. Quoted by Leon Morris, *1 Corinthians*, p.17.
7. W.M. Ramsay, *Hastings Dictionary of the Bible*, 'Corinth', vol. 1, T. & T. Clark, 1898, p.482.
8. R.G. Gromacki, *Called to be Saints*, Baker Book House, USA, 1977, p.113.
9. The Greek word *kubernētēs* (steersman) appears, in its Anglicized form, in the English language. *Cybernetics* is the science of systems of control and communications in animals and machines.
10. E.A. Nida, *op. cit.*, p.9.
11. *ibid.*, p.35. Wife-lending among the Eskimos is an important technique for gaining prestige.
12. *ibid.*, p.95.
13. Michael Griffiths, *Shaking the Sleeping Beauty*, Inter-varsity Press, 1980, p.57.
14. E. Butterworth & D. Weir, *The Sociology of Modern Britain*, Fontana, 1970, p.317.
15. Richard Hoggart, *The Uses of Literacy*, Pelican Books, 1958, p.80, 81.
16. E.A. Nida, *op. cit.*, p.256.
17. *ibid.*, p.39.
18. Richard Hoggart, *op. cit.*, p.88.
19. K. Heasman, *Christians and Social Work*, S.C.M. Press Ltd, 1965, p.91.
20. D. Bartles-Smith & David Gerrard, *Urban Ghetto*, Lutterworth, 1976, p.55.
21. D. Martin, *A Sociology of English Religion*, Heinemann, 1967, p.105.
22. Roger Lloyd, *The Church and the Artisan Today*, Longmans, 1952, p.20.
23. Roger Sainsbury, *From a Mersey Wall*, Scripture Union, 1970, p.74.
24. J.H. Bavinck, *An Introduction to the Science of Missions*, Presbyterian & Reformed Pub. Co., 1961, p.80.
25. E.A. Nida, *op. cit.*, p.23.
26. See: Charles Bridges, *The Christian Ministry;* C.H. Spurgeon, *Lectures to my Students;* C.H. Spurgeon, *An All-Round Ministry;* Richard Baxter, *The Reformed Pastor;* W.G.T. Shedd, *Homiletics and Pastoral Theology;* H. Sugden & W. Wiersbe, *Confident Pastoral Leadership.*

27. See Leon Morris, *Ministers of God*, I.V.F., 1964, p.70 ch. v., 'Presbyters'; Errol Hulse, *Reformation Today*, Jan. - Feb. 1977, 'Reformation of the Eldership', p.11.
28. John Wesley, *A Plain Account of the People called Methodists*, Epworth Press, 1951, p.11.

Chapter 9

1. But see A.W. Pink *An Exposition of the Sermon on the Mount*, Baker Book House, 1950, p.43.
   Pink contends that the words, 'You are the salt of the earth' apply to God's ministers in particular and not to God's people in general. His argument is not convincing.
2. H.F.R. Catherwood, *The Christian in Industrial Society*, Tyndale Press, 1964, Introduction, p.xii.
3. W. Hendriksen, *Matthew*, Banner of Truth Trust, 1973, p.282.
4. K. Heasman, *Christians and Social Work*, S.C.M. Press, 1965, p.98.
5. 'The gentleman depicted entering a meeting in state (James 2:2), is clearly of Roman equestrian status, as the gold ring must imply. It need not mean that he belonged to the metropolitan aristocracy, however, and even if he did, he might still be a *parvenu* among them as the equestrian insignia could be awarded to freedmen to distract attention from their origins. But it is much more likely that the writer is thinking in terms of the big businessmen of the eastern cities who were certainly familiar to his readers, if not included among them (James 4:13). Such persons were not concerned with political careers in the capital; the equestrian insignia were useful to them simply as a mark of their being millionaires.' E.A. Judge, *The Social Pattern of Christian Groups in the First Century*, Tyndale Press, 1960, p.53.
6. J.A. Motyer, *The Day of the Lion, The Message of Amos*, IVP, 1974, p.94: foot-note.
7. Alan Storkey, *A Christian Social Perspective*, IVP, 1979, p.181.
8. *ibid.*, p.183.
9. *ibid.*, p.185.
10. Roger Lloyd, *The Church and the Artisan Today*, Longmans, 1952, p.36.
11. H.F.R. Catherwood, *op. cit.*, p.26.
12. *ibid.*, p.7.
13. J.A. Motyer, *op. cit.*, p.132.
14. For a detailed exposition of the biblical teaching on 'work' see John Murray, *Principles of Conduct*, ch. iv, 'The Ordinance of Labour', Tyndale Press, 1957, p.82.
15. A. Dallimore, *George Whitefield*, vol. 2, Banner of Truth Trust, 1980, p.149.
16. See Kathleen Heasman, *Evangelicals in Action*, Bles, 1962.
17. John A. Simpson, *The New International Dictionary of the Christian Church*, Paternoster, 1974, article on Lord Shaftesbury (1801-1885), p.900.
18. John R.W. Stott, *Christian Counter-Culture*, IVP, 1978, p.66.
19. W. Hendriksen, *op. cit.*, p.283.

Chapter 10

1. George Haw, cited by E.R. Wickham, *Church and People in an Industrial City*, Lutterworth, 1957, p.175.
2. See *Christians in Industrial Areas*, Autumn 1980 issue. This 'correspondence' journal appears three times in a year. Its material is supplied by its readers. It provides a 'clearing house' of Christian thinking about the particular needs of urban and industrial areas — general articles, particular themes, book reviews, readers' letters, etc. The Autumn 1980 issue is wholly given to the matter of Government responses to urban deprivation. There are a number of contributors. The content of the journal provokes thought on issues which Reformed evangelicals tend to neglect. Views expressed in the journal often indicate a 'wider-than-evangelical' outlook. Editor: Rev. Bryan Ellis, 31, Peterson Road, Wakefield, W. Yorks.
3. David Sheppard, *Built as a City*, Hodder & Stoughton, 1974, p.88.
4. E.R. Wickham, *Church and People in an Industrial Society*, p.217.
5. A.A. Hoekema, *What about Tongue Speaking?*, Paternoster Press, 1966, p.137.
6. J.G. Vos, 'The Use and Abuse of Church History', *Banner of Truth*, March 1969, p.23.
7. R.B. Kuiper, *The Glorious Body of Christ*, Banner of Truth Trust, 1967, p.84.
8. H.L. Ellison, in *Men Spake from God*, Paternoster Press, 1952, p.27, says, 'It seems likely that the 120,000 persons that could not "discern between their right hand and their left" are the younger children of two and three and under.'

    Apparently following this line of reason, Dr F.A. Tatford, in *The Prophet who deserted*, Prophetic Witness Publishing House, 1974, p.68, says, 'There were 120,000 there who had not yet reached the age of discretion, so the total population (i.e. the complex of Greater Nineveh) must have been at least 600,000.'
9. Raymond Brown, *Let's read the Old Testament*, Victory Press, 1971, p.159.

Contents analysis

1. Urban people: the working classes

Is it right for Christians to think in terms of 'class'?
Who are the working classes?
What do we need to know?
Working class views of the church

2. In darkest England

The legacy of history: an unbridgeable gulf?
  The general picture
  A man for the masses
  What about the Baptists?
  The true perspective

Exploring and explaining the 'unbridgeable gulf'
  Progressive industrialization
  Urban revolution
  Ecclesiastical inflexibility
  Social migration
  Religious formalism
  Ministerial professionalism
  Introverted evangelism
  Cultural estrangement
  Economic parochialism
  Recreational diversions
  Undisguised snobbery
  Social injustice

Concrete jungles and crumbling communities
  Streets and roots
  Changing values
  The grey desert
  Dimensions of deprivation
  Power and the professionals

Contents analysis

    Glimpse of a ghetto
    Spiritual darkness
  Where have all the Christians gone?
  The doors are closing

3. Battle for the mind

  Language forms: concrete and conceptual: the distinction explained
  Biblical languages: Hebrew (concrete) and Greek (conceptual)
    Original revelation
    Universal transmission
  Concrete and conceptual: New Testament analysis
    How Jesus taught
    How Paul taught
    Knowledge and experience
  Language and learning
    The limitations of logic
    Reason and impression
    Intelligence
  The mind and the media
  Decision-making
  Mental descipline

4. A message for the millions

  Thinking scripturally
  The message we are called to proclaim
    A gospel for the working classes?
    Confusion and its causes
    One gospel
  The people we are concerned to reach
    Do we practise unfair discrimination?
    New Testament God-fearers and working-class church-goers
    Preachers or witnesses?
    Features of New Testament evangelism among the Gentiles

5. Winning them wisely

  Plain speaking
  Instruction and persuasion
  'Publicly and from house to house'
  Salvation and solidarity : the influence of 'the group'
  Sunday Schools
  Reaching young people
  Creation and the city
  Ten questions

6. Lessons from Lystra

   Three sermons from the book of Acts
   How we know that God is there
   Good news for the workers
   Ritual or repentance?
   Spotlight on superstition
   'Human like you'
   The Most High God
   Signs of the times

7. Growing together

   What is an indigenous church?
      Self-support
      Self-government
      Self-education
      Self-propagation
   A lesson from John Wesley: the importance of 'the group'
   An all-round teaching ministry
      Paul's example
      Expository preaching
      Shared experience
      Catechetical teaching
      A place for questions
      The benefits of two-way teaching

8. Building an indigenous church

   Persuading and helping Christians to live locally
      Why do they go?
      Why should they stay?
      How can they stay?
   Corinth, culture and class
      What is culture?
      Culture in a New Testament urban church
         Testing the phenomena
         Steering the church
      Some cultural criteria
      Culture in a contemporary urban church
         Testing the phenomena
         Steering the church
         Right about race?
   Home-grown leaders
      Plurality of indigenous leaders
      Diversity of spiritual gifts
      Continuity of biblical teaching

Contents analysis

　　　Reservoir of corporate wisdom
　　　Preservation of spiritual unity
　　　Promotion of pastoral efficiency
　　　Development of spiritual maturity
　　　Ministry of mutual encouragement

9. Salt where it counts

　　　The urban Christian in an industrial society
　　　A friend of the lonely
　　　A defender of the powerless
　　　A champion of the oppressed

10. How long till harvest?

　　　Responsibility ... yesterday?
　　　Reformation ... today?
　　　　Biblical principles
　　　　Worship and culture
　　　　Church history
　　　Revival tomorrow?
　　　　The city God spared
　　　　The society God changed
　　　　The servant God used